Insiders and Outsiders

New Directions in Anthropology
General Editor: Jacqueline Waldren

Volume 1
Coping with Tourists: European Reactions to Mass Tourism
Edited by Jeremy Boissevain

Volume 2
A Sentimental Economy: Commodity and Community in Rural Ireland
Carles Salazar

Volume 3
Insiders and Outsiders: Paradise and Reality in Mallorca
Jacqueline Waldren

Volume 4
The Hegemonic Male: Masculinity in a Portuguese Town
Miguel Vale de Almeida

Volume 5
Communities of Faith: Sectarianism, Identity, and Social Change on a Danish Island
Andrew S. Buckser

Volume 6
After Socialism: Land Reform and Rural Social Change in Eastern Europe
Edited by Ray Abrahams

INSIDERS AND OUTSIDERS

Paradise and Reality in Mallorca

Dear Paula
Now you will have
Deia in Rochester and
learn all our secrets
Much love
Jackie
Deia 10/97

Jacqueline Waldren

Berghahn Books
Providence • Oxford

First published in 1996 by
Berghahn Books

Editorial offices:
165 Taber Avenue, Providence, RI 02906, USA
Bush House, Merewood Avenue, Oxford, OX3 8EF, UK

Library of Congress Cataloging-in-Publication Data

Waldren, Jacqueline, 1937–
Insiders and outsiders : paradise and reality in Mallorca / Jacqueline Waldren.
p. cm. -- (New directions in anthropology)
Includes bibliographical references (p.) and index.
ISBN 1-57181-889-8 (hardcover : alk. paper). -- ISBN 1-57181-890-1 (pbk. : alk. paper)
1. Deià--(Spain)--Social life and customs. 2. Deià--(Spain)--Ethnic relations. 3. Aliens--Spain--Deià. 4. Visitors, Foreign--Spain--Deià. 5. Tourist trade--Social aspects--Spain--Deià. I. Title. II. Series.
DP402.D395W3 1996
946'.754--dc20 95-42239
CIP

Cover photo: *Catalina de Ca'n Deya* by Heiner Schmitz

British Library Cataloguing in Publication Data
A catalogue record for this book is available from the British Library.

Printed in the United States on acid-free paper

Contents

ACKNOWLEDGEMENTS

This book is based on the personal experience I have shared with the people of Deià, Mallorca over the past thirty-five years. Fieldwork at home when one has made her or his home in another place presents problems and advantages. The most difficult problem I had was in trying to separate myself from the people and activities I was describing. My particular relationships with the various people and groups I have tried to describe undoubtedly affect my presentation of their lives, but I hope the variety of perspectives I bring to view enriches rather than detracts from the insights offered.

My interpretation is socially situated in a variety of changing circumstances and derives from observation, participation, and experience. My life and work overlap with much of local life and the shared activities, discussions, joys and pain, agreements and arguments, different perceptions and interpretations of events are what have made this book possible. My research involved neighbours and friends, trying to understand the manner by which each was making some sense of earthly existence. From the beginning it was clear that I was dealing with various conflicting and often incongruous aspects of Deià life and would have great difficulty in making a coherent presentation.

The last few lines of a poem by Robert Graves called 'The Devil's Advice to Story-Tellers' gave me the confidence to keep trying:

> Sigh then, or frown, but leave (as in despair)
> Motive and end and moral in the air;
> Nice contradiction between fact and fact
> Will make the whole read human and exact. (1972:59)

I hope that those who consider themselves Deianencs, long-term Deià residents, seasonal visitors, and tourists gain some additional understanding of one another through these pages. They are the people who made this work possible, whose similarities and differences have shaped the village as it is today. I am especially grateful to my daughters, whose experiences of growing up in Deià are reflected throughout this book and to Magdalena 'de Son Bauça',[1] Margarita and Magdalena 'Burota', Tomeo and Antonio 'Trona' who never tired of my endless questions and seemed to derive great joy from sharing the details of their lives and that of their families, friends and neighbours with me. Many of those who helped me most are no longer alive to share the outcome of their generous hours spent teaching, explaining, advising, and opening their worlds to me. Many Deianencs, Maria 'de Ca'n Blau', 'Mestre' Toni, and Toni 'Ferrer' will live on in these pages. Peter and Godfrey Lienhardt, my teachers and friends, who taught me to listen as much to silence as to words and to understand the richness of everyday social life, will always be remembered.

My thanks to my supervisor, Peter Riviére, and to colleagues at the Institute of Social Anthropology in Oxford for their teaching, support, constructive criticism, and patience. My special thanks to Gae Eisenhardt for her technical expertise, Bel Moll for including me in so many university activities, brother Ken for his inspiration, our mother Rosa, whose curiosity and vitality keeps us all going, and to my husband Bill, who helped me to turn problems into challenges. His enthusiasm and dedication to life and work inspired me to pursue this study of Deià.

Note

1. De Son Bauça, Burota, Trona are not surnames. They are descriptive names used to identify individuals in terms of their House of birth or other family characteristics. See Chapter 3.

INTRODUCTION

This book is about the village of Deià on the island of Mallorca where the indigenous population has lived side by side with increasing numbers of resident and visiting foreigners over the past 150 years. It is about coexistence and the process of forming personal, social, regional, and national identities in a period of accelerated social and economic change. The changing concepts of insiders and outsiders in this small village, and the conflicts and resulting compromises that have occurred, have provided a sense of history that allowed various groups to define, develop, adapt, and sustain their own sense of belonging to a community where different cultures, values, and aspirations have been a constant threat to any shared concept of local life. As the inside and outside influences mixed, merged, split, or confronted one another, lives, values, and experiences were affected. Opposition has provided a purpose to those who have formed the village over time, aiding them in constituting relationships and formulating a sense of identity and in preserving and maintaining some semblance of solidarity despite the changes they have undergone.

Social and political life in Deià today is based on the adaptation of old models to fit new conditions and modern aspirations. The local population has found that it can balance a sense of tradition with modernity by maintaining the image of paradise that has attracted so many outsiders. Drawing on traditional aspects of their past, insiders have found ways to combat the disruptions caused by outsiders; their sense of place and a consciousness of local distinctiveness are products of their relations with the outside world rather than the result of isolation. What has occurred in Deià over this period illustrates how this particular community learned to gain full advantage from the economic opportunities opened up by foreigners without losing the fabric of social relations, the meanings and values of their culture.

What initially occurred in Deià is being repeated in one form or another in many parts of the world today. People perceived as outsiders, seeking rural beauty, tranquillity, and a return to nature, have moved into villages, converting old houses into facsimiles of what they once were (with a few added modern conveniences), or highly altering and modernising interiors, while maintaining the external continuity of the traditional (local) architecture. In some areas the occupants commute to a nearby town or city to work during the week, revel in their new-found joys of nature on the weekends, and soon act as though they know more than the locals about what is best for the place (e.g., Elmdon, Wales, Isle of Man, Inner and Outer Hebrides, Brittany, Provence, Costa del Sol).

In some places, foreigners developed local properties and attracted more outsiders to purchase them. Absentee owners lived and worked in other countries and escaped to their island retreats for their holidays, which could range from two weeks to three or four months each year. Often dependent on local people to look after their properties, symbiotic relationships developed between locals and some outsiders.

In Deià, like Tangiers, Saint Tropez, Arles, Martha's Vineyard, Tahiti, or Goa, a few foreigners who felt they had discovered what they perceived as 'paradise' settled in to pursue the arts: painting, writing, composing or performing music, observing and appreciating the wonders of nature and creativity. Paradise meant different things to each person but common themes seemed to include a place that combined nature's bounty, earthly pleasure, social harmony, free will and expression (e.g., Rousseau, Milton, Gauguin). When we speak of paradise we are considering questions of philosophy, creation, nature, or identity perhaps in contrast to technology, progress, or science. The search for meaning in earthly existence led some to seek answers in distant places. They learned local languages and customs, established residence, and pursued their idea of idyllic existence in paradise.

Travellers in large numbers are now called tourists, and accommodations have been expanded in all of these areas. Thirteen million tourists visited Mallorca in 1995. Local people in each area are differently affected by the changes that have occurred. When development has been financed by outside firms and created for the needs of foreigners, many locals are displaced. Some have benefited, at least materially, from the influx, but many believe that the process of restructuring their lifestyles and values to cater to outsiders and their own increased desire for material goods has caused them to lose much of their quality of life. Men and women have emigrated to towns, cities, or resort areas to take up a variety of jobs that require them to learn different languages, concepts of time, gender, and culture. In some areas, the fabric of social life has become almost threadbare except on annual village festival days when local sons and daughters try to return from near and far.

As global communications bring the most remote[1] areas closer and closer together, local identities seem to be more tenuous. The idea of a European Community is seen by the people of some countries as a threat to local and national identities. Community studies, ethnic, regional, and national identities have been the focus of anthropological research in many parts of the world; in Spain, where this study took place, we can draw from a vast amount of research, especially since the death of Franco, the establishment of social democracy, and the division of Spain into seventeen autonomous regions.[2] Most of these studies are concerned with understanding local continuity, while outsiders are often ignored or seen as intrusive and modernisation is blamed for the disappearance of local culture.

This study of Deià offers a long-term perspective on the process of identity recreation at various periods. The people of Deià have been able to enjoy the advantages of modernisation and in the process have revived a respect for traditional values and customs by restructuring concepts of insiders and outsiders in terms of changing circumstances. The manner in which this village has adapted to the influx of foreign residents without losing its sense of identity offers an example that could be useful to other areas that are or will be experiencing similar changes.

Deià is a relatively small village for Mallorca. It is the fifth smallest of the fifty-two villages on the island. If one looks at the population statistics for 1900 (900) and those of 1993 (562), one would assume that like other rural villages on Mallorca and throughout Western Europe, Deià was a dying village. Actually, Deià's population has been increasing steadily since its low ebb of 450 in 1960. In the chapters that follow, it will become evident that the village has been able to continue as a community with its own symbolic boundaries and identity not despite but because of the presence of outsiders. This was not the case in other areas of the island.

Over the past twenty-five years an entire service sector has been created to deal with the massive influx of seasonal visitors to Mallorca.

Prior to this time, there had been a large peasant sector and a small but powerful group of large landowners and religious authorities who exercised social control. Migration from the rural areas to the city or newly developed coastal resorts has brought about a decline in agricultural activities, turned small villages into dormitory towns, and led to an enormous increase in those employed in the service sectors.

In most areas, development was initiated and financed by foreign companies to meet the necessities of foreign-organised tourism. Seafront properties were purchased and developed along most of the southern and eastern coasts of the island.[3] Hotels, bars, restaurants, cafés, and souvenir shops replaced the tiny kiosks that once supplied tepid drinks to local Sunday picnickers. Other areas of the island developed aspects of folklore, geology, or history to attract tourists for a few hours each day, while an increasing number of complementary services – cafés, restaurants, banks, and souvenir shops – were added for the tourists' convenience. Deià's closest neighbour, Valldemossa, has capitalised on the three-month visit of George Sand and Frédéric Chopin in 1838. Sand's critical descriptions of the people have immortalised her extremely frustrating experience and turned the rooms she and Chopin are said to have stayed in into one of the island's major tourist attractions. Other towns have introduced excursions to natural caves, which have been decorated with coloured lights and classical music to accompany the guided tours.

Unlike these other parts of the island that have been completely transformed by tourism, Deià appears to have remained an 'idyllic' mountain village untouched by the ravages of time. The manner in which this village has dealt with change over the past century reveals a subtle, creative, manipulative reordering of old and new conditions while maintaining the image of a 'traditional' village. The village projects an ethos of related people, houses, and families, of shared space and familiar activities carried on within an ancient landscape. Within this 'image of paradise', the realities of everyday life, work, sustenance, pain and pleasure, cooperation, disagreements, gossip, and competition are combined with generations of shared experiences of new and different relationships.

Foreigners in search of unspoiled beauty and tranquillity discovered Deià during the last century. The arrival of a small number of strangers into their village added to the interests of local life. Some local men gained power and prestige through their dealings with these foreigners. Foreigners could purchase land only in the name of a local person and relationships of mutual interest and respect developed. When only a few foreigners lived in Deià, they were reliant on the local people for access to most goods and services, and relationships of interdependence developed. Foreigners were seen as gentlemen: hosted on a visit, accepted over time as *senyors,* and easily drawn into the existing social hierarchy based on land ownership. Some of the local peasant population, once dependent on the fluctuations of the agricultural seasons, began to supplement their incomes by providing services for these foreigners. But it would take almost a century before most of the local people would derive some personal benefit from the increased demands for their products and services.

As increasing numbers of foreigners arrived in Deià, they began to turn to other foreigners for advice instead of relying on the local people. The symbiotic relationship of locals and foreigners that had been beneficial to both groups was no longer possible. Five or ten foreign eccentrics added entertainment and distraction but two hundred foreigners was another experience altogether. More foreign visitors and residents meant more local people could experience prosperity, but it also meant an alteration in the social relations between the two groups. Foreigners no longer represented the wonders of an outside world once thought unattainable by a local person. On the contrary, they now posed a threat to the local 'inside world'. The presence of another group that could threaten their very existence strengthened cohesiveness and drew – and continues to draw – locals together despite individual differences.[4]

In the local terminology, people are categorised as *Deianencs*, *Forasters*, and *Estrangers*. In the strictest sense, Deianencs are those born in the village of Deià, the natives or insiders. Forasters are Spaniards from other villages or mainland Spain. An estranger is a stranger; estrangers are strangers, foreigners, outsiders, persons from other countries. In this study of Deià, I will endeavour to describe the way in which these terms are used, how people label and group one another, and how they determine these labels. I will develop the argument that these terms are basically circumstantial. People categorise one another according to the situation and the desired results. Categories are important but they do not interfere with ongoing social relations. These terms are only headings under which people are described, and they are contracted, expanded, and reinterpreted to fit the constantly changing 'reality' of the society. Boundaries and definitions are shifted to meet the needs of the moment.

The category Deianenc includes the generations of men and women born in Deià and wed to others from Deià, affines from other Mallorquin villages or from mainland Spain, Spaniards who reside and vote in Deià, and may be extended to include children born to foreign parents in Deià and foreign-born residents who act in the interests of the village. Locals feel both respect and resentment for those who cross social boundaries. The ideal of being the same is very difficult to maintain. The definition of a Deianenc is directly tied to the conception of the village as shared space, time, related people, activities, and behaviour. Deianencs are defined by the space and are at the same time the defining consciousnesses of the space (S. Ardener 1965). The fluidity of this category is essential to the continuation of the space known as the village.

The significance of being a Deianenc, an insider, once meant that one had a birthright, a family, a home, which gave one a sense of belonging more than others who moved into the village from outside. But today, with half the houses in the village owned by foreigners, some of whom have resided there for over forty years and whose children have been born and brought up in the village, they too can claim to be Deianencs. Foreigners and locals share many aspects of village life and are competitors for the same resources. Competition for land, houses, consumer goods, jobs and services has replaced the interdependence of the earlier years.

During the past decade, the increasing number of foreign-owned properties, the impact of local council decisions on areas of foreign interests, and the inflated prices of Deià houses beyond the means of young, local buyers are some of the reasons that may have caused Deianencs and foreigners to reinterpret their relationships with one another and the village they share. The meaning and use of the term Deianenc and estranger have developed to their fullest and most manifest forms during the past ten years' coexistence with increasing numbers of foreigners. The terms are being elicited to articulate symbolic boundaries between those who form the village and make decisions about its future development, and those who merely live there.

This book has developed from the perspectives of local informants and is intended to shed some light on the 'world of experience' that allows Deianencs to differentiate themselves from others. I hope to reveal a multiauthored dialogue between locals and foreigners, old and young, which reflects the fluidity and complexities involved in concepts of insiders and outsiders.

The first chapter will present the realities of paradise: the place, the people and their history. The island of Mallorca has been a trade centre and stopping place throughout the centuries. A sense of local identity has developed over time in contrast to the many outsiders with whom locals have shared their village.The necessity to identify themselves as separate from others within the same setting has always been prevalent. Accounts of the Moorish occupations, the conquest of the Moors in 1229, and events throughout the next seven centuries all record confrontations between insiders and outsiders. The local Deianenc population is contrasted to the Moorish occupants of the ninth through thirteenth centuries, then to the Aragonese and Catalan conquerors who were represented by Cistercian monks in the fourteenth and fifteenth centuries, to the Church and the Valldemossins in the sixteenth through eighteenth centuries, and to large landowners, workers from the mainland, Spanish officials, and foreigners during the nineteenth and twentieth centuries.

The various oppositions among the separate Balearic Islands, Catalonia, and mainland Spain also reveal diverse levels of antagonism or cooperation at different periods. The political turmoil of the first half of the twentieth century emphasised being Spanish, rather than Mallorquin, and forced regional and local identities to go underground. The continued surveillance of local communities by members of the Falange during the Franco regime and the suppression of regional identities during this period may have subdued the assertion of local identities, but they were subtly expressed at every opportunity through rituals, modes of address, clothing, gesture, food consumption, etc. By the time democracy was introduced, the formerly well-kept and productive land, forests, olive trees, stone terraces, and citrus trees (once the source of local pride and identity) were in various stages of neglect. People were too busy (or too old), agriculture had become unprofitable, while tourism in all its forms (accommodations, services, food, transport, fuel, etc.) offered the kinds of security that most people wanted. Pride and identity had to be derived from other aspects of life.

The second chapter, 'Conceptions of Space', describes the village through the various perceptions of the people that live in it. To a Deianenc the village is not just a place; it is generations of kin, recognised members of local households, and the reality of everyday existence in familiar surroundings with others who share one's activities, beliefs, rituals, and values. It is the vantage point from which an insider forms his or her view of the world.

The foreigner describes the village from a distance: an outsider's view of beauty and tranquillity; an idealised setting that satisfies personal needs and provides an economically viable alternative lifestyle or an investment; a paradise where dreams and reality blend together and where many like-minded persons live with whom to share these expatriate experiences.

Chapter 3 presents the social structures and values around which life develops. Separate households are grouped together under the name of 'one House', which not only indicates shared property and the problems that it engenders but becomes a metaphor for social relations past and present. This part records the struggle for coherence in a changing world through the social evolution of the household, the family, and the value system. Increased incomes and interaction with foreigners have allowed individuals and groups to develop new avenues and relationships that reduce internal pressures and divert social conflicts. Unlike many studies of villages that relegate the study of the present to the last chapter and endeavour to present the past as though it were more exotic,[5] purer and wiser, or richer in ceremony, rituals, and symbols than the societies of today, this chapter deals with the process of change that is now part of the present. Change has been occurring throughout the period discussed in this volume. In Deià, the desire for modernity, increased demand for material goods, more free time, easy access to distant places, and global communications offered advantages that, when combined, made local social life more varied and simultaneously stimulated a revival of interest in traditional culture.

In Chapter 4, we will see how people have learned to incorporate change by selectively maintaining those traditions that can be adapted to the new requirements. Tradition is not inherited; it is a name given to something constantly being made. The Deianencs have been able to adapt, absorb, develop, or reinterpret change in local terms. The struggle for coherence in a changing world involves faith, reflection, and reevaluation of personal and social identity. By the continued use of old and the invention of new nicknames, House names, and various forms of address, the insiders have continued to define the place, status, and relationships of one another and each outsider in their society.[6] Deianencs have developed a creative means of coping with differences and the pressures of change. Those who most object to change are the foreigners who are actually responsible for bringing the changes.

Chapter 5 adds some perspective to the terms 'insiders' and 'outsiders' and endeavours to show the changing attitudes that affect the use of these terms in different situations. Outsiders-Insiders do not just define one another. As Strathern wrote for Elmdon, 'some people belong to the village in a way others do not. Outsiders who assume the village is a unity see residence as community but locally perceived social boundaries delineate separate functioning entities within the larger society' (1981:94). After more than a hundred years of coexistence between Deianencs and foreigners of all sorts, it is more a question of degrees of insideness and outsideness. The regular use of the terms Deianenc and estranger to distinguish insiders from outsiders is a local manifestation of the general pattern provoked by the national constitution of 1981, which divided the country into seventeen autonomous regions and forced areas to turn inward to rediscover local and regional identities in contrast to the rather contrived 'unity of Spain' so long espoused by the Franco government. Outsiders-Foreigners offered a contrast against which the insiders could articulate a local identity. Lacking legitimate citizen roles within the village, foreigners could be grouped together as 'outsiders'.

In Chapter 6, we will see how the village has been 'paving the way to the future' since the last century. Expansion of any sort, either housing development or the opening of new roads or improvement of old ones, has been a major source of disagreement between various individuals and groups throughout the history of Deià. It was only with the new democracy that various public political confrontations were made possible, and these were often between foreign residents and local voters concerning the future developments of roads and housing in the municipality. From the foreign resident's point of view, a new road or an improved old one devastated the landscape and opened the village to too many people, but from the local point of view, roads provided easier access to and from the village and many advantages for Deianencs and their families. It became evident that each group had quite different concepts of what 'the village' was and how it should evolve in the future.

In 1982, to counterbalance the intrusion of outsiders in village affairs and to try to stay the acquisition of more village lands and houses by foreigners, the categorisation of people as Deianencs and estrangers, as synonyms for insiders and outsiders, became widespread. It gave the locals a way of saying that heritage, birth, and kinship symbolised the relationship between themselves and their village and that only Deianencs held the power and authority for making decisions about that village. Deianencs became the term that expressed the solidarity and self-governing potential of the new democracy.

For centuries, Deianencs had served and supplied the product Deià as identified and desired by outsiders. The outsiders resident in the village wanted Deià to remain unchanged so that they could continue to live their ideal lives in paradise. What they did not consider was that their residence had begun to make a marked economic and social impact on the local economy. No longer just peasants but acquisitive individuals and families, the Deianencs were in a position to reidentify the product Deià in their own terms. It was time that their needs and those of their children were foremost. They were concerned with improvements that would provide employment and housing in Deià for Deianencs. The outsiders' criticism created antagonism and resentment where symbiosis once existed.

While so many areas of Mallorca have been altered beyond recognition by outsiders and tourism, Deià has been able to maintain village continuity visually, culturally, and socially by adapting and reinterpreting traditional activities, attitudes, and values to meet the demands and aspirations of modern life. The selective use of traditional relations and symbols has marked the community's response to changing political and economic conditions and opportunities. Reliance on tradition reveals history as a legitimator of action and expresses and symbolises the social cohesion of the village as an enduring combination of land, kin, Houses, occupations, and shared experience, in contrast to the outsiders who in ever increasing numbers have settled in Deià.

Outsiders maintained the material symbols of the past while the locals were struggling to find work and have enough to eat. While Deianencs were putting work, time, and energy into improving and modernising their lives and homes, foreigners were buying up the past as enthusiastically as the Deianencs were putting it aside. By the time there was work for all and rewards were many, Deianencs were ready to reinterpret their own past. They were able to capitalise on the qualities that had attracted outsiders to their village. Deianencs selected those that fit their present needs and would allow them to accommodate change. The very symbols of the material past – wooden-beamed stone buildings, tiled floors, olive-wood furniture, agricultural implements, clay pots, fireplaces, and wood-burning stoves, once devalued by their parents but purchased and restored by foreigners – were adopted by young Deianencs to express their collective identity. The home became a key symbol of renewed local identity, drawing both from the past and the present, the outside and the inside, for ideas and artefacts. On the inside of local houses were found the recontextualisation of their worlds and values.

This selective tradition is a form of cultural self-identification that serves as a base for collective identity: an assertion of a sense of solidarity through the symbols of everyday life. It is not just a reaction to social change but an element in determining social action. Family, neighbour, and religion are very different institutions from what they were in the past. Yet they form the basis for most social associations. Nuclear and extended families have become more important while neighbour relations have altered considerably. People are identified by House names which reflect the activities, occupations, and lineage of generations of occupants. The names of streets and different areas of the village refer to historic events and personalities that are part of Deià's past. These familial and community linkages have been gradually rearranged to promote current aspirations while maintaining the idea of life as the interaction of the generations.[7]

Vatican II and post-Franco democracy have greatly altered the religious rituals associated with ceremonial occasions but the celebrations continue to reaffirm familial and community ties. In Deià today, both religious and calendrical rituals mark locality and other aspects of community identity. The structured forty-hour work week has made every weekend a celebration instead of the periodicity associated with church festivals. Religious services have become celebrations of the community. Heightened social life once associated with the sacred has become more secular and matter of fact. The sacred has become popularised and membership in the religious community is another expression of identity.

By using the categories of Deianenc-Estranger, the local population is expressing symbolic boundaries. Insiders are those who understand the meanings behind the symbols. The concepts of insiders and outsiders are based on a perceived social distance between those who understand one another through a common language, traditional associations, shared knowledge, and experience, and those who lack these qualities. The insiders maintain an image of a traditional people in a traditional setting and an ethos of continuity and timelessness. This image is an effective device behind which changing attitudes and material acquisitions can be assimilated. Insiders have drawn ideas and practices from the outside for many years. By marking at least some parts of their social life as unchanging and invariant, they have been able to respond to innovation and change by bringing the changes inside their homes and families without disrupting the appearance of the social order.[8]

Rather than collapsing under pressure or giving up their culture and community to outsiders, Deianencs have found ways to resist total change by revitalising their own cultural heritage within the changed conditions brought on by the continuous presence of outsiders. By maintaining a semblance of traditional life they retain a sense of continuity, a personal and social security based on previous generations' experiences.[9] Changes in ideas, values, attitudes, and behaviour can be understood in terms of generations, as Lison (1983) has so well documented for Galicia, but I believe that what we find in Deià is not clear differences from one generation to another but rather a sharing, a borrowing between generations, a reinterpretation in new terms of their combined history. The current generation could not be as independent as they have become without the infrastructure provided by their parents and the state. Young people are not turning away from the previous generation; they are drawing on the emotional support of parents and grandparents and invigorating the present with their renewed appreciation of the past. A life cycle marks not just individual growth but stages in the process of socialisation. In Deià we find the generations crossing, separating, informing, reintegrating over time.

The village has prospered and been able to evolve new attitudes and aspirations within the time-honoured institutions of marriage, home, and family. Women and men pursue careers, education and recreation are given high priorities. Deianencs have developed a secure framework on which to base their future and have learned to appreciate the past as the source and legitimation of their community. They want to reclaim the material symbols of that past before they are completely lost. Landownership, once the basis for social status, the source of life and individual identity, has become a commodity sold to the highest bidder. Deianencs identify those who belong and remind everyone else that belonging cannot be purchased; that no matter how much foreign wealth one invests in Deià, no one can buy the birthright that only Deianencs share with all the generations before them.

This assertion of solidarity may be short-lived. At the current rate of inflated property values, locals cannot afford to buy houses in their own village, and heirs to a Deià property will not be able to afford to keep the house in the family as they once did. The shares will be too high for any one sibling to buy out the others. Many of the oldest Deianencs are widows or widowers who have no children. Their heirs are their godchildren or other relations who often live outside the village, and it is likely that these heirs will prefer to sell the houses they inherit to the highest bidder, who may well be a foreigner. To try to balance this, the village has begun a project to build sixteen subsidised flats which can be purchased by Deianenc first-time buyers. There are already far too many names on the waiting list and the manner of selection has not been decided. However, it seems clear that the largest houses in the village are or will be owned by foreigners.

Deià has become one of the most popular and at the same time expensive resorts on the island of Mallorca. This may be the result of the symbiosis of insiders and outsiders who over the last century learned to complement the separate interests of each and gain the full advantage of their respective goals. It is also due to outside developers and local officials working together to exploit the very qualities people associate with Deià and to sell them to the highest bidders. Insiders are those who want to maintain the 'ethos of a traditional village' while opening the way for more investment that will produce jobs, housing, and livelihoods for their children and grandchildren. Some outsiders want to maintain their existence in paradise by halting change while others have begun to participate in the changes. Is there a means to encompass the realities of progress with the ideals of paradise?

Notes

1. Edwin Ardener has written a great deal about remote areas. I refer here to his suggestions that 'the age of discovery showed us that the remote was actually compounded of imaginary as well as real places, yet they were all of equal conceptual reality or unreality before the differences were revealed. A place is remote to those who have not been there, but to those within it is just another place' (in Chapman [ed.] 1989).
2. Valuable anthropological research on Spain has been done by British, American, Spanish, Dutch, Swedish, Portuguese, and researchers of many other nationalities. I have cited only the works most relevant to the issues under discussion.
3. Until the 1950s, large landowners divided their various properties among their children. The males were always bequeathed the agricultural and productive lands while the girls were often given large sea-front properties. These areas were not particularly valuable and were seen to provide a backup for the women who often married the sons of other landowners. In the late 1950s, large foreign companies offered vast sums for these coastal properties and many Mallorquin women held large amounts of capital which allowed them to assume important economic power in the early years of tourism.
4. Pitt-Rivers noted that 'Tensions of the internal structure are projected outside the group where they serve as an exterior threat, to strengthen the group's solidarity' (1954:29).
5. Maurice Bloch's interview in *Anthropology Today* (vol. 4, no. 1, February 1988) suggests that the 'exotic' only exists in remote areas of the world. I believe that this study of Deià as well as many of the articles in the *Journal of Social Anthropology of Oxford,* Michaelmas 1988; R.T. Antoun 1968, Bestard 1986, and many other European ethnographies, show that even the most complex and

cosmopolitan societies have developed 'exotic' forms of communication which warrant specialised anthropological studies.

6. Anthony Cohen recognised a similar phenomenon in his work on Whalsay, a fishing village in Britain. He writes that 'the changed nature of things is masked by the retention of the symbolic expressions in idioms derived from their historical character' (1982:35).
7. This has been expressed over and over again in the literature on Spain: i.e., Ortega y Gasset, Brenan, Paul, Atholl, Thomas, Lison Tolosana, Pitt-Rivers, Kenny, Brandes, et. al.
8. This phenomenon is not new. Hugh Thomas described Spain in his classic study of the Civil War as follows: 'Isolated by good fortune and by geography from the so-called "world's game" of European and great power rivalry since 1818, it has more lessons to offer other people than it has to learn: above all it has grasped more successfully than other nations the art of combining progress with the persistence of tradition' (1961:x).
9. Abner Cohen's discussion of what I have called selective tradition is useful here: 'Some patterns of symbolic action can be survivals from the past and others called traditions are of recent origin and others are being continuously created for new or old purposes' (1974:36).

1. The Realities of Paradise

The setting of Deià has been described by scribes, poets, and travel writers as 'a paradise imbued with magic and mystery'. In reality, the municipality of Deià extends over 1,511 hectares (151 square kilometres). It is the fifth smallest of the fifty-two municipalities on the island of Mallorca.[1] Mallorca is the largest of the Balearic Islands, which include Menorca, Ibiza, Formentera, Cabrera, and a number of tiny uninhabited islets. The Balearics form a province made up of all the islands of this archipelago, but each of the islands has its own history and characteristics. The Balearics are an autonomous region of the Spanish nation since 1980.

Deià is on the mountainous northwest coast of the island, twenty-eight kilometers from Palma, which is the largest city and capital. It is in the northern Sierras, known as *Serra de Tramuntana* (Mountain of the North Wind), a Jurassic limestone mountain range running from northeast to southwest along the western coast of the island. The village of Deià is situated in the valley below the mountain known as *Es Teix* (after the yew tree, *Taxus baccata*). Surrounded on three sides by mountains and on the west overlooking the Mediterranean, Deià lies between Valldemossa (nine kilometres to the south) and Soller (nine kilometres to the north) on the main Palma road, which winds through the mountains along the precipitous coastline to Deià, then turns and bends through the mountains to Soller.

Commencing at the 1,365 metre height of the Teix is the *Torrente Major* (major stream), which cascades from October to April through the valley where the nucleus of the village lies and down a narrow gorge to the cove below. Other springs flow into the torrente along its course and provide Deià with an abundance of water most of the year. Access to this water is more complicated as all water rights are privately owned. The almost constant heat of the summer months begins to cool in September and occasional rains fall through March. The Mallorquins have replaced the Catalan word *tardor* (autumn) with two springs: *primavera d'estiu* (spring of summer, September–November) and *primavera d'hivern* (spring of winter, December–February), and all assure one that winter does not exist in Mallorca. The winter is short – lasting two or three months – and the temperature seldom goes below 0° C (Bonner 1980).

From the pine and oak forests on the surrounding mountains the descending landscape is covered by olive, carob, almond, fig, pear, plum, orange, and lemon trees growing along terraces supported by dry stone walls. Between the trees, vegetables are grown, and water flows from the reservoirs built at varying intervals to catch the flow of water from the mountains.

The village church and cemetery rise above the valley on a hill, *Es Puig*, 211 meters above the sea. Stone houses with ceramic tiled roofs, wooden shuttered windows, surrounded by vines and gardens, are clustered together along the hillside that borders the main road and descends into the valley below. Large *fincas* (farming estates), some with watchtowers, can be seen within the forests above the road and dot the landscape at various points along the cliffs above the sea.

The paved highway runs through the village, past the hamlet of Llucalcari, and on to Soller. Smaller paved roads wind up the mountainside, circle the church, and descend into the lower parts of the village. Dirt roads lead to the more isolated farms. The cove can be reached by a rocky footpath or down the hairpin-curved, paved road.

Enclosed by mountains on three sides and open to the sea on the fourth, Deià is subject to remarkably different weather conditions from those in Palma, Valldemossa, and Soller. Frequent winds from distinct directions are common and the Mallorquin *vuit vents*[2] (eight winds) are well known by all who live in the village.

The People

The population of Deià in the latter part of the nineteenth century was about 900 inhabitants. The developed area of Deià, which is considered the village proper, occupies only a small portion of the municipality, and until 1930 over half of the population lived and worked on the outlying fincas. Agriculture was the main occupation and cultivations included olives, carobs, grape vines, and fruit trees. The five shopkeepers, three café owners, three barbers, five ironmongers, five fisherman, and two carpenters working in the village, and charcoal-makers, woodcutters, and lime-makers who lived seasonally in the surrounding mountains, all combined agricultural work with these activities (Salvador 1955).

Today, only one of the eighteen olive presses that processed the olives into oil, once the main livelihood of the village, is still operative. In many areas of the village the olives are left to fall from the trees or be eaten by birds. The mule carts once driven by singing drivers as they moved from one area of the village to another transporting charcoal, crates of olives, sacks of lemons or carobs have been replaced by unmuffled motorbikes, cars, and coaches as local traffic has become completely motorised. But the rushing of the stream, the singing of birds, and the sound of the wind through the trees is still discernible despite the noise of modern transport and technology.

The 1993 census lists the resident population as 562 persons. Four hundred thirty-one are Spanish (58 percent were born in Deià, 28 percent in other parts of Mallorca, and 14 percent are from the peninsula), and the other 131 are foreigners, many of whom live on retirement or other forms of income from abroad. Twenty-eight percent of the Spanish are retired, 19 percent work or sell goods outside the village, and 53 percent live from work in Deià. Of these 53 percent, 15 percent work in agriculture, 12 percent work in industry or crafts, and the other 26 percent work in the service sector (hotels, cafés, bars, restaurants, transport, housekeeping, caretaking, gardening, construction, etc.).

The Deianencs speak Mallorquí, a dialectal variant of the Catalan language, which preserves many aspects of early literary Catalan, and was the language spoken by all classes on the island from the time of the conquest by combined forces of Catalans, Aragonese, Genoese, and troops from Southern France in 1229 AD until 1717 when the *Nueva Planta*, a royal decree, abrogated the Catalan constitution and Mallorca was declared a territory of the Spanish Crown. From that date until Franco's death in 1975, Spanish (Castilian) was the official language of the nation. Nevertheless, Mallorquí was spoken among the locals in rural villages despite the declaration by the Civil Governor of the Provence in 1939, which stated that 'only in the intimacy of one's home can regions preserve their own dialect, the street belongs to the state, the school belongs to the state, offices and commercial life are also of the state'. Local languages and dialects were kept alive in the villages throughout this long period.

Foreigners were always spoken to in Spanish, and it was extremely difficult to convince Mallorquins that one was really interested in their language. I spoke Spanish when I arrived in 1959, and it was quite difficult to convince the locals over the years that I was interested in learning to speak Mallorquí. Hearing it in the shops and cafés one gained some understanding, but it was only when my children began to speak it with neighbours and friends that I too was allowed to share in the conversations. Most mainland Spaniards who have lived in the village for some time and especially those married to Deianencs speak some Mallorquí. Three adult foreigners and most of the foreign children that have been born in the village or have lived there any length of time speak Mallorquí, especially since it has begun to be taught as a second language in the schools.[3]

Many Deianencs over forty learned French while visiting or working in France, from relatives, or at school. A few Deianencs under forty speak English, which they learned mostly from British and American friends with whom they were brought up in the village. Younger students are now learning English at school, practicing with local friends and summer visitors. German has been learned by a few who work in the German-owned hotels in the village. Teenage girls, who might once have gone to France to help relatives in their businesses or with domestic chores and learned the language while working, are now visiting foreign friends in Germany or England and taking language courses. This change in focus on learning different languages reflects the impact of the outside on the inside over the years. A language learned for economic reasons made it possible to welcome foreigners in Deià and has become a social and political asset over time.

Background

The Balearic Islands lie northeast by southwest, midway along the western reaches of the Mediterranean. Mallorca is 167 kilometres from the Catalan coast of Barcelona and equidistant from the south coast of France (315 kilometres to the north), the island of Sardinia (320 kilometres to the east) and the north African coast (310 kilometres to the south). With an area of 3,740 square kilometres Mallorca is the largest of the Balearic Islands.

The geographical location of the island is interesting in its relationship to the mainland. The individual islands form a series of stepping stones that would have allowed early navigators to sail easily from one island to another by means of landfall navigation without ever losing sight of land. Braudel describes the effect on the Balearic Islands of their strategic location in relation to the outside world:

> The Balearic Islands have always been of considerable importance; an entire shipping sector revolved around them.... That the sea surrounds islands and cuts them off from the rest of the world more effectively than any other environment is certainly true whenever they are situated outside the normal sea routes. But when they are integrated into shipping routes, and for one reason or another (often external and quite gratuitous reasons) become one of the links in a chain, they are on the contrary actively involved in the dealings of the outside world.... (1975:149)

The prehistory and history of the islands highlight commerce, conquests, the defeat of some invaders, and the occupation of the island by diverse foreign groups who laid claim to the territory over the centuries. It is presently believed that prehistoric human arrival on the islands occurred around 5000 B.C.E., but earlier evidence may be found as excavations continue around the islands (Waldren 1982). According to Pericot (1972) some of the earliest written references to the Balearics appear in texts by Diodorus, Polybius, and Strabo written in the early centuries C.E. Diodorus wrote that

> Mercenaries were recruited from *Gymnasia* by the Carthaginians for their campaigns on Sicily. The Greeks called the islands *Gymnasiae* because the inhabitants went unclad in the summer time but the native and the Romans named them *Balearides* from the fact that they hurl large stones with their slings, the best of all mankind.

The name *Baliares* was first used by Polybius in the second half of the second century. This seems to be the rendering of the native name, and may be derived from the Greek *Balein*, meaning to throw from a sling, or the Basque, *balar*, a sling-thrower. Strabo wrote that

> It is said that 'gymnetes-light armed foot soldiers' are called 'balearides' by the Phoenicians, and that on this account the Gymnasias were called Balearides.

Balearic sling-throwers were included among the mercenaries Hannibal enlisted from all over Hispània, when preparing his campaign in the second Punic War. They protected Mallorca from conquest until 123 B.C.E., when Cecilius Metallus managed to defend his ships from the stones of the islanders' slings by covering them with skins. This practice of slinging survived well into the sixteenth century: twenty *balisteros* (slingers) are among the men of arms noted in the census of Deià taken in 1585 (Pons 1976). In 1593, Binimelis wrote that

> Accuracy of aim was inculcated into the very young by the heads of households who followed the practice of lodging a boy's daily rations of food in the high branches of a tree, leaving him to bring it down by sling and stone or go hungry. (Pericot 1972:16)

The history of Mallorca for several centuries under the Romans was a tranquil one; the land underwent remarkable development and foundations were laid for roads, agriculture, and industry. During the Roman occupation, Christianity spread, as is documented by historical accounts, some inscriptions, and the remains of early Christian churches.

In 426 C.E., Vandals plundered the islands and, in 483 C.E., the Balearics formed a province as a dependency of the governor of Sardinia. They were again invaded in the sixth century by Byzantine forces. Together with reconquered Spanish territories and Ceuta they were formed into a second Mauritanian province. St. Isadore and other texts of the period use the names *Maiorica* and *Miniorica*, but others call the islands the *Aphro-disiades*, a name derived from ancient Greek (ibid.).

There is an account of the first Moslem that plundered the island in 707 C.E., but Rossello Bordoy (1968) maintains that the Balearics were not annexed by the Caliphate of Cordoba until the beginning of the tenth century. During the next three hundred years, various houses of Moslem rulers controlled Mallorca. The name of *ad-daya* (see below) appears on the eleventh century records of Moslem territories. The text by Abi Bahr al-Zuhri, written sometime in the twelfth century, gives some idea of island life at that time:

> This island is well nourished by products from its lands, but the inhabitants do not know the fruit of the olive, except imported ones, and they have few figs. They cultivate cotton and linen, but are unacquainted with silk or its products, except for what they import from Andalucia and Syria. They have many sheep, and goats are few in number. They have many bulls, cows, horses and mules. On this island there are no wolves and the sheep can wander freely without a shepherd.... (Barcelo 1975:6)

This medieval period on Mallorca is referred to in the literature as 'the dark ages' as there has been little research done on the Moslem occupation of the islands during this period. There are enigmas concerning the Arabisation or Islamisation of the Mallorquin populace and many questions to be asked about the survival of Christianity during this period. Based on studies from mainland Spain, where the rapid Moslem occupation was followed by the accession to Islam of large numbers of the population, we see that those that became Moslems did not do so out of fear or threat of violence. We can assume, then, that forced conversion to Islam or persecution of non-Moslems was not a feature of the Arab occupation of Spain. Those who did not convert from Christianity or Judaism to Islam became known as *Mozarabs* and continued to adhere to their former faiths which they were allowed to practice, while becoming loyal subjects to the Moslem rulers (Lourie 1970:644). This would seem to suggest that there was some cooperation among the indigenous people and the conquerors. Certainly, on Mallorca, the names of some of the villages (i.e., Binisalem, Binibeca, and Valldemossa, which derives from *Wade Musa* or valley of the muse), the vast irrigation systems, the forms of cultivation, the instruments of tillage, the draw wells and reservoirs, as well as some of the melodies sung by peasants in the fields are survivals from the Moslem period which continue in use today.

Conquests

Mallorca's early history was marked by a series of colonisations which ended in the thirteenth century when King James I of Aragon (Spain itself was not yet a united country) conquered the island and eradicated any vestiges of previous rule. Between 1229 and 1231 C.E. the history of the Mallorquin society begins. It is a story of conquest and a colonisation that immediately generated a series of problems and contradictions that seemed insoluble for the conquerors and, in time, have strongly conditioned the Mallorquin historic process in specific ways. Until the mid-twentieth century, an exceedingly large landless peasant sector (70 percent of the population) was subject to the inflexible dominion of large landowners and religious pressure for social control (Soto 1982).

The conquest of Mallorca had the character of a business venture aimed at economic and political expansion. Each of the participants received a portion of land commensurate with the risks taken (Segura i Salado 1979). After the King's portion, the next largest went to Nuño Sanç, Count of Rossellon and Sardinia, and included ten of the largest areas on the island among which was Valldemossa. Within Valldemossa was the hamlet called Ad-daya, more or less the same size as today's municipality.

The name of the village is of uncertain etymology. *Aldea* and *alqueria* are the Castilian and Catalan words for a grange, farm, or hamlet, generally a good distance from neighbours. The name appears in Moorish records from the eleventh to the thirteenth centuries as *ad-daya* or *ad-deya*. In Arabic *ad* means 'the' in combination with certain letters and *daya or deya* means a small village or hamlet. It has been suggested that the name stems from the Latin name Didius or Didianum, and in some Latin documents the name appears as Deiàno. Another suggestion is that it derived from an Arab lineage called Deya or Daya that might have owned this area before the Catalan conquest. In records from the Moslem occupation, there were two other small villages called Ad-daya on the island and one in Menorca. The most likely explanation is that the Catalan-speaking conquerors kept the Arabic descriptive terms and used them as a proper name, adding the Catalan descriptive term, Aldea. The whole name Aldea Ad-daya, was probably shortened to the name Deià or Deya (Catalan or Spanish) sometime in the fourteenth century.

Nuño Sanç distributed the land of Ad-daya among certain persons who had helped him in the conquest in exchange for their creating a village and paying an annual rent consisting of one quarter of the produce collected from the land. In 1239 Sanç founded the monastery of St. Bernard of the Royal in Palma and gave the rights over the rents from Ad-daya to the Cistercian monks.

The monks sent a representative to oversee their interests, organise the properties, legalise sales and purchases, and administer justice. This representative was given the title *Batle* (Mayor). His ample powers conflicted with the powers of the royally appointed Batle of Valldemossa under whose jurisdiction Ad-daya had been included by royal charters. During the thirteenth to fifteenth centuries, the workers of Deià provided most of the taxes paid by Valldemossa to the General Council of the Catalan-Aragonese Federation. The conflicts between the monks, the Valldemossa landowners, and the workers from Deià continued for centuries, and people from Valldemossa are still referred to as *pagès amb corbates* (peasants who wear ties and consider themselves gentlemen).

Some historians describe the monks as feudal lords, men who ceded portions of land on conditions of vassalage or homage, but the Mallorquin form of land control has been referred to by most local historians as a *senyorial* regime rather than a truly feudal system because it involved mercantile as well as agricultural interests (P. Montaner 1975; J. Portella 1979; Moll i Suau 1986).

These monks were the true founders of Deià. They owned the entire area of Deià including the hamlet called Llucalcari and Miramar in Valldemossa. In apportioning the land they attracted people to settle there permanently, ceded land by contracts to managers and workers, and gave the people who had been under Moorish rule an opportunity to work their own parcels of land toward the purchase of their freedom.

Present day land tenure is still based on the systems established at that time. Lands were granted in *alodio* (from the Latin *allodium*, a possession not held by tenure to a superior lord) and *emphyteusis* (permanent rights over land use in exchange for annual payment).The alodio was introduced in the thirteenth century by Jaime I to encourage repopulation and cultivation of neglected lands. Owners could rent their lands for minimal sums and indefinite periods to whoever was willing to cultivate them. The rentee could sell his rights to that land at any figure commensurate with his improvements to and investments in the property and its current market value. The owner retained the right to a slight increase in rent *un laudemio* (5½ percent) from the new tenants each time the property rights were sold. This form of contract is still operative and has benefited the tenant rather than the landowners as rental properties change hands for vast sums and the owner receives only the stipulated percentage.[4] In both alodio and emphiteusis, it seems use and usufruct were transferable. There was strict control over the land, which made the peasant dependent on his landlord. This was not, however, a dependence that limited his personal liberty; rather it pre-empted his potential for expansion or ownership of land held by senyors.

Those who owned or held lands in alodio or emphyteusis usually hired a manager or tenant farmer to oversee the work, hire labourers, and be in charge of the lands. Various forms of contracts were made and personally negotiated on St. Michael's Day (September); payment was both in money and kind and the arrangement involved a series of rights and obligations on the part of both parties along classic patron-client lines. Five- to eight-year contracts (the most common contracts were for six years or six harvests) stipulated the conditions of land usage. Payment procedures were based on *censos* (a fixed sum to be paid each year for the use of land) or *àmitges* (contracts for the use of lands with products, gains or losses from cultivation being divided in half with the landlord) (Segura i Salada 1979; Pons 1976; Rossello Vaquer 1980). Those who rented the land were responsible for hiring daily workers and supervising them. The hierarchal structure of social relations was clearly established. Senyors lived between the village and the city, were exempt from taxes, and acquired their livelihood from the labour of others. Among the *pagésia* (peasants)[5] there were those who managed the lands (*els amos*) and those hired by the year (*missatges*) or on a daily basis (*jornalers*). At the lowest end of the social scale were lime and charcoal-makers and wheat-growers (*roters*), who worked, seasonally, on the poorest lands high up the mountainside.

During the late thirteenth century, more olive trees were planted in many parts of the island and especially on the mountainous areas of Valldemossa and Deià. Negotiable cultivations supplanted subsistence farming (small land-holdings producing enough for an extended family), and wheat, olive, and grape cultivation replaced those crops which needed irrigation. Dry stone-wall terracing was extended throughout the area.

The prosperity of the islands during the thirteenth and fourteenth centuries was due precisely to the fact that the interests of the city and the country not only coincided but complemented one another. From the land came a great deal of what the city marketed. The connection was not only economic but also political. The judges of the city held jurisdiction over all of the island and any conflicts of interest between the rural peasant classes (*pagés i minestrals)* and the city residents (*ciutadans i cavallers*) were dealt with by these judges (Quadrado 1930).

Agriculture was the source of the island's wealth but, although it was the labour of the rural workers that provided that wealth, most of it went to the landowners, senyors, and nobles, who lived in the city of Palma. The workers received only a miserable daily wage. There was a great deal of lending and borrowing among the workers in Deià when it came time to pay the censos and other taxes imposed by the King, the Church, the landowners, and Valldemossa.

Problems were exacerbated each year when the city-based nobles and senyors (exempt from taxes themselves through royal decree), sent Jewish 'bankers', known as *Chuetas,*[6] to collect funds from the rural workers toward the repayment of *censals*. Censals were loans made to the city administration by large property owners, clerics, and rich Catalans resident in Palma. The interest on the amount loaned was guaranteed to be paid each year and this continuously increased the tax burden on the rural workers. The city relied on the country workers to repay these loans, although they derived little or no benefit from them. As taxes increased, anger and resentment against the city grew stronger and was directed at the Jews who were referred to as the King's treasure-keepers.

They were important to the economic life of the islands and generously provided with privileges. They handled precious metals and were often accused of false coinage. In 1391 labourers from all over the island descended on the Jewish quarter in Palma and attacked the residents.

There were two more attacks on the city by rural workers during the fifteenth century. Then, in 1521, the revolts known as the *Germanias* (The Brotherhood Revolts) began. The Germanias, often represented as a social revolution of workers against feudal oppressors, were fought to alleviate grain shortages and ecclesiastic powers and to combat the injustices of tax exemptions granted to the *Mascarats*, who were the privileged nobles, large property owners, managers, and ecclesiastics who caused the peasants to bear the major tax burdens. The wealthy and powerful men in Deià at this time were among those called Mascarats.

During their brief control of the island, a cabinet formed of thirteen *Germanets* (Brothers) cancelled all interests due on the censals. As a result of the Germanias, taxes were restructured according to wealth instead of the arbitrary way they had been in the past. Taxes on necessities, such as wine, meat, cloth, salt, and the milling of wheat into flour, were removed. Just two years later, in 1523, the Germanets were conquered by forces sent from Catalonia by Charles V and the social reforms and tax adjustments were immediately reversed.

Thirty percent of the island's population was lost in the fighting and, with the plague that same year, village populations suffered even greater losses. Deià was not as badly affected as other villages, some of which lost as much as 50 percent of their populace. An icon of *Sant Sebastian* (made by L'Adria) was donated to the church of Deià in gratitude for their being saved while so many in the neighbouring villages of Valldemossa and Soller died (Rossello Vaquer 1980). This wooden sculpture still stands in the Deià church and continues to be the focus of prayers for the health of family members.

The monks, who continued to dominate all aspects of Deià life, moulded the moral, religious, and material values of the early inhabitants. They established a monastery in their mountain retreat of *Ca l'Abat* (House of the Abbot), which is located on the outskirts of the village, and called it *Monasterio del Santisima Virgen Maria* after their patron. They also established the three devotions that are still dominant in Deià today: Santisima Virgen Maria, Sant Bernardo and Ramon Llull.[7]

Celebrations on St. Bernard's day have taken place at Ca l'Abat every year since the thirteenth century. In 1497 a small church was established on *Es Puig*, the highest hill in the center of Deià, with St. John the Baptist

(Sant Joan Bautista) as the patron of the village. However, it was subject to the whims of Valldemossa and its priests until 1883 when the Deià church became independent and could have its own priest in residence to perform regular masses, baptisms, marriages, and funerals.

Between 1450 and 1500 finca owners ran into economic difficulties and were forced to sell off large land-holdings to pay debts. These properties became investment sources for urban merchants. The term *possessió* was used to describe these new properties. A possessió was a large portion of agricultural land owned by one person but part of a larger complex known as a finca. The finca was an entire estate and could be divided into a number of possessios. Isabel Moll writes that 'the possessió was the unit of production of the economic structure of the island during the fifteenth to the nineteenth centuries' (1985:8).

Deià formed part of the *Universitat* (separate administrative entity or corporation) of Valldemossa. Deianencs paid the major portion of taxes received by Valldemossa and were described by a city notary of the period as 'rich people who lived very well' (Segura i Salado 1977:4). Of the 178 persons that had to pay taxes in 1570, only 52 or 29.21 percent were from Deià; but those Deianenc taxpayers contributed 55.53 percent of the total taxes. Without the Deià taxes Valldemossa would have been in a sorry state. Most of the fincas in Valldemossa were owned by persons exempt from taxes or by men who resided outside the village. The taxes on these properties were paid by the finca workers to the owner's place of residence rather than to Valldemossa (Segura i Salado 1977:7).

In Deià the acquisition of extensive properties and the extension of water to these properties allowed the monks to improve the lands and reap the rewards. However, the monastery contributed nothing to the costs of maintaining the village. Exempt from *tallas* (taxes levied by the village), the monastic holdings were a great preoccupation to the people of Deià who saw themselves as *quatre pobres* (four poor ones). Between censos (yearly rentals on agricultural land) censals (yearly payments on loans), tallas, and water negotiations, everyone in Deià was contributing to the Cistercian synod (Pons 1976).

Deià, no more than a hamlet, had no powers to counteract the injustices they suffered from the city, the Valldemossans, and the monks. Deià finally gained its independence from Valldemossa by a royal decree in 1583: 'A handful of earth was spread about the area of Deià and an unsheathed sword, for cutting trees and as a symbol of true possession, was handed over to the new Deià Council by the King's representative' (ibid.). The newly formed Council was made up of the major landholders in

Deià. In the 1570 census Jaume Rullan, Mayor of Deià is listed as 'the richest man in the Universitat de Valldemossa', and councillor Joanot Mas Roig of Es Moli in Deià, is the 'ninth richest' (ibid.).

At the first meeting of the Deià Council the members decided to buy wheat and dispense it through the City Hall 'to assure provisions for those who can't get to the city to negotiate for themselves'. Although this action was presented as a way of showing consideration for those who had less than themselves, it was, at the same time, a means to keep out middlemen. This is a vivid example of the control these landowners assumed over every aspect of village life. Control of production and employment through the ownership of land, often a result of inheritance or seniorial rights to rents, made possible the continued domination by these landed senyors for generations to come.

Water rights, which were held by those who owned the estates where the springs originated, had to be negotiated. Promises were made and often broken, and the spring that supplies the area of Llucalcari with water is still referred to as *Ses Mentides* (the lies). The spring was the subject of disputes over water from 1480 to 1583 between the inhabitants of Son Coll, on one side, and those of Llucalcari, on the other. Even today, there are regular disputes over water. All water rights in Deià are privately owned by the heirs to fincas or by those who have acquired rights to them as heirs to the tenant farmers who ran the fincas where the springs commence.

During the sixteenth through the eighteenth centuries, corsairs (Barbary pirates representing Turkey, Algiers, or Morocco) and pirates who held no allegiance to any country were assaulting the coastal areas of Mallorca. Watchtowers were built on the large estates, next to the church and on the prominent points along the sea cliffs so that knowledge of approaching ships could be quickly passed on to villages. 'Smoke by day and fire by night' were the means of sending signals. Deià was a common stopping place and there are many stories still told to the young today about the sacking of houses and the abduction of a village woman who was never seen again. A favourite threat to small children is 'be good or the Moors will come and take you away'.

While the Moors, corsairs, and pirates were greatly feared and posed a constant threat, the *bandoleros* (highwaymen) were referred to by the people as *es pan nostra de cada dia* (providers of sustenance to the poor). These highwaymen were heroes to the peasants, who revelled in the stories of riches being taken from the grand estates and distributed among the poor. These difficult years were made all the worse for the population of landless peasants by the incorporation of Mallorca into the Spanish state in 1715. Philip V issued an edict known as the *Nueva Planta* (1717) in which he revoked all the *fueros*[8] held by Catalonia, the Balearic Islands, and Valencia. Moreover, it brought to an end the Catalan constitution and revoked the right to speak the Catalan language and to practice its customs. Town and country were more divided than ever before. Peasants were not only subject to the dominance of the senyorial classes but the Spanish state now imposed further obligations, including taxation and conscription.

During the eighteenth century, the Cistercian monastery acquired most of the large fincas that had been built during the fourteenth through sixteenth centuries in Deià. Heirs of those who had acquired and developed these properties met with difficulties during the latter years of the seventeenth century. Outstanding censos, taxes, and poor crops had caused them to incur large debts which could only be met by selling some of their holdings. In 1778 *La Real Sociedad Economica Mallorquina de Amigos del Pais* (The Royal Economic Society of Friends of Mallorca) was established to give advice on agricultural, commercial, and industrial matters. It was also to provide loans for land purchase or anything else that might contribute to the growth and welfare of the island (Salvador 1959:136).[9]

The *Ley de Cortes*, issued on 20 October 1820, deprived monastic orders and other non–tax-paying persons of dominion over any Spanish lands. This was intended to raise needed funds for the new Spanish State and to break the aristocratic and church monopoly on land-ownership. In 1821 Ca l'Abat and all of its properties were auctioned; only tax-paying citizens were permitted to bid, clearly excluding *manos muertas* (dead hands or persons who were exempt from taxes). A Palma businessman bought four of the largest fincas in Deià and one in Valldemossa (Ca l'Abat, *Son Canals*, *Son Bauça* and *Sa Torre*). However, Ferdinand VII, on the throne again after a three-year absence, rescinded the law and decreed that everything enacted by the Constitutional Government from 1820 to 1823 was null and void. All the Deià lands belonging to the monastery before 1820 were reclaimed. Finally, in 1835 convents of less than twenty-four members were dissolved and their goods turned over to the government.

In 1851 the *desmortizaçión* laws decreed that those who had purchased or reclaimed ecclesiastic properties could keep them in *tuta conscientia.* Inheritance by the *hereu* (primogenitor) was outlawed under these laws and the practice of partiple inheritance began. Despite the new law, in Deià and other parts of the island estate owners found ways to keep their properties intact. One strategy was to leave the largest properties to one's grandson. The primogenitor would remain the guardian of this property until his son became of age. Smaller mountain properties and less valued coastal lands would be distributed among the other siblings. In this manner, the property remained in the same family for at least three generations (Moll 1979). In some cases, *parcel.las* (portions) of smaller properties were sold off to local peasants in order to raise funds to buy sons out of the army or pay debts from poor investments. These parcel.las became small domestic properties where the *casa* (house) was the unit of residence and production. Although most of these early peasant landowners had to combine work on the fincas with the maintenance of their own lands, this period saw the beginning of change in the island's social and agricultural patterns.

Peasant producers planted more commercial crops and wine, almonds, vegetables, fruits, and potatoes were marketed by the small landowner along with the olives and carobs from the fincas. Some peasants (*pagés rics*) became rich through lending others money to make their yearly land payments (censos). When the borrower could not repay the loan, his small portion (parcel.la) of land would become the property of the lender. The borrower would then become an employee on the land he once owned (in emphyteusis). A new class of bosses, 'els amos' (managers), and another of 'pagés' (workers) developed within the peasant ranks.[10]

Contact

Economic activities in Deià were always part of the wider island and mainland networks. In 1767 olive oil (mostly from this mountain region) made up 89½ percent of the total Mallorquin exports. Textiles and fruit (especially citrus) began to be exported to France in 1820 by means of a steamship which travelled three times weekly between the neighbouring town of Soller and Sete, France.[11] Deià producers sent their fruits by middlemen or took them themselves by mule and cart to Soller. An epidemic in the 1860s, which destroyed a great deal of the orange and lemon crops in Deià and Soller, allowed Spanish mainland producers to move into the French market.

In 1872 the French wine crisis (all the vines were destroyed by phylloxera) brought about a great demand for Spanish wines. Deià developed viniculture during this period. When this demand declined at the end of the nineteenth century, almonds became the most exported product. Locally grown figs were eaten fresh or dry and fed to the pigs which were in great demand in Catalonia. Pigs, which were bred on the larger fincas, could be let loose in the forests to feed on acorns and carobs after which they would be transported to Palma and shipped to the mainland. Mallorca supplied major quantities of fruit, carobs, and pigs to mainland Spain and France during the last half of the nineteenth and well into the twentieth century. Soller and Deià were major producers of Mallorquin olive oil, which was a valuable trading commodity within the island. Oil producers were considered rich men. Oil was used not only for cooking, but also for light, soap, cleaning, medicinal purposes, lubricants, etc.

Soller continued to be the main market for Deià goods, and lasting relationships between Deià and the neighbouring villages were formed. If marriage partners could not be found in Deià, one looked toward Soller and then to more distant villages. Young women, usually from the plains of Mallorca, would be brought to Deià by the finca manager to help with the olive crop. They were housed on the fincas and paid in oil and some cash. There were dances and other social activities during the olive season, and when the girls (known as *gallufas*, female olive pickers) returned to their villages some had made *promèses* (promises to wed).

Books about travelling to Spain (and other European countries) were quite the vogue in the nineteenth century. Although references to Mallorca had been made earlier, the first complete book dedicated to the island by a foreign author was *Souvenir d'un voyage d'art à Majorque* by Laurens, a writer and artist from Montpellier. Published in 1840, it presented the wonders of Mallorca to a European audience. Framed as a story of a voyage, it presents philosophical reflections and personal confessions inspired by the beauty and calm he found. It painfully reminded George Sand of her previous winter there and is said to have prompted her to retrieve her notes from that trip and write *Un hiver à Majorque.* Sand and the composer Frédéric Chopin had come to the island for ninety-six days in 1838.

In her book Sand describes the Mallorquin people and their society in some detail. Although her observations are blurred by her personal reactions and the hostility she provoked from the people she met, her writing nevertheless reflects some aspects of nineteenth-century life on the island and should be included among the early tourist literature. She describes the difficulty in finding lodging and the formality of introduction: 'One has to carry letters of introduction and recommendation to twenty of the more important local personages who have been given several months warning, unless one can face the prospect of sleeping in the open air.' She empathises with the hopeless task of the peasant labourers 'trying to survive in Majorca where as throughout Spain corruption is still the ruling power'. She laments the lack of oxen, horses, cows, and fertilisers, and attributes the salvation of the Mallorquin peasant to 'the hog':

> It is entirely thanks to the hog that I could visit the island ... with the export of hogs, civilisation has made its impression on Majorca. A handsome steamer was bought in England, which weekly conveys two hundred pigs and a few passengers as well. (1848:38)

Throughout the book she implies that some outsiders have tried to civilise the Mallorquins, but that their efforts have been in vain. This perception of civilisation coming from the outside was shared by locals. Cabanyes, a Spanish author writing in 1837, points out the local response to the arrivals and departures of the steamship: 'the port is full of people rushing to see this new invention so seldom seen in this isolated land.' The arrival of the steamship seemed to give those who lived in the city a new form of entertainment. Vuiller, writing in 1893, notes that 'the pier was packed with people and horse-drawn carts were parading back and forth with no other apparent reason than to show off. There was light, colour and movement, a vibration of life in full beneath a blue sky and a city bathed in sun'.

George Sand describes the relationships she observed between nobles and their staff and the effects of parcellisation on the land:

> When one wonders how a rich Majorcan can spend his income in a country bare of all luxuries and temptation, the answer is found in the houseful of good for nothing loafers of both sexes, who occupy a wing of his mansion set aside for this purpose, and as soon as they have spent a year in his service, enjoy the right to be lodged, clothed and boarded for the rest of their lives. Those who wish to excuse themselves from this serfdom may do so by resigning certain benefits; but custom sanctions their continued morning visits to take chocolate with former comrades, and their sharing, like Sancho at Gamache's residence, in all the festivities of the household.... It happened, however, that certain rich Majorcan landowners, observing that their expenses were on the increase and their assets on the wane, decided on a remedy. They leased part of their estates to selected peasants on a life tenure, and wherever this measure was tried the earth which had hitherto seemed cursed with bareness, brought forth plenty ... and after

> a few years both contracting parties found their financial situation eased. (ibid., pp. 40–41)

Sand's attitudes and behaviour seem to have challenged every value sacred to Mallorquin society at the time. Her hosts apparently saw her as 'an adulteress, a pagan and an inept mother'.[12] A popular journalist of the time wrote that

> Sand, disillusioned in her search for the rustic ideals romanticised by Rousseau, wrote scathingly of the inhabitants of Mallorca. As she was one who received favours as dues, who publicly jeered at the faith and quaint customs of villagers, it should surprise no one that her house was avoided by most people and that she was pointed out as one accursed of God. To Majorcans any woman who dressed in trousers, smoked cigarettes, exposed her children to the fatal disease of her lover and, to top it all, never went to mass, was the devil's own handmaiden.... (Quadrado 1841)

Ferrá suggests that 'During their stay in the monastery a lively enmity sprang up between the foreigners [Sand and Chopin] and the Valldemossan peasantry. On Sunday mornings the peasants found a way to satisfy the 'glory of God' by banding together and making sure no one would sell the couple fish or eggs or vegetables save at outrageous prices. The slightest observation from the couple drew a – 'So, your worship does not want it?' – 'giving themselves the airs of a Spanish grandee' (1948). The locals were not unaccustomed to class distinctions but were offended by the lack of respect for God or man.

Luis Salvador of Austria,[13] descendant of one of Europe's oldest royal families, arrived on the island in 1867 under the guise of one 'Ludwig Graf von Neudorf' and checked 'discreetly' into one of the few inns in Palma. According to his diaries he travelled around the island by mule, spending nights in the open air or in a room of a *predio* (Castilian for 'rustic property') by the kind invitation of a peasant. He made notes and sketches everywhere he went. 'The presence of this young foreigner was noted by the people of the villages he visited, unaccustomed as they were to the sight of visitors; few would suffer the hardships that travelling incurred in those days...' (ibid.).

The Archduke returned to the island in his yacht *Nixe* five years later to purchase one of the most beautiful residences in Mallorca, Miramar, which is located between Deià and Valldemossa. Miramar was made famous in the thirteenth century by Ramon Llull and is linked with the richest spiritual heritage of the island. The Archduke then proceeded to purchase all the lands on either side of Miramar. 'He paid willingly and splendidly even when the smallest landowners asked double the value of their lands.' He restored, adorned, and enlarged Miramar, combining artefacts collected on his travels around the Mediterranean with those he discovered and purchased in Mallorca. Some additions had a definite Italian influence, especially in the north wing and along the west facade. He added a marble temple shrine in the garden and two lookouts with a panoramic view of the sea and mountains. From these lookout points can be seen the valley of Deià, the rocky peaks of the Teix behind it, the coastal hamlet of Llucalcari to the mountains of *Cap Gros* in Soller, the *Cavall Bernat*, the heights of *Balitx*, and the massive *Puig Major*. He had paths cut through the forest and along the cliffs to areas that opened onto views of sea and endless horizons. This and the other estates he bought along the coast (*Son Galceran, Son Gual, Son Marroig, Son Ferrandell, S'Estaca, Sa Pedrissa, Son Gallard,* and *Son Moragues*) led him to maintain a number of large households and staffs. He opened the first hospice on the island, *Ca'n Mado Pila*, where he provided travellers with bed and linen, wine and bread for three days. Some of the first guests in the Grand Hotel that opened in Palma in 1898 took excursions to Miramar. The new Palma-Valldemossa-Deià-Soller highway begun in 1905 brought a great many more visitors to the area and to the new inn.[14]

The Archduke's ethnographic interests led to the creation of the Museum of Agriculture and Industry at Son Moragues where foreign visitors could see the products of the island and their manufacture. Traveller, artist, natural scientist, writer, aristocrat, poet, and landlord, he found 'the splendid landscape filled with magic and poetry' and sought to 'ennoble' the past by gathering all the information he could about the islands. His seven-volume *Die Balearen* (The Balearics Described in Word and Picture, 1869) is a valuable catalogue resource for Mallorquin geography, archaeology, natural history, ethnology, history, legends, social and artistic life, and customs from the eighteenth to the twentieth century. His descriptions of activities which are no longer practiced is an invaluable record of those times. In recent times, the events and customs described have been imbued with symbolic value and used in the process of renewing Mallorquin identity.

The fact that the Archduke 'felt more at home in Mallorca than anywhere else in the world' is evident in his writings. From 1872 to 1913 he entertained royal and creative guests, some of whom later made literary and artistic contributions to the increasing number of works inspired by Mallorca, i.e., Gaston Vuiller, Rusiñol, Sargent, Ruben Dario, Unamuno, et al. There are a number of Deianenc men and women over eighty years of age who can recount stories of their encounters with the Archduke, and they especially remember the annual Sant Antonio festival when young people from all the villages in the area – Valldemossa, Deià, Soller, Biñaraitx and Fornalutx – were invited to a party at Miramar. The eccentricities of the man as well as the vast amount of food and drink made a great impression on these young people.

During the nineteenth and well into the twentieth century, the activities of the people of Deià and Valldemossa remained tied to the land – to the cultivation of the olive, fruit trees, pigs, and sheep. Within this complex structure of landowners, tenants, employees, and day labourers, land remained an important instrument of social dominance. The Archduke's acquisition of properties during this period was both beneficial and disruptive to owners and workers alike. There are conflicting opinions about his social, economic, and ecological contributions to the area. Some say that his purchase of the large estates and his refusal to allow trees to be cut down, birds to be hunted, or the fruits of the forests to be collected put many out of work and food. On the other hand, his acquisition of so many properties necessitated employing tenant farmers and the maintenance of many traditional social patterns and activities. His idiosyncratic behaviour and reputed practice of employing his *droit de signeur* are still part of local legend.

Prior to his arrival, day labourers, stone masons, small landowners and seasonal workers had begun to emigrate to the Americas. During the first half of the nineteenth century, the island had developed an active navigation industry with shipbuilding and commerce. Fruit, *sabo d'oli* (soaps made from the residue left after pressing the oil from the olive), *aiguadent* (liquor), *flasadas de llana* (woolen cloth), almond oil, and essence of orange blossoms for perfume were shipped regularly to South American ports. After 1868 the *febre d'or* (gold fever) attracted more men to South America and provided money which was reinvested in Mallorca. Banking, industrial development, the creation of mercantile companies and small businesses took precedence over investment in the countryside. Rural properties were sold to finance these new ventures. The impact of the Archduke's purchase of many of these properties on the social and economic relationships in Valldemossa and Deià is still evident today.

There has always been an ambiguous attitude toward strangers. No one could ever be sure that the stranger in his or her midst was not the bearer of good fortune. The Archduke expressed this when he wrote that

> The Mallorquins' innate good nature makes them all the more sensitive to those less fortunate than themselves. It is a question of honor for the Mallorquins to greet a stranger, and share with him the goodness and beauties of their island. All foreigners, even those completely unknown, represent welcome visitors.[15]

The struggle to overcome obstacles and adapt to circumstances is a theme that runs through the Mallorquin *Rondalles* (Myths and Legends) which were collected and published by the Archduke and then again by Mossen Alcover a few years later. This oral tradition, which was recorded verbatim by the Archduke, was altered by Alcover, a priest, who tried to clean up some of the more risqué language and thus lost some of the colloquialisms of the period. The language as recorded by the Archduke contains some of the richest collection of expressive words in Mallorquin. The *Rondalles* have been told to children through the ages but have been especially popularised these past ten years to provide a particular 'local heritage' for the islands. Island history has been highlighted in contrast to Spanish history since the Balearic Islands have become an autonomous region within the Spanish nation.

Padre Ginard points out in his analysis of the *Rondalles* that there are many themes that are not particularly Mallorquin and were most probably from foreign sources and assimilated by the local culture. However, the origins of the symbols used to evoke local identity need not be verified in order to be accepted as relevant to the Mallorquin past. Many of the stories concern heroes who rise from humble origins to a higher destiny through the aid of strangers. The hero is often the youngest child in a family. On his route he must overcome obstacles and pass tests. Generally, he needs help and his benefactor comes disguised as an enigmatic, contradictory, or unvalued person: a stranger, a poor person, an old lady or man, a mother and baby, or as a giant, a bird, or a horse. By obliging these unconventional people or creatures the child finds the way to his goals, while the false hero (usually his elder brother) fails through impatience and arrogance (J. Grimalt 1975; Sabrafan 1982).

Perhaps the *Rondalles* can help us to understand the ease with which the Archduke was drawn into local life. He employed Deià people on the various farms he acquired where they saw aspects and styles of living they had never before observed or experienced. He bought properties to protect the trees from being cut down and allowed his forests to become thick and overgrown. He learned all about the way Mallorquins cultivated and cared for trees and forests, but he chose to have his lands less economically productive to retain what he considered the 'natural beauty' of the area. He was a senyor, and senyors had always done things differently from the labourers; that was their privilege.

The Archduke's extended stays and involvement in so many aspects of local life made the stranger in Valldemossa and Deià far less strange. The differences that at first perplexed and shocked locals were turned to admiration for a man who could contribute so much information on the Balearics and spread the image of the islands in different languages throughout Europe. He was given the title of *hijo adoptivo de Mallorca* (an adopted son of Mallorca) in 1878 and was appointed the first Honourary President of the *Fomento de Tourismo* when it began in 1909. As Enrique Lazaro noted:

> The eccentric Archduke was a gift from heaven, like the sea in Deià, the cliffs in Valldemossa or the rare fascination the landscape exercises over the imaginations of foreigners. In his writings, the Archduke reflected on the island life that helped him to forget the uncomfortable aristocratic trimmings he had left behind. He discovered like many expatriates that there was no better country than the one they invent for themselves abroad. There are no tourists like him today, nor legends to match the cultured, womanizing, extravagant shadow this man cast over the islands. (Diario de Mallorca, 4 April 1994)

By the turn of the century, the number of foreigners began to increase and, like the Archduke who came to find a beautiful unspoiled landscape, they discovered Deià and stayed. A guidebook from 1898 described the beauty of Deià and notes that 'One of its chief characteristics is its collection of strange and eccentric foreigners.' Foreigners were housed in one of the three small pensions or found rooms above family homes or managed to rent a vacant house. A new and different system had to be devised for these non-producing tenants to pay for their lodgings and the services provided by the newly formed peasant landlord. It could not be based on *mitges* (halves) or censos nor on improving the land, but had to be calculated in cash. The foreigners who arrived in this period were well dressed, like senyors, and were treated with respect and tolerance. Letting to foreigners gave increased cash, status, a new topic for gossip and curiosity. The foreigners had no choice but to adapt to the socio-cultural ambiance around them. They were dependent on the goods and services the local people could provide.

By the turn of the century, 'Contraband' networks had developed within the village and between villages. The working people and the smaller landowners began to experience a control over their own lives rather than being completely dependent on landlords. There was hope that the social and economic imbalance might one day be altered. The relationships that developed in these smuggling networks were to form a dominant role in the years ahead. The need to cooperate in order to make a profit forced peasants and tenants to rely more on one another than on their landlords. They were no longer willing to work long hours just for the benefit of others. An old man who participated in these activities said: 'The apostles sacrificed themselves for all. I don't want to be an apostle.' He was tired of putting all his labour into activities from which he derived little profit. The gain from smuggling tobacco and 'colony cash' earned in South America began to show in increased building and land purchases within the village.

Life in Deià was dictated by the seasons, the crops, saints' days and the fiestas that accompanied them. On Sundays all the young would walk along the main road, in close sight of their elders. Most of the families were large and many, including their school-aged children, walked to the surrounding fincas during the olive season and worked 'from sunrise to sunset'. Men waited daily in *Es Porxo* (the central area of the village by the City Hall) for the tenants of the large fincas to collect them to work their lands. Women worked with men during the harvests, baked bread weekly, and with water drawn from wells within their houses or from nearby fountains they washed clothes in vats of boiling water and ashes.[16] After their experience with the Archduke, the Deianencs saw the arrival of a small number of foreigners into their village not as a disruption but as an addition to their lives. The Deianencs were not threatened by these outsiders; on the contrary, they were viewed as adding to the social and economic life of the village.

The Twentieth Century

Travellers arrived in great numbers during the early part of the twentieth century and the term 'tourists' began to be used. The *Fomento de Tourismo* was founded in 1909 to promote tourism on the islands. There was a gradual change in the employment structure with some peasants gaining access to small and medium-sized properties, and others moving into the service economy (Rossello i Verger 1981). Industrialisation allowed leather goods production to increase to meet tourist demands, and cut gloves were sent to Deià where many of the women who once worked the land with their fathers or husbands stayed at home to sew gloves. The income from glove making was much greater than any earnings women had previously made working the land.

Robert Graves arrived in Deià in 1929 with his friend, the American poet Laura Riding. Although there were three pensions by then, he preferred to rent a house. He was befriended by Joan Marroig – known in the village by his nickname *Gelat*, based on his family's transporting *gel* (ice) from the city to Deià on top of his bus – a well-known figure in Deià business and politics from 1920 to 1940. He held the tenancy of five of the largest estates (*Es Moli*, *Sa Pedrissa*, *Ca'n Fusimanya*, *Ca'n Valles*, and *Son Rullan*) and employed thirty or forty Deià men. Graves described him in his diary of 1930 as 'One of the most intelligent and ambitious of the village men, who owned land, many of the local water rights, ran a taxi service from Deià to Palma and supplied the village's first electricity'. Foreigners could not own property at this time so all of Graves's purchases were made in Gelat's name. He was closely involved in all the business dealings of Graves and Riding, and he supervised the building of their house outside the village nucleus, which Riding (with the help of Gelat) named Canelluñ.[17] Graves invested in a new water turbine generator which Gelat installed, and in 1934 they bought the land in front of Canelluñ and built the first road down to the sea. There was talk of a hotel being built but money ran out (O'Prey 1982).

Graves wrote that 'In 1929 Spain had been under the dictatorship of Primo de Rivera – but the village took no notice, except to add a strip of Republican purple to the red and yellow Spanish flag at the Casa Consistorial – and when in July, 1936, the Revolution broke out, nobody thought that it would affect Majorca'. A note in his diary from July 1936 relates that 'Mallorca has not recovered from the crash of the Credito Balear Bank, and talk of "Red Riots" by the Daily Mail has frightened off a lot of tourists. Deya is suffering from there being no demand from Barcelona for gloves which are made here by the women. But no real poverty anywhere, just anxiety' (ibid).

Graves's friend Gelat backed the Republican government elected in February 1936 and in May he was appointed Mayor of Deià by the Governor General of the island. By 20 July 1936 it was obvious that Mallorca would support Franco and that anyone who did not go along would be harshly treated. The Balearic Islands were claimed to be one of the 'Thirteen Fascist Provinces' and Gelat and the other leftist Mayors on the island were ordered to hand power over to some 'non-politico' (ibid.). They soon 'changed coats' and regained their local power base. The Civil War did affect Mallorca but Deià was one of the more fortunate areas; a few people were imprisoned, but no one was killed. Detailed accounts of the build-up, the war, and the aftermath in Mallorca have been written by Bernanos (1938), Massot i Muntaner (1978), and many others. Schalekamp (1976) has recorded some impressive conversations with Mallorquin survivors of those years.

In Deià, I was told Falangists made it a policy to check the church rolls, and anyone absent paid with imprisonment (many men say they have not attended church since this time except on very special occasions). Food producers had to turn over large amounts of food to the military and everyone had a terrible time hiding enough for their family's survival. Those who lived on the outlying fincas helped those within the village. Some of the tenants on the fincas were able to put aside quantities of oil that were extremely valuable trade items after the war.[18] Contraband activities helped the people feel they were 'outsmarting the law'. They felt it was an expression of their anger at a time when nothing else could be done.

Although a few foreigners remained on the islands during the years of the Civil War, Graves left Mallorca in August 1936 and was unable to return until 1946. He spent some of that time with Gelat's sister and her family in France and received news of the activities going on inside Deià. He was told by one woman that 'after the war no man would be honoured who had not been in prison'. Only one Deià man was sufficiently committed to the opposition to warrant that experience. He managed to avoid death by evading the authorities and spending the latter days of the war in a cave in the mountains above the village. Most other Deianencs rather passively (some say superficially) acquiesced to the authority imposed on them. There were many *denuncios* (denunciations to the authorities of one local citizen by another) but none led to prison. There are still a number of families in Deià where brothers do not have any contact with one another nor with any members of their respective households due to the differences brought on by the war. People prefer not to discuss the war, but when encouraged some men recalled their postings to other parts of Spain, their loneliness and hunger. Most, however, remained on the island and admitted seeing 'terrible things' but preferred to forget the details.

Graves returned in 1946 and, except for brief journeys abroad, made Deià his home. During the Franco regime, when the government-appointed mayor of Deià was concerned about rulings affecting the village, he often asked Graves, who was an island celebrity by this time, to intervene with the Palma governor; and if Graves and other foreigners objected to some decisions made within the village he might, once again, use his connections in Palma to intervene in village politics. Graves formed a number of close relationships with village families was a welcome addition to village life. He (like the Archduke before him) was made an *hijo adoptivo de Mallorca* (an adopted son) in 1969. He had been responsible for the arrival of many of the foreigners who passed through Deià, and some of those who resided there at different periods came to Deià through some interest in or connection with Robert Graves.

It was the mid-fifties by the time the village began to prosper with agricultural innovations, credit from the government, and the beginning of mass tourism. There were few consumer goods available, and people said that 'no one lacked what they didn't have'. The young began to emigrate to the service sector, and 'cheap' labour had to be brought in from the peninsula for the olive harvest. The tenant farmers (els amos) were the important men in the village at this time. They held control over lands, water, oil, and access to work.

By the sixties, when I settled in Deià, the demands for the traditional products from the rich forests of the Teix – charcoal (used to cook and heat), pine, and oak wood (for beams and furniture) – were decreasing rapidly, replaced by butane gas and imported woods from the mainland. It had become more profitable to raise pigs in artificial conditions than in the forests, and the market for olive oil produced on an artisan basis (picked and pressed by human labour) was not competitive. Social security payments, initiated under Franco, made employing large numbers of labourers prohibitive. Smaller families reduced the number of 'unpaid labourers' that tenants had relied on in the past.

The development of tourism allowed young people to move into the cities and other developing tourist areas to find work. They were able to move away from family agriculture to become wage labourers; the work day was structured by the clock instead of the rise and setting of the sun, and they could count on a fixed salary at the end of each week or month. More foreigners seeking the peace and tranquillity of the countryside came to the island to purchase property. Relationships between Mallorquins and their foreign neighbours led to exchanges of information about available houses and land. A local friend would get the best price possible for his new foreign friend and other reciprocal gestures followed. One German couple bought a property in the name of their Mallorquin friends with whom they shared it. The Germans lived in it for three to six months of the year, the Deianencs the other months. Their relationship was much like that of the patron-client relationships of the senyors and tenants of the past except that, since these senyors had no children, the Deianenc family would be the heirs to the estate they worked. Again and again, we see foreigners performing the role of benefactor as expressed in the local legends.

During the summer of 1960, there were twenty-five or thirty foreigners in Deià who spent their days at the *cala* (cove) and evenings in the village cafés. Few Deianencs came down to the cala during the week, except the fishermen who sat by their huts repairing their nets. There were two cafés at the cala, one built on the cliff and run by a fishermen and his family, and the other a tiny kiosk in the rocks which dispensed wine and spirits. On Sundays the youngsters from the village would come down to the cala for a swim or to fish off the rocks.

There was one bus a day to Palma that left at 7:30 A.M. and returned at 3:30 P.M. The electricity was still supplied by the generator Graves had helped to buy. The lights came on at 7.00 A.M. and went off at 10:00 A.M. and from 7:00 P.M. until 10:00 P.M. they came on again. If the lights ever came on at other hours, one knew that either the proprietor's wife was listening to the radio or using her new electric iron (the only one in the village), or that a baby was being born or someone was ill or had died. The same midwife was on hand to deliver two generations of children and few people died who were under eighty years of age. Everyone knew just about everything about everyone else in the village and news about the arrival of a few new foreigners circulated within hours. Engaged couples courted for six or eight years and married when they had a furnished accommodation to move into. The church was full at morning mass when the priest who had been in residence for over twenty years presided, and there were dozens of mothers and children to help the nuns decorate for fiestas. There were five or six cars and three lorries in the entire village. The Guardia Civil had a small office in the village and patrolled the coast in the evenings. Many men were still involved in contraband networks.

The diminishing importance of agriculture in Deià can be gleaned from City Hall records dealing with payments of taxes on rural rustic properties. The payments from agricultural lands received in 1976 represented only 1.45 percent of the taxes paid that year. With fewer people available or willing to work in agriculture, the land held little value. However, during the past twenty-five years, the demand for that land for speculation or for construction of secondary houses has augmented the value of rural lands enormously (1970 to 1995).

In 1981 a small terrace with three or four lemon trees and one carob tree produced more income than an entire mountainside of olive trees.

The harvesting can be done by one man in a few days and the prices paid for lemons and carobs increases considerably each year. In 1987 lemons were thick on the ground with trees laden and only one or two men bothered to harvest them. If an owner hired one man to work along with him, they could have picked 9,000 pesetas worth of lemons. By the time the owner had paid his helper the day's wage of four thousand pesetas (500 pts. an hour), his bags, transport, and food, he would have been left with about 2,000 pesetas for his day's work. Two thousand pesetas a day would be equivalent to half of the minimum wage and far below the average wage of a full-time employee in the service sector. The only people that can afford to do agricultural work are those who own the land and their own house and either have no children or no longer have children in school. In most instances this means extended bachelorhood, limited marriage potential, or the over-fifties and retired people.

The terraces of olive trees, once the mainstay of Deià life, are now potential building sites. Most of the demand for land comes from outsiders. Two hundred four owners of 263 houses in Deià make their permanent residence outside of the village. One hundred thirty-five of these are Spaniards who live most of the year in Palma, Madrid, Barcelona, Valencia, and France. Sixty-four are foreigners and five are mercantile companies composed of Spanish and foreign shareholders. The Register of Urban Properties (*Cadastre de riquesa urbana d'Hisenda*) of 1981 listed 301 proprietors owning 425 houses. The census listed only 146 resident householders. Numerous city dwellers, artists, and writers have purchased or rented houses for their weekend or holiday retreats, and a high number of houses left vacant by Deianencs who have emigrated to other towns and countries accounts for the low number of permanently occupied houses.

Matching ownership records with tax records shows that 65 percent of the houses (which represent 80 percent of the assessed value of village property) are owned by persons who live outside the village municipality. Deianencs own only 34.5 percent of the houses in Deià (which are equivalent to 19.9 percent of the village property assets). This suggests that Deianencs own fewer houses than outsiders and that those houses are more modest. In terms of land and house-ownership much of Deià belongs to 'outsiders'. This is not a new phenomenon. The history of Deià since the thirteenth century is one in which the majority of land and houses in the municipality have always been owned by people who reside most of the year *fora vila* (outside of Deià). During the thirteenth through the eighteenth centuries, most owners lived in Palma while during the nineteenth and early twentieth centuries some owners lived further away in South America, Puerto Rico, Cuba, and France. Most of these owners were Catalans or Mallorquins, and many of them were related to the early settlers of the area or themselves were Deià born. Young men or women who had been sent to the Spanish colonies to earn a living their natal village could not provide were able to acquire houses with their 'colony cash'. The purchase of houses and estates by foreigners began slowly but accelerated as twentieth-century travellers began to seek 'unspoilt landscapes' for their artistic and literary pursuits. By 1981, 133 of 566 residents of Deià were foreigners, and they owned half the houses in the village. New houses have been built during the 1980s and 1990s, but the resident foreign numbers remain about one-third of the population.

Today, there are more jobs available in the village than people to fill them. The two hotels and numerous bars and restaurants have all had to seek employees from neighbouring villages and the mainland. Some Deianencs care for the residences of absentee foreign owners, as well as their own small gardens and orchards. There are three active fincas that produce barely enough for the tenants to live on and a few enterprising workers who manage to make a living from collecting and processing olives in season and doing other odd jobs, such as pruning trees, clearing and burning weeds, that most Deianencs don't want to or are unable to do. There is a bank, a water-bottling factory, a pharmacy, and a butcher shop. There are numerous cafés, bars and restaurants, grocery stores and boutiques, some foreign owned. The only people at daily masses are widows and elderly women. Sunday mass is better attended, and a few foreigners participate in the choir. Until 1987, the nuns at the local convent took care of cleaning the church and gathered flowers from around the village for each Sunday mass. The tasks they so humbly completed are now being performed by elderly religious women (*beatas*). A church committee was organised to see if they could generate a little more interest in church care and activities. During 1988 the permanent priest was replaced by visiting priests who divided their time among the neighbouring parishes of Fornalutx, Biñaraitx, four churches in Soller and Deià. The dominant role of the church in local life may have declined, but it remained a focus for Deianenc identity. The village was not going to be made a peripheral parish after centuries of independence. The committee complained bitterly to the Bishop of Palma and managed to get a permanent priest appointed in 1989.

The number of 'tourists' resident in the village at any one time is restricted by the number of beds available in the pensions, the hotels, and the houses to let and usually does not exceed 1,000 (nonetheless, during June to September this triples the normal population). Communications made possible by radio, television, newspapers, magazines, and planes brings ideas, news, images, and people across borders, seas, and oceans. The outside world with its different people, customs, values, and material goods is a familiar part of Deià life. Most families have refrigerators, indoor plumbing, televisions, telephone, and at least one car (some have one for each family member over eighteen years of age). Electricity is supplied by GESA, the national electric board; rubbish is no longer disposed of in the torrente (the stream that runs through the village) but collected by a village van five times weekly during the quiet season (October to May) and every day during the tourist season (June to September) by the *municipals* (council employees) who also serve as village police during the season to regulate parking and late night noise levels from the bars.

In 1977 the first mayor and council to be democratically elected since 1936 made it clear that 'belonging' to the village in a legal sense was reserved for Spanish nationals who become *empadronado* (registered) in the village. Empadronado was often extended on paper to include foreign residents (to increase the total population count), but no voting rights accompanied this listing. However, since 1992 Common Market members have had the right to vote in foreign municipal and national elections; although few have used it.

Foreigners who reside most of the year in Deià have participated directly or indirectly in village activities since the turn of the century. The descriptive terms available in Catalan or Spanish to describe strangers, foreigners, or outsiders are limited to *estranger* and *foraster* or *estranjero* and *forastero* respectively. Foreign residents, like Deianencs, are referred to by the name of their house, their surname, or their village nickname, which is a clear indication of the village's recognition of their presence and participation in some aspects of village life. But since the new democracy, Deianencs have begun to describe themselves in contrast to outsiders in general. Foreigners, once valued as conveyors of culture, cash, and entertainment, seem to be less valued than in the past. The foreigner, once an addition to the limited socio-economic life of the village, is no longer seen as an individual but as part of a group, 'the force from outside', which has entered the village and brought about change in every aspect of Deià life. Long term non-Spanish residents of the community, once encouraged to take an interest in decisions affecting village affairs, are no longer particularly welcome at council meetings.

Recently the terms Deianenc, estranger, and foraster have been used to draw a distinction between those 'inside' – the Deianencs – who can share in the decision-making activities of the village and those 'outside' – foreigners – who have no legal role in village activities. The use of these restrictive categories gives no indication of the history of the relationships that exist between some local families and foreign residents in the village, or the essential part these relationships played in Deià's past. The categories imposed by language and nationality are only headings within which the people label one another, but the variety of concepts pertaining to these categories suggests that these terms or labels have become impediments to understanding the way people actually experience one another and what they mean when they use the terms Deianenc or estranger.

Notes

1. The Castilian-Catalan spelling (Mallorca) is used throughout except in direct quotes where author has used English (Majorca) spelling.
2. Vuit vents are the eight winds that affect the local climate: Tramuntana (North from over the mountain), Llevante (East), Migjorn (South), Xaloc (Southeast), Ponente (West), Gregal (Northeast), Mestral (Northwest), Llebeig (Southwest).
3. In 1977 regional languages were to be taught at least three hours weekly in junior schools and in increasing amounts during successive years. The end result was that many schools today teach at least some (if not all) subjects completely in Mallorquí/Catalan, and in both the University of Palma and the University of Barcelona more lectures are given in Catalan than in Castilian. Exams may be taken in either Spanish or Catalan (allowing for participation by students and professors from other parts of Spain).
4. *El Dia* from 18 January 1984 reported that 'the alodio is condemned to extinction but still holds until an adequate replacement can be designed to cover the interests of all those concerned'.
5. Peasant does not refer to a unity or a single class. Shanin discusses this in *Peasants and Peasant Societies* (1963). Ortiz also discusses the complexities of this term in *The Peasantry As a Culture* (1971). The use and meaning of the term 'peasant' in Deià will appear in various contexts at different points in the present work.
6. *Chuetas* or *Xuetas* is the Mallorquin name given to the Jews of Mallorca who converted to Catholicism during the fifteenth-century Inquisition (on mainland Spain converted Jews were called *Marranos*). Although they made a great show of Catholic piety, Xuetas were shunned by all other Mallorquins. In Catalonia the descendants of converted Jews merged with the general population

within two generations; but this never happened in Mallorca. Those identified as Xuetas by their family names and trades are still shunned by many Mallorquins as somehow responsible for Christ's crucifixion, and are debarred from becoming priests, nuns, or until lately, army officers. While writing this book, I overheard a mother say to her son: 'You couldn't consider marrying her, she is a Xueta.' See Braunstein 1956, Bucholtz 1960, Colom 1985, Forteza 1986, K. Moore 1986, or B. Porcell 1987 for various descriptions and interpretations of the activities and people included in this group.

7. Ramon Llull was a Mallorquin 'mystic' and philosopher. His youthful folly and lust were followed by his conversion and 'heavenly illumination'. Consumed with missionary zeal, and with the aid of the King and the monks in Deià, he founded a teaching college at Miramar to school young friars in the Arab language 'for the conversion of infidels'. Llull himself mastered Arabic and travelled through the Moslem countries converting them to Christianity until he was stoned to death by a mob at the age of eighty.
8. *Fueros* were special rights to have their own laws and customs granted by monarchs to warriors who helped them conquer new territories. These applied to Catalonia (Mallorquin and Catalan spelling – *Catalunya*), the Balearic Islands, and Valencia.
9. The Royal Economic Society of Friends of Mallorca was composed of the Bishop of Mallorca, the Captain General of the Balearics, Count Cifuentes, most of the richest Castilian nobles resident on the island, and various well-known priests and lawyers. Their activities included the establishment of an Academy of Art and schools where grammar, arithmetic, and calligraphy were taught to all ages and classes. They initiated road improvements, export arrangements for agricultural goods, etc. (Salvador 1985:136).
10. A typical purchase of a *parcel.la* at this time was based on a *hipoteca* (loan) made by the owner of the land or a third party. The borrower agreed to pay a 3 percent interest on the capital until the time that the full amount could be repaid, and collateral was based on 'all of one's present and future goods' (*Inventorio De La Documentacion De Las Contaduras De Hipotecas Tomo II, no. 592 – Indice Antiguo de Fincas urbanas y rusticas de Deya, 1843*).
11. Soller orange-growers would accompany their produce to France, set up a stand to sell it on the docks, and return on the same boat. As the demand increased, a few Soller men opened warehouses and remained in France to receive the Soller fruits. I have been told that orders for fresh fruit from distribution networks that now range from Barcelona to Cologne, Germany are still made in Catalan.
12. It should be noted that the number of foreign female visitors to the island in 1860 was just eleven, so that the village's experience with foreign women was very limited at this time.
13. His various titles included: Archduke Luis Salvador, His Imperial Highness the Royal and Serene Archduke of Austria; Luis Salvador of Hapsburg Lorraine and Borbon; or third son of Leopold II of Tuscany and Marie Antoinette of Borbon, daughter of Francis I, King of Sicily, sister to Marie Christine, wife of Ferdinand VII, and past Queen of Spain.
14. A recent biography notes that these were Palma businessmen and their mistresses who welcomed this out-of-the-way place for their rendezvous (J. March 1986).
15. It would be difficult to maintain these standards today when visitors number in the millions.

16. *Sa bugada* refers to the weekly or fortnightly washing of linens. This chore required the heating of a large tub over hot coals and the use of ashes as a whitening agent. Sa bugada is synonymous with gossip as an entire day could be spent by groups of women sharing in this chore, and it was a great opportunity to exchange all the latest news. The reference is still used today by older people when talking about women who spend time together talking about others.
17. The meaning and various spellings of this name are discussed in Chapter 5.
18. Elliot Paul's *The Life and Death of a Spanish Town* is a vivid portrait of that period on the neighbouring island of Ibiza. Hugh Thomas 1961, Duchess of Atholl 1938, Lyttleton 1974, et. al., have written in more detail about the Civil War on the mainland with some references to Mallorca.

2. Conceptions of Space

Description

Along the highway from Palma to Soller, just past Miramar, the site of Ramon Llull's thirteenth-century school for Oriental languages which was later acquired by the Archduke, the sign of the *Terme Municipal de Deià-Benvinguts* (Welcome to the Administrative Territory of Deià) marks the boundary between the municipalities of Valldemossa and Deià. Deianencs are extremely proud of this sign which welcomes travellers to 'their village'. From this point on, they will point out each house and give its name, history, and several anecdotal stories about people associated with it, especially if the house is one of the twenty estates (fincas) that were once the main source of employment for the people who came to work in the hamlet and who later formed 'the village' of Deià.

Twisting and turning, the two-lane highway passes the finca of Son Gallard where the highway narrows into a single lane for about one hundred yards and widens out again as it passes *Ses Cases Noves*.[1] This narrow stretch of highway[2] was the last reminder of the rigid senyorial class[3] and the powers they held over workers and officialdom. When the rest of the road was widened, the highway department was told by the owner of this narrow stretch that he would be pleased to give up a few feet of his terraces if the department replaced the walls on either side. The department, however, was only willing to replace one wall. Sheep, the tenant farmers' source of income, graze on the terraces below, and with no wall to keep them enclosed they might wander onto the road. The farmer held his ground to protect his interests and livelihood against bureaucratic interference.

The forty to fifty tourist coaches that daily bring visitors from other parts of the island to see the cells in the Valldemossa Carthusian Monastery[4] where Frédéric Chopin and George Sand spent their *Winter in Majorca* must follow this winding road to Soller. The magnificence of the gnarled olive trees, some of the oldest on the island (870 to 900 years) growing on the terraces that descend to the cliffs above the expanse of the Mediterranean and up the surrounding mountainsides, makes this one of the most spectacularly beautiful coastal scenes on the island. A village farmer returning from a trip to mainland Spain remarked that 'all the olive trees there were the same. Here each one is different…'.

Son Rullan[5] is a finca high above Ses Cases Noves which overlooks the highway, the vast expanse of Deià, and the sea below. Until a few years ago, driving along this road in the autumn one would pass women and children in their brightly coloured sweaters and straw hats as they bent beneath the olive trees to collect the fruits. The olives were later pressed into the rich olive oil so desired by the Mallorquins, which was the main source of income for the fincas in this area. Today, these fields are used for grazing sheep, who take shade from the summer sun beneath the olive groves whose neglected fruits fall to the ground. Only a small portion of them can be collected by members of the sharecropper's family. The cost of employing men or women to pick olives is prohibitive. The girls who once were available and willing to work for a small wage and a few litres of olive oil have moved into service jobs in the growing tourist industry.

The road curves downhill and reveals the estate of Son Marroig. The name Roig (red) appears among the Provincial noblemen who accompanied Jaime I in the conquest of the islands in 1229. Tax records from the Monastery of Ca l'Abat list '12 lluires paid by Masroig in 1370'. In the sixteenth century a tower was built, specially equipped for defense with loopholes and embrasures, from which the estate could be guarded as its proximity to the sea made it vulnerable to attacks from Mediterranean pirates. The property also included the Foradada, a rock islet with a massive hole through it and one of the outstanding landmarks on this section of the coast.

In 1870 the Archduke purchased this property. It was improved and has been maintained and opened to the public as a museum by his heirs in this century. An often repeated story tells of a peasant who remarked to the Archduke that he had paid an exorbitant price for this property. The Archduke replied: 'I have not even paid the price of the hole in the Foradada.' One might suggest that the Archduke's sense of beauty and spatial dimensions has established the focus for the images captured by the majority of tourists. The highway department constructed parking areas near his favourite lookout points. Anyone driving along these roads wishing to take photographs finds the best spots indicated by a camera sign next to these parking areas. For those who do not take photographs, postcards of the Foradada and the estate are available in most kiosks along the way. So many of these postcards have been sent around the world that when people come to visit they say the scene looks 'just like the postcard'.

Further along the highway the finca of Sa Pedrissa (the rock) and its tower, known as the *Torre de Deià*, mark the descent into the valley of Deià. Here one finds a striking view of the village church perched on a hill and the many stone houses built on the surrounding terraces. The lands of Sa Pedrissa extend down to the sea and a stone footpath leads to its orchards and the cove below. This was another of the fincas purchased by the Archduke. The road curves and twists past a few more named houses and the finca of Son Bauça with its round tower. The finca dates from the fourteenth century; the tower was a sixteenth-century addition. The finca and three other named houses are approached by a small access road which descends sharply off the main road. This is one of the few fincas in Deià that is still occupied by the descendants of the original owners. The descendants held diverse privileges of exemption from taxes until the nineteenth century and played a dominant role in the history and political life of Deià.

Back on the main road one passes *Sa Siki* which is perched precipitously on the north side of the road, having been separated from the fountains from which it derives its name by the construction of the highway. A plaque on the side of Sa Siki reads *Provincia de Las Baleares, Partido Judicial de Palma, Pueblo de Deya. Partidos* are the districts into which provinces are divided for judicial purposes throughout Spain. Beyond Sa Siki lies *Ca'n Renou* (House of the Noise) a large house and lands recently converted into eight flats by the owner.

Ca'n Quet, across the highway and once part of the adjoining finca of Es Moli (the mill), was sold separately in 1934. It was converted into a *residencia* (lodgings) and a restaurant by an Englishman in 1935 and bought a few years later by a Deianenc who gained his restaurant experience in

France. It remained a restaurant and residence under various managers until 1983 when the heirs sold it to the present owners of Hotel Es Moli (see below). They have modernised the restaurant while the residence has been converted for use by the hotel personnel who come from the mainland. Below Ca'n Quet a small road descends to the area known as *Es Clot* (the hollow), the lowest and oldest part of the village of Deià. This was the only access road to the village before the highway was built.

Following the main road again, it passes by Es Moli, one of the three flour mills in Deià until the 1930s. Es Moli, once an active finca, went bankrupt in 1934 and was bought at auction by a Palma businessman. The fall of the Banco de Credito Balear in 1929 had terrible repercussions in Mallorca. As a Mallorquin-owned bank, it had deposits from the island's small businessmen and returning emigrants. In December 1934 all payments were suspended. Then *Banca Agricola,* which had mostly peasant holdings, folded as did the railway company. Local men say that 'Only the peasant who stored his savings in mattresses and inside of wicker chairs was left unscathed'. Es Moli was rented in 1954 by a Danish couple who ran it as a guest house until 1960. It was then purchased by a German company and converted into a four-star hotel with 167 beds, an olympic-sized swimming pool, and a private beach along the coast to which hotel guests are transported by coach twice daily. The gardens of the hotel are said to be among the most beautiful on the island and were created and maintained by a Deianenc gardener who was employed by the various owners of the finca until 1983.

The next house along the road is *Ca'n Pere Juan*, and around the turning we encounter *Ca'n Caleu* and a sign indicating the *casco urbano*, the developed area or urban centre of Deià. The casco urbano, or village nucleus, lies at Km. 4, in the middle of the great expanse of mountains, terraces, and sea which make up the 1,511 hectares of the municipality of Deià. The developed area of Deià known as 'the village' occupies only a small portion of the municipality (3.8 of 151 kilometres). This is the centre for local administration, education, medical assistance, church, and shopping. The creation of their own village in 1583 did not alter the living arrangements of most residents. Until 1930, two-thirds of the population of Deià lived outside the village nucleus on the various fincas where they were employed. The census for Deià shows a marked increase in local village houses and occupants between 1930 and 1940 by which time three-quarters of the population lived inside the village nucleus.

Perceptions

The physical geography of the urban centre known as *el poble* (the village) can be mapped and measured as described in the previous paragraphs, but the perception of 'the village' held by the people living within and around this geographical nucleus suggests that description and interpretation will differ markedly according to the age, gender, nationality, and interests of the person giving the information. Experiences of residence and occupation also influence peoples' perceptions of 'the village'. The ways people order, value, and express (often as much through actions as in words) their knowledge of their 'worlds of experience' differs markedly between locals and foreigners.

An eighty-four-year-old Deianenc man, who worked most of his life as a charcoal-maker on the lands high on the Teix, left his house each week late Sunday evening and returned on the following Saturday. Some Saturday evenings he would join the other young men of the village carrying contraband tobacco from the cove of Deià through Es Clot and up the mountains over the Teix, 'for a little pocket money and my own bit of tobacco'. To him, 'the village' of Deià is the expanse from mountains to sea, the lands he and others worked, familiar names of people, houses and land-holdings.

A bachelor fisherman who is sixty-eight years old has slept in his fishing hut by the sea 'every night since I was born'. He and his brother come 'up to the village' daily to sell their day's catch of fish, to have their midday and evening meals with their sister, and to visit with friends and family. He draws a clear distinction between his house 'in the village' and his *casita* (small hut) at the cala (cove). His widowed sister lives in the village with her children in nearby houses and like them he is 'of the village', but he lives outside the physical space known to him as 'the village'.

A woman in her thirties who was brought up at Son Bauça (an estate and small cluster of houses outside the urban centre of Deià) used to come 'into the village' to go to school each day and then 'home' to Son Bauça. Since marrying twenty-nine years ago she has lived 'in the village', but said she will never be 'at home in the village' like she is at Son Bauça where the members of the four families living there venture unannounced in and out of one another's houses, help themselves to a piece of fruit, or go to the refrigerator for a snack. 'We were not relations but we were like one big family.'

To each of these people the area known as 'the village' represents different geographical dimensions but the notion of the village as a social reality is shared by all. The different categories by which people group one another – family, kin, friends, or neighbour – become submerged within the common social experience of 'the village'.

An American who has resided in the village for thirty years said he felt he entered the village when he drove beneath the towering pine by Sa Pedrissa and saw the church perched on the hillside in the distance. Other foreign residents gave similar descriptions of the physical entity of the village and its surroundings: the stone houses built on terraces, the mountains, the olive trees, the hills, the streams, the pink hue of the mountains as the sun set each evening. They shared an idealised concept of landscape and timelessness somehow devoid of people. When people were included they were other foreigners.

Santiago Rusiñol, a Catalan humourist, writer, and painter, presented his perception of Deià in his book *The Island of Calm*:

> Deià is a little model Bethlehem with the church standing up on the summit, a row of cypresses in front, and a handful of houses scattered round it as if thrown there by accident. Below, others and still others, like the steps of a staircase, one on top of another.... We must explain here that in this village, as in many others of the island (with apologies to those who live in them) the human figure is of least importance. The man does not detach himself from the landscape. That is why a country village always seems uninhabited. The scenery in these villages is so vast and grand that the men who dwell in them, pictorially, do not exist.... It is a village which seems to say to us 'Here I am complete like a wonderful still life (*reredo*) so that when you see me you can pray to me or paint me'. (1958:139–42)

Many people from the city of Palma, mainland Spain, and more distant countries share this distanced perspective portrayed by Rusiñol. Like most foreign residents they describe Deià from outside – a socially distanced personal view of geography and architecture from which they derive emotional, intellectual, and spiritual inspiration. Deià, for most who were not born or brought up there, exists only as they perceive it, a paradise for rest and relaxation or an exotic landscape designed to test their creative abilities, to discover or soothe their 'soul'. Tales of witches, Diana cults, and energy forces coming from the mountains abound among the foreign colony. The 'mystic' quality of the setting and the effect of the phases of the moon on all forms of life have been popularised by Robert Graves in *The White Goddess* and in his poetry and prose.

The harshness of the landscape leaves little leisure for mere admiration for those who must wrest a living from the land. Deianencs appreciate and resent their environment. They appreciate its beauty and its climate. They appreciate its textures, the contrasts of stone and earth, mountains and sea. It is conducive to producing ample crops but it requires many months of arduous labour and more months of waiting to collect and process the products.

The year is structured by the religious festivals that mark out the seasonal cycles on which the agricultural workers are so dependent. They are no less aware of the effects of the moon on the planting and growth of plants than are the poets. There are innumerable sayings that point out the peasants' concern with the moon. The experienced peasant always plans his activities around the phases of the moon. He finds a great difference between the waning and the crescent moon. '*Plantes de fruits enterrats com patatas, cebes i alls … en Lluna Vella, els treballs s'han de fer en el sembrats i les que 'A l'air tenen els seus fruits, tan desitjats: sien pedres, melons, blats … amb Lluna Nova, convenen.*' 'Plants that ripen underground like potatos, onions and garlic should be planted with the old (waning) moon and those that have their fruits in the air (above the ground) whether they be with stones (peaches, plums, apricots, etc.) melons or wheat do best planted with the new moon' (Vila 1984). Many older men informed me that 'Trees cut with the full moon dry better and make the strongest beams for house building'.

Over the past thirty years, the climate and the setting of Deià have attracted sufficient numbers of people from outside the village to offer most of the villagers another and less arduous means of income to supplement the diminishing returns from agriculture. As the hours of sunshine increase each day the locals begin to open the houses of summer residents who will be arriving in the next months. As long as there is sun the village will be filled with visitors from abroad.

Although the qualities of sun and moon, mountain and sea are perceived differently by the locals and the visitors, these are nevertheless the elements that bring them together in Deià. The Deià summer 'community' is quite different from the winter 'community'. The small number of residents in the winter is vastly increased when the summer comes. Family members who reside in France and other areas of the island all try to be in Deià for the annual fiestas of *Sant Joan* (St. John's Day) in June. By July, school and work holidays begin and the numbers of foreign visitors increase filling every available bed in private homes as well as all the hotels and pensions.

A description of the village is not the straightforward task one assumed at the outset. As I have lived here for thirty-five years, my perceptions are undoubtedly a conscious and subconscious mixture of my personal experiences as a participant in some of the activities and associations of both Deianencs and foreigners who refer to Deià as 'their home'. A description today must take into account the different perspectives of those residing in the village. The local Deianencs have a rather all-encompassing concept of 'their village' while foreign residents have formed a different image; and travellers, tourists, or visitors may have altogether different impressions. Anthony Cohen summed this up admirably when he wrote: 'The conceptual constructions of the village are such as to keep the communities apart as worlds of meaning in the minds of the members' (1986:82). The paradise described by locals, foreigners, or visitors over the centuries is dependent on the realities of each person's experience. Work, personal histories, memories of drudgery, oppression, or challenges affect each person's perception. By taking all of these different perspectives into consideration we begin to recognise how the use of terms like Insiders and Outsiders comes about and on what levels, if any, conceptions merge and at what points they are very far apart.

Space, Time, and Gender[6]

Continuing our tour of Deià from the boundary indicator of the casco urbano (urban centre), one follows the highway past the stone washstand built at the foot of the hills beneath the Teix and filled with fresh waters flowing from the primary stream on its descent through the valley of Deià down to the sea. A stone stairway next to this washstand leads up the hill to the area known as *Es Reco*, past *Ca'n Oliver* (also known as *Pension Miramar*).[7] At this point one can go uphill to the large house of *Ca'n Bilona* and the pine forests above or descend via the access road that passes the cluster of houses known as *Sa Vinya Vella* and connects with the main highway. Another stairway across the highway below the washstand leads down to *Sa Font Fresca* and connects with a new access road constructed in 1982, which passes by a number of houses and joins the road to the lower village, Es Clot. Another stairway, *Sa Costa d'en Topa* connects Es Clot road up to Es Porxo and continues up the *Carrer de Ses Monjes* to Es Puig. These stone stairways are each *set palmos* wide (seven palms – equal to seven times the width of a stretched hand calculated at approximately 20 cm per hand, therefore 140 cms), the width needed for a mule carrying filled bags on each side. They are known as 'the donkey steps' by most foreigners. These stairways were once the only access to the village nucleus, and through the village from Palma to Soller.

Men and women who live in various parts of the village nucleus delineate the major areas by the above references which have been used for generations and are usually based on recognisable features of that specific area: Es Reco (the corner); Sa Vinya (the vinyard); Sa Font Fresca (the fresh fountain) – water was drinkable; Es Clot (the hollow, pit, ditch, or grave) – the lowest part of the village; Costa d'en Topa (the way to the top); Es Porxo (the porch);[8] and Es Puig (the hill) – the highest point of the village where the first small church was built in the fifteenth century.

The highway beyond the washstand bordered by houses on either side is an area referred to by older men and women as *Sa Tanca* (the enclosure). This entire area was an enclosed field until the turn of the century when portions were sold for building plots. These lands were purchased by men who were tenants on the outlying fincas. The first building, completed in 1905, was a grocery and café still known as *Ca'n Pep Mosso*, followed by six other houses each connected to the previous one's western wall and forming a continuous line along the street.

These are large houses by Deià standards, having three or four floors, with large rooms, cellars (where carts and mules were kept), and attics (where foodstuffs were dried and stored). The two lower floors have large, shuttered windows that face north and south. These houses have large, finely furnished entry halls where family relics and religious objects are stored in olivewood chests and lush plants are on display behind the polished glass-paned doors that open onto the street. The actual living space is neatly hidden from street viewers by a lace curtain or an inside door.

As the composition of families living under one roof changed, upper floor rooms were converted into flats for married children or let to foreign visitors. One enters a Deianenc's house by tapping lightly on the door and opening it while saying, '*Ave Maria Purisima*' (religious references are commonly used in greetings). Front doors are always left unlocked while someone is in the house so that acquaintances have easy access to the inside. These salutations evoke a commonalty, a relationship and an association of people over time. A sure sign of a stranger is a formal knock on the door.

This area has replaced Es Porxo as the main commercial area of Deià. Many foreigners refer to it as the High Street or Main Street. Here one finds a grocery, bakery, pharmacy, cafés, restaurants, a bank, an insurance office, an art gallery, three boutiques, and a carpenter's shop occupying the street-facing rooms of these houses. This is the public centre of village activity with women going to the grocers, men on their way from the café to their work, children passing to and from school, coaches transporting tourists to other parts of the island, private cars going to Palma or Soller, and a few foreigners having drinks on the café terrace. The five fisherman who once sold their day's catch here as well as a small butcher's shop stopped trading a few years ago. With only frozen fish or meat available in the village, many families make weekly trips to Soller or Palma to shop in the covered markets or at one of the city's supermarkets.

Foreigners – men, women, and children – move in and out of the bars, shops, and cafés at any time, on any day, and seem to make little or no distinction between daily and weekend space, time, activities, or clothing. Some are in communal space all their waking hours. The café is the meeting place when 'home' is a small room or house. The spatial connotations of the locals are quite different. Deianencs observe a fairly gender- and age-specific, regularly patterned spatial orientation. Weekly activities are prescribed and restricted by occupational demands. Weekends are more loosely structured and activities vary according to the season of the year. Although few men or women work in the fields any more, seasonality still affects their activities. During the summer months, June through September, children have school vacation. There are many more foreigners in private houses and hotels and a variety of available jobs. In summer there are also many more village fiestas and family visits from those who live outside of Deià. In autumn men go into the mountains to pick *setas* a wild mushroom; in winter they hunt birds and rabbits and go fishing when the weather permits. Family outings include excursions to other parts of the island, summer swimming, picnicking, etc.

Until the past few years, most women's weekly activities were centered around the maintenance of their house and family but nowadays more and more are going out to work. Certain spaces and times are special and require appropriate behaviour and attire. A woman's age affects her spatial orientation and her manner of weekday dressing. Until 1985, women whose children were in school all day might take in washing or go out to work a few hours cleaning foreigners' houses, but today they prefer to work in one of the hotels. This entry into different domestic spaces brings women in regular contact with outsiders and provides them with insights into the private lives of people from different backgrounds and experiences who would otherwise be seen only in public situations.

Women from Es Clot complain that now that they have no shops nearby they have to come into town to do all their shopping. This requires them to change clothes a few times a day. They feel one must put on a proper dress and shoes (leather not cloth) to go uptown, and since the shops don't have fresh goods until after ten in the morning, they have to change in and out of their housedresses at least twice each day to begin their domestic chores, go shopping, come home, and do the cooking, cleaning, etc.

Older women put on their best coats and walk up to the church every evening for six o'clock mass. On weekends women's spatial trajectory increases and intersects much more with the men's movements. Most women go to church and the hairdressers, and a few go to market day in Soller or Palma, to all of which they wear 'proper clothes': skirts, sweaters, dresses, and leather shoes. Women over fifty are usually driven to town by their husband, daughter, or son.

Unmarried girls do not want to work in private houses, but they may work in the water-bottling factory or one of the hotels. They prefer to work in the company of their peers rather than in a situation where they feel subservient. They will drive their car or motorbike to work rather than walk. While middle-aged women at home or work wear simple dresses or nylon smocks and house slippers, young girls assert their independence from conventional dress and wear trousers for leisure (preferably blue jeans), a uniform for work in the hotels, and high fashion on special occasions. Local fashion consciousness has always drawn from the latest fashion trends. Fashion magazines have been the source of style for Deià women since the 1920s. Many women showed me photographs of themselves in beautifully designed dresses. Long before 'ready-made' clothes were available in the city shops, village dressmakers were copying the latest Paris fashions for women to wear at annual fiestas.

There is often conflict between young girls and their mothers about what is considered proper clothing for weekends and what the girls consider fashionable. Levis 501 red label jeans, frizzy hair, and worn leather jackets are *de rigueur* for the girls, but mothers make sure that the jeans are washed and ironed and the shirts are starched and pressed, which actually negates the carefree appearance the girls are seeking to present. Foreign-style dress tends to be much scruffier, more bohemian than the locals and much the same for all occasions. With the new five-star hotel, local boutiques have been set up and some foreign visitors and residents are now much more fashion conscious. In fact, one of the differences between new and old resident foreigners is their manner of dress.

School children in blue and white smocks are accompanied by their mother or older brother or sister to school and home each day until they are about six. Then, if they do not have to cross the main road, they can manage on their own. Later there will be visits to friends' houses in different parts of the village. At this stage they will begin to refuse to wear their school smocks and insist on wearing what the older children wear, which these days tends to be track suits.

Young children are the ones most likely to cross the real and imagined boundaries between foreigners and locals as they wander into foreigners' houses to play with schoolmates. Boys and girls seem to play together easily until they are about seven years old. Then their modes of play separate them. Recently, the boys of nine to eleven have begun riding their bikes swiftly down the Es Clot road and returning along the main road. This route marks out the wider boundaries of the village where their activities take place. At twelve years of age they begin to go to school in Soller and their horizons expand. Unlike the larger groupings of boys, girls tend to form close ties with one or two others and play closer to home.

Men's spaces encompass greater distances as they travel by motorbike or car to work, bar, and home again. Men of working age go out to work early in the morning, return to their houses for the midday meal, and go back to work in the afternoon. One can discern workers who have come from outside the village. At lunch they either eat packed lunches from home on the work site or join others in one of the local cafés where special workers' menus are prepared. Most men, local and from farther away, stop at the bar before and after meals. During the week, working men are almost always unshaven. They wear old flannel shirts and hand-knitted local wool sweaters, baggy trousers, flannel slippers or rubber-tyre soled shoes, and a *boina*, the Mallorquin name for a beret.

Older retired men dressed similarly to workers trace the boundaries of the village as they walk along the main road almost every day. Bent over or supported by a walking stick, they all try to follow the village doctor's advice that walking is good for them. Old cronies meet up at various spots along the way, catch up on all the latest gossip (it is misleading to believe that only women gossip), and continue to the end of the built area of the village and back again. They will stop at the bar for a coffee or soft drink on their return and sit and watch or join the middle-aged and younger men playing cards. The younger men may have the day off or have office jobs (which finish at 3:00 P.M.). In contrast to the workers' dust-covered clothes, men who work in offices wear clean jeans, open-necked shirts, and sweaters, either hand-knit or bought. Their clothing too is subject to a mother's, wife's, or girl friend's scrutiny. The movements of young men and women are those most likely to cross the boundaries from village to town and back again. Most eighteen-year-olds have access to the family car or have been given one of their own, and on the weekends they take groups of friends to the discos in Soller, to the beach or plaza. These gender- and age-related spatial trajectories suggest that a person's concepts of time and space alter during the life cycle and are varied for men and women.

Spatial Connotations

A guided tour through Deià reveals the development of the village over time, the changing perceptions of those who live there. Es Porxo, one of the few straight streets in the village, runs parallel to the main road. A wide expanse of cultivated terraces and a tiny stream separate the two areas. The *Ayuntamiento* (City Hall) is on Es Porxo. In the middle of Es Porxo is Ca'n Valles, a mansion built by the Archduke for his secretary who was from Deià. The house is presently owned by a Catalan family that uses it occasionally in the month of August. This house, with its fine paintings, carpets, furnishings, and cultivated gardens, is cared for by a Deianenc who weekly opens the windows to air the relics inside while he maintains the cypress-lined paths and gardens. This house is a reminder of the social differences that in the past dominated Deià life. The fences that enclose it and separate it from all the neighbouring houses frame it in a time warp. Without inhabitants, it is no longer part of village life – just a remnant of Deià history.

Today, Es Porxo is a residential street. Children play on it, tourists wander about, peering at houses with closed windows and shutters where people are out to work. At the entrance to Es Porxo there is a paved road that ends at Es Puig and passes a municipal park built by the town council in 1979. The park has swings and a small playing field surrounded by stone benches forming an amphitheatre. It was built on the west side of the hill, which had always been left free of houses. In 1978 the new mayor instigated an 'urban development scheme' and acquired the land for the City Hall in exchange for permits to a local estate owner to build a water-bottling factory and six houses. Older people said 'this is an unnatural growth of the village because the site is *fora vila*, outside the village nucleus. It is an unhealthy place to live. It is exposed to the eight winds, humidity and lacks sunshine most of the year. Furthermore, the houses will face the sea and have their backs to the village. Village houses face one another'.

The annual celebration of Sant Joan, the village saint's day, has been held in the park since 1979. Before then, the fiestas had been held on Es Porxo. At first, many people said the park was outside the village and held no connection with the shared space, people, history and traditions with which Deianencs identify their village. But each year, as the traffic increases through the village, the park is becoming more and more accepted as a place – perhaps the only place – where activities can be carried on without the noise and disruption of cars, motorbikes, claxons, children and grown-ups going to and fro. A local theatre group, *S'Eregall* (the Winding Road), has performed different plays at each year's fiestas, folk dance classes meet there weekly, and the amphitheatre has been integrated into village space through these regular activities.[9]

A stairway leads from Es Porxo to the recently built doctor's office, up to the *Estanco* (tobacco shop and grocery) and the post office. The Estanco or Tabacalera S.A., the tobacco monopoly of Spain, is licensed to sell stamps while the post office only dispatches and delivers the mail. Four large houses line the road up from the Estanco. Beyond it, two new access roads open to the north. Twelve houses were built on these two new streets during the 1980s. They are part of the urban development plan introduced by the mayor in 1978 which encouraged building within the urbanised areas of the village. The houses have three to four bedrooms, sitting rooms, modern kitchens and baths, garden areas, etc. Although they were built with foreign buyers in mind, quite a few of the houses have been bought by young Deianenc couples who have done very well in business over the past few years. They have created a new neighbourhood of local people. This area, once referred to as fora vila by older people, has become an accepted part of everyone's concept of the village mainly due to the number of locals that live there. This is a telling example of how conceptual boundaries are expanded over time.

The streets have been named *Carrer d'en Sant Joan* and *Carrer d'en Roberto Gravés* commemorating the residence of these well-known art and literary figures in Deià. Approval to use the names was not requested from the families concerned and there were no dedication ceremonies when the name plaques were installed. The Graves family was especially dismayed at having a new development bear Graves's name as he had always made a great effort to have building restricted on that side of the village. Nevertheless, the name remains.

The Estanco road ends at Es Puig where the *Plaça de l'iglesia* is surrounded by houses and the final ascent leads to the church and cemetery in which generations of Deianencs and a few foreigners are buried. On the north side of the church is a house called *La Posada* (the inn or guesthouse). This house was built by the owners of the estate of Es Moli. It was used by family members to freshen up before attending church and for receiving guests after services.[10] Although it was a common practice for the owners of the large fincas surrounding Deià to build a posada in the village, this is the only one left. This posada was bought by the Archduke and used for the *cuarentena*, the forty-hour vigil maintained in the church prior to the celebration of Ascension. Robert Graves purchased it in 1934 and used it as a guest house until his son married and made it his family home in 1965.

On the east side of the church there is the priest's house and a second house, both owned by the diocese. The present priest set up a local ecclesiastic museum that holds a rather eclectic collection of church relics, including silver candlesticks and drinking vessels, some paintings of saints, a Byzantine cross of unknown origins, and a few archaeological artefacts donated by the mayor's grandfather. The cemetery is on the west side of the church and the area behind and below it is free of buildings. The cemetery, set on the top of the hill overlooking olive-tree covered terraces, rugged stone outcroppings, and the descent into the valley down to the sea, was enlarged to accommodate eight tombs. A number of houses have been built down by the cove during the past ten years but the village nucleus is set a good distance from the sea. Until recently, Mallorquins, as in general the Spanish, did not like to live near the sea as it was considered unhealthy (Salvador 1981).[11]

The road descending from Es Puig and the Carrer de Ses Monjes continues down via the Costa d'en Topa and meets the road which descends from the main road and continues past the cluster of houses known as *Ca'n Pintat* and *Ca'n Xesc*, over the stream to *Ca'n Carindo, Ca's Fornés, El Museu, Ca'n Borino, Ca'n Bujoca,* and down past the area of *Ca'n Boi* to Es Clot, assumed to be the area of the oldest houses and the original nucleus of 'the village'.

The entire area from Ca'n Boi up to Ca'n Pintat is referred to by most people over sixty as Ca'n Boi. All the land in that area was owned by the four brothers who lived in the house called Ca'n Boi. They were described as *pagés rics* (rich peasants) because they owned many hectares of land and three or four pack mules. They were known as 'the bank' because anyone who needed to borrow money to purchase seeds, pay outstanding debts or censos knew that they could depend on Ca'n Boi. The brothers would make loans charging only 1 percent to 3 percent interest and the borrowers were permitted to pay back in small sums through the season. Some of the lands that belonged to Ca'n Boi and extended up into the mountains and down by the coast were acquired in lieu of unpaid loans.

The roads and streets once known by names derived from familiar areas and landmarks; i.e., Ca'n Boi, Sa Tanca (a large enclosure), Carrer de Ses Monjes (the Street of the Nuns), or Plaça des Puig (square on the hill) have been renamed at different periods. Under Franco, street names in villages and in the city were changed to reflect the regime: José Antonio, General Goded, Generalisimo Franco, et al. The village mayor of Deià in 1974 managed to include most of the Catholic hierarchy by choosing the following names: Pio XII, Bisbe Simon Bauça, Beato Ramon Llull, Virgen de Lluch, Reverendo Jeronimo Pons, Sant Sebastian, and one more, Felipe Bauça, a mapmaker who had the same surname as his, Bauça. The political orientations and changing interests of Deià mayors can be seen in the themes they choose to commemorate with street names. The preferences of the first democratically elected mayor in 1979 seemed to be for cultural figures.

Over the past decades, each street and section of road has been given a separate name (often with no reference to the previous names) and the oral mapping and naming which preserved notions of property divisions, family histories, traditions, and shared conceptions of space are now used only by older people when they are queried about the village past by grandchildren (or curious anthropologists). Through the years fences, gates, and walls have been built to delineate boundaries between properties once understood by means of inherited knowledge of where one's property began and ended and to whom each area, from mountain to sea, belonged.

There is a notable association between the descriptions of the village and the age of the person giving the information. Men and women over fifty used the oldest references to describe areas and landmarks. They often explained how a street or path looked prior to the changes they have seen take place during their lifetimes or been told about by their parents. People between twenty-five and forty said their parents told them about places, houses, streets, etc., which had been previously known by other names and they themselves used a mixture of past and present descriptions. Young people, under twenty-five, tended to use present-day names for streets, landmarks, and area descriptions. By the time the present generation of school-aged children are adults describing their conceptions of the village, they will automatically include the park and new road and street names as though they had always been there, because for their lifetimes this is the case.

Upper and Lower

Es Clot is the 'fertile crescent' of Deià where the waters from the mountain streams Sa Siki, Es Moli and the major stream (Torrente Major) converge. The number of houses in this relatively small area far exceeds any other grouping in the village. Many of the people living higher up in the village have their orchards, which they say go back many generations, in this area. Retired men and women make an effort to maintain these orchards and, despite age, arthritis, rheumatism, or other ailments, they continue to plant, weed, and collect fruits and vegetables for their own use. They say their continued efforts are purely a social obligation, but it does provide them with both physical exercise and some small addition to their table.

The clusters of variably sized houses in Es Clot form streets with doorways facing one another or outward toward the street. Those living in such close proximity meet up with one another many times in the course of a single day: on their way to the local grocery, at the washstands, hanging laundry, watering gardens, or popping in and out of one another's houses to borrow some sugar, offer a freshly cut bouquet of flowers from their garden, or stop in for a cup of coffee and a chat. The women say they have been taught always to keep their hands busy and spend a relaxing afternoon – after a hard day's work cleaning their house, doing laundry and preparing a cooked lunch – in the small areas in front of their houses crocheting, knitting, or embroidering surrounded by neighbours similarly occupied. Much like the girls who grew up at Son Bauça, the women living in Es Clot know everything about one another's private lives, houses and their contents. People who live in different parts of the village nucleus delineate the major areas of the village in terms of upper (*dalt)* and lower (*abaix)*. Abaix refers to all the houses below the centre. Often the name Es Clot is used to indicate the entire area of the lower village. Thus, one would say, 'I am going to Es Clot' rather than to the lower village. The term dalt is used mainly by people who live in this general area known as Es Clot. One who lives in the upper village would not use this term. He or she would use the specific area or place name to describe their destination: 'I am going to the doctor's office or Sa Vinya or Es Puig.'

The use of the term dalt by one section of the village more than another suggests the importance of the location of one's house in each person's conception of the village and his or her place within it. The word dalt implies: of considerable altitude, superior to the middle, the most elevated part (figuratively) of a class, a state, or knowledge. It is a vertical dimension. *Baixa* implies: inferior in respect to other things; vulgar or inferior in quality; an inferior place; the lower part; decrease in the value or price of something; of little height. *Dalt a baix* is a local expression meaning opposite extremes (Arimany 1965). Going 'up to the Church' has both literal and figurative connotations.

The use of these terms contains a value judgement concerning the geographical space in which people live their lives and surely affects their attitudes about themselves and the place of others within the village community. The descriptions of the village by people living in Es Clot show that they recognise the full interpretation of the terms. Most of the advantages of living in Es Clot are expressed in contrast to life on Es Puig; neighbours are nicer in Es Clot (than on Es Puig). It is cooler in the summer (than on Es Puig) and good fountains and water supplies are nearby (unlike the dry Es Puig where some houses must pipe water from across the village at Es Reco, having had to collect it in buckets before it was piped).

Es Clot may be described by some who live elsewhere in the village as damp and dark in the winter, cut off from the centre, etc., but those who live in Es Clot are quick to cite advantages that outweigh these minor inconveniences: closeness of neighbours, open relationships, cooperation, etc. If someone who lives in the upper village goes to Es Clot, everyone in Es Clot knows where they went and what they did. The upper village does not take such notice of those from Es Clot as most amenities and public life take place around them.

There are many observable differences between the upper and lower village. The main road to Soller runs through the upper village and the people that live there are more accustomed to a variety of people passing through their neighbourhoods. The houses in the upper village are much larger than those in the lower part. Most upper village houses have three or four floors, front- and back-facing windows, large front doors, and entryways facing onto wide streets or roads. Most of Es Clot houses are built against terraced walls and many of the terraced houses – with only small windows and doors to let in the daylight – are built along narrow intersecting streets and passageways.

Everyone agrees that Es Clot houses are the smallest but they are also recognised as the oldest houses in the village. Although houses obviously increase in size as one ascends the hill from Es Clot to the centre of town, social distinctions between the upper and lower areas are not clearly articulated by the residents of either geographical area. However, subtle remarks and comparisons are commonplace. The size and number of houses in each area, the surface area on which they are built, the proximity of one house to another, and the relationship between the households in each area suggest a difference in social organisation within each named area. However, there are also many similar characteristics in each area and between areas which override the distinctions of upper/lower when village or community membership is in question.

These named areas evoke historical moments and economic, social, religious, and political activities that everyone has heard about or experienced. They coincide with the Deianencs' ordering of space and his or her individual conception of the village, which includes family, house, neighbours, shared values, beliefs, and activities over time.

Changing Perspectives

Until fifteen years ago, a dominant feature of the named areas of the village was the proximity of kin. When a son or daughter was planning to marry, parents were able to acquire a nearby house vacated by a Deianenc who had moved elsewhere or they could convert a second or third floor of their home into a flat or build on adjoining land. In 1956 thirty-six of the forty houses in Es Clot were inhabited by parents, siblings, and children of six Deianenc families.

It is evident that the people who lived in each named neighbourhood (*redol*) distinguished themselves from those living in other areas of the village by subtle reciprocal activities and the degree of neighbourliness. The concept of neighbour differed in each area depending on the number of kin living nearby, on the proximity of houses, and on the gender, marital status, age, occupation, and nationality of the occupants of each household. People who live in close proximity to one another are sometimes called neighbours but as Juliet du Bouley noted in regard to *Ambeli* (Greece), 'neighbours is a precisely termed but uncertainly defined relationship between particularly the women of the houses concerned'

(1979:13). Neighbours in the Basque areas of France (Ott 1981) or Spain (Greenwood 1976) are subject to more structured relationships.

Through the 1970s the residents of each named area would light a bonfire to celebrate the village fiestas of Sant Joan, another on Sant Antoni, Christmas Eve, and Good Friday to express each neighbourhood's identity and community cooperation. However, as the number of Deianencs in each area declined, there were fewer and fewer people to organise the bonfires and share in the traditions. A woman who lived in the Font Fresca for fifty years expressed this change when she said she had to move away because 'there were no more neighbours there'. Although there were three foreign families in the adjoining houses, she no longer had any 'Deianenc' neighbours.

Today, there seems to be a preference toward letting to visiting foreigners. The reasons given are (1) that short-term contracts to foreigners allow regular rent increases to keep up with the cost of living, and (2) one can gain access to one's house, if needed, at the termination of the contract. Many homeowners prefer to have their houses empty half the year and let them only during the season at very elevated prices that a yearly tenant would not pay. This way they can look after their houses and gardens during the winter months and gain a bit of cash to supplement their pensions in the summer.

Until the 1960s buying, building, or renting a house was not terribly prohibitive for a Deianenc; but when larger numbers of foreigners began to settle in Deià and buy or rent most of the available properties, prices rose beyond the means of most Deianencs. The few locals who did own properties preferred to speculate on development or hold out for the highest bidder.

Letting to Mallorquins or permanent foreign residents for long periods means that one's house is tied up for years and rents are held down. Innumerable houses have been let for over fifty years to Deianencs, and two foreign women still pay rents of one to three pounds sterling agreed upon, verbally, at the time of the original lease. Selling an occupied house entails rehousing the occupants or paying for their resettlement as well as depriving an often long-known or even related person of his or her home. Nowadays, contracts are made for eleven months with renewal clauses stipulating increases according to the cost of living indexes.

The boundary indicating the end of the urban center is back on the highway, below the fincas of Son Canals and Son Moragues, two large estates which formed part of the earliest village of Deià and employed twenty or thirty men to work the lands, make lime and charcoal in the mountains, and process the olives each year in the olive presses on the properties. These fincas ceased to operate as productive estates in the late 1970s. Each was maintained by a married couple with one or two children who barely managed to eke out a living from their small herds of sheep and meagre harvests. In 1982 both fincas were sold to a consortium – a group of German, English, and American investors organised by a German architect and developer – for about forty million pesetas each (approximately £200,000 each).

Over the next two years the interiors of the main houses once occupied by the senyors and the smaller adjoining quarters of the tenant family were converted into a hotel with seventy deluxe rooms within the original structure, and a thirty-four foot swimming pool in the newly landscaped gardens. Development of hillside houses and hotel extensions followed. The beauty and continuity of the estates has been maintained while they have been adapted to the requirements of a discerning class of tourists – those who can afford the luxury within the ancient walls. The old building that housed the olive press, with its rustic beamed ceiling and stone walls, has been converted into an elegant restaurant where linen tablecloths, silver dishes, and candelabras are combined with the stone and wood to create an atmosphere of rural opulence never before experienced by anyone in Deià. Large paintings of Robert Graves adorn the walls while inside the hotel one can see a collection of paintings by foreign artists who resided in Deià over the years.

Most Deianencs were pleased with these new developments. Older men said agriculture was a dying occupation, 'young people don't want to be tied to the land as we were'. Other Deianencs knew the hotel would bring more jobs for the youth of Deià and visitors who would spend time and money in the village. Some foreign residents were concerned that the hotel would attract a different sort of visitor to Deià, raising prices in the village and crowding 'their paradise'. When *La Residencia* opened in June 1984, it employed fifteen people of whom six were Deianencs and two were foreigners born in Deià. The other seven were from Soller. Although there are still many critics (especially among the long-term resident foreigners), *La Resi* has become a place to which both foreigners and Deianencs take visitors for a special treat. The hotel attracts guests from Germany, England, Spain, and America. Providing only breakfast and a very expensive restaurant, hotel services had to be augmented by village development. A number of new restaurants were opened in the village to cater for the increased number of people from the hotel who dine out in Deià.

Urban development has also increased greatly since La Residencia was built in 1984. The urbanised area of the village continues to expand as investment from outside increases. Mountain areas made accessible by new roads offer picturesque spots for development. Expansion within the confines of the village is being encouraged by the local council and there seems to be little objection. A new school, football pitch, and tennis courts have been built below the water-bottling factory, houses have been built in Es Reco and a water-purifying station has been installed on the mountainside descending to the cala. Building is allowed in areas once protected or considered rustic. The urban area of the village has been redefined to include a number of housing developments begun in the 1960s and never properly classified. Houses can be built on agricultural lands within the village and around fincas. New neighbourhoods are springing up on terraces that were once covered with orchards of thousand-year-old olive trees. Large plots of land are required for each house and new estates are appearing on the landscape. The major investors in these private homes and developments are 'outsiders'.

The picturesque village in the mountains of Mallorca, which has been depicted by artists and writers and was home to an agricultural populace now oriented toward the service industry, seems to be inhabited today by groups of people with quite different conceptions of the village in which they live. When decisions about the future of the village are to be made, conflicts of interest become political issues. The minor internal squabbles of village politics are being absorbed in a mounting desire to unite Deianencs against opposition from outsiders. As Pitt-Rivers wrote so many years ago, 'The recognition of foreigners as part of the social milieu allows them to be used as scapegoats which implies a degree of proximity and cooperation' (1954:143).

It seems that the concept of the village has as much to do with the nature of local social organisation and ideology as it does with geography. It is with these concepts in mind that I have attempted to describe some aspects of Deià. The concept of the village is not a general geographical location or an administrative label casco urbano but a composite of known space which holds vertical time, people, associations, and activities. The conceptual boundaries of the village expand and contract in different contexts. These boundaries can include family members who live in Palma and as far away as France, while some people who live in the mapped area of the village are not conceived of as 'of the village' at all.

The village is not a fiction in which time is compressed and rearranged, distanced from reality and absent from quotidian concerns.

Neither is it a bounded entity nor a mere physical space; it is a social dimension which encompasses the living and the dead, the past and the present, the outside and the inside, the private and public, the spiritual and secular in an ever changing cycle from generation to generation.

Notes

1. The contraction *Casa (de)* meaning House of combines with the definite article and is reduced first to *Ca* and then contracted as follows:

   Ca'n before a name introduced by *en* (personal article m.)

   Ca's before a name introduced by *es* (ref. pron.)

   Ca'l before a substantive introduced by *el* (*Ca'l Bisbe* – the Bishop's House

   Son (contraction of *ço que és d'en* – that which is of*)* is used before the name of a large estate, possession, or finca. It has been said that the original divisions of land by Jaime I are denoted by *Son*, i.e., *Son Bauça* – lands of the Bauça family

   Ses before names of groups of buildings, lands, etc., as in *Ses Figueras* and *Ses Casasnovas*.

   The Catalan masculine article *el* appears before words that begin with consonants and *l'* before vowels. The masculine plural article is *els*. The feminine singular article before consonants is *la* and *l'* before vowels. The feminine plural is *les*. In Mallorquí the usual article is not *el* or *la* but *es* (masc. sing.) and *sa* (fem. sing.) or *ets* (masc. pl.) and *ses* (fem. pl.). The only time *el* or *la* is used is with substantives, *el Bon Jesus*, *la Mare de Deu*, *el Abat*, etc.
2. Highway versus road: I have used highway and main road interchangeably based on the meaning of *carrer* (Catalan), road, and *carretera* (Castilian), highway, or main road; and *camino real* or royal road; and *cami d'el rei,* road built for the King's visit, a reference commonly used by older people in Deià. The royal road or highway was built at the beginning of the twentieth century.
3. The owner of this land was the Count de Fontaner who tried to use his position to influence the highway department. The department felt they were avoiding favouritism by denying his request. Either way, his power was acknowledged. Epilogue: the Count died in 1986 and before his estates were sorted out the Highway Department arranged to widen this area of the road. By the end of 1987 the curves had been replaced by a ruler straight, complexly engineered asphalt highway.
4. The rooms or cells shown to the public since 1963 are completely different from those which Chopin and George Sand actually inhabited. They had two rooms on the north side of the monastery which were very dark, damp, and sparsely furnished. The present rooms are on the south side of the building and open onto lush gardens through long windows which shower bright light onto the entire space now cluttered with pedestals, cases, busts of Chopin, and a piano with a plaster cast of a hand (Chopin's hand?) on the keyboard.

5. This is one of the oldest fincas in Deià. There are documents dated 1355 that register the return of the hamlet of Son Rullan, from the monastery to its previous owners, the two Muntaner brothers (Seguro i Salado 1979:29).
6. I did not realise that this is similar to the title of Henrietta Moore's book, *Space, Text, and Gender*. I chose this title for a seminar given in 1984, prior to the publication of the above.
7. Miramar is a common name used for pensions and this one has no relation to that of the Archduke discussed earlier.
8. When the City Hall in Deià was enlarged in 1875, the Archduke acquired the pillars that formed Es Porxo (the porch of the first city hall built in 1583) and placed them in the entrance of Sa Pedrissa with a plaque explaining their origin.
9. Deià's local theatre company was invited to perform in Soller's central plaza in 1987. Despite microphones (which they had not needed when the play was performed in the Deià amphitheatre), it was almost impossible to hear any of the actor's lines over the noise from the plaza. The plaza was filled with people watching the play, but the open theatre area is surrounded by cafés where others sit drinking and talking and where motorbikes go careening by.
10. In Pina, a village on the eastern plains of the island, the Ribas de Pina family still hold prayer meetings at their finca on the edge of the town. In Deià, the finca-owning families were the main contributors to the church funds and the organisers of religious activities: outings, processions, etc. Today, the heirs of Son Marroig are still greeted with special courtesies, and their presence at funerals is always noted by the villagers.
11. Some say that the location of villages was based on its defensibility from invasion; others say that mosquitoes and disease were the reason for building villages on higher land away from the sea.

3. The People
Changing Composition

Family and House

In Deià 'casa' means not only house but the people in it and family. A *llar* or *fogar* (Castilian *hogar)* is the hearth symbolising the smallest and most intimate domestic group with which individuals identify. The earliest census records not persons but *focs* (fires or hearths; metaphorically those who share a common fireplace). The large farming estates of the past had various hearths: one in the main house for the owners, another for the tenant farmer's family, still another for the labourers, and one for the shepherds. In historical records and the early census (*padrons*) of the village, payments to landlords, *fogatges*, were based on focs. When I use the terms domestic group or household they are synonymous with the metaphorical meaning of foc.

A domestic group is most often formed from family members but other arrangements are possible. The essential difference between the reference family and that of domestic group or household is that family, while referring to kin relations, need not imply a residential unit. By contrast, a domestic group shares a residence but need not be kin. At present, there are at least twelve different types of domestic group (household) arrangements in Deià. Except for a few households that are composed of unmarried foreign couples, friends, or employees, my use of the term household or domestic group implies members of a single family or various families living together in one building.

The term House (casa) can encompass the smaller parts which are the various households that have developed from the core House. Capital H in House stands for the House as a metaphor for social relations (e.g., House of Windsor). A House name evokes associations of kinship, work, spatial orientations, social class, economic, religious, and political affiliations past and present and differs from a house (a building) in which a single domestic group resides. (This will be discussed more thoroughly in the last section of this chapter.) Usually, only one child stays in the core House, brings his or her spouse to that house, and works with the parents. Other brothers and sisters marry out and join other Houses, set up their own households, or might remain in the core House. Each of these may or may not become a separate economic unit but it remains sentimentally part of the core House. Therefore, one can say that a House is made up of many households. Ideologically, it is perceived as a whole despite the fact that it may be composed of many different physical structures.

As in Latin, *familia* (family) can mean a fusion of kinship and coresidence. Family includes the members of one or more households usually associated with two core Houses. This dual connection is recognised in the surname given to the progeny of a newly formed household. Surnames are composed of paternal patronym followed by maternal patronym. A child's surname, by combining the two families' patronyms, recognises the union of his or her parents and their respective families.

The term family refers to many different groupings. Depending on the circumstances, the number and distances of relations included among those considered family will increase or decrease. There are no specific terms to distinguish kin from family. One's 'close' relatives are referred to as *mi familia familia* or *es meus parents*, meaning parents, siblings, bilateral grandparents, aunts, uncles, and cousins. Beyond this point, people to whom one traces some relationship are referred to simply as *familia* or *parents*. Most people are familiar with, at the least, their third bilateral cousins.

The Civil Code defines the family as a nuclear group: a man, his wife, and their legally recognised children. However, in emotional, social, or religious terms family is an elastic term which can encompass very few or very many people. For inheritance purposes, the family is restricted to the group recognised by law or those referred to by the village as 'of one House'; whereas for funerals, distant relations are notified and all are considered family. At weddings the familia familia of each of the partners become 'the family' and people are 'forced into a careful defining of their social relationship through material exchange, both symbolic and substantial' (Brandes 1975).

Ideally, family members are those with whom one is most relaxed and at ease and with whom one can share the joys and sorrows of life. The ideal is seldom reached. In fact, the individuals that make up the family of 'one House' are those most commonly involved in conflicts. The properties of the House are often the basis for discord between its members. The grouping together of different households under the name of 'one House' points up the shared property that binds them together and sometimes drives them apart. Inheritance disputes are a major source of family discord. While parents are alive siblings make an effort to remain congenial. If contact between sibling households breaks down completely after the parents' death, it is almost always due to a dispute over inheritance. Two sisters who live in divisions of their core House have not spoken for thirty years due to a squabble over twenty centimeters of an internal wall between their houses. Some parents seek to prevent these family breakups by planning ahead. One woman very cleverly divided all of her property into equal parts (rooms, furnishings, lands were all evaluated by a professional). Five *lotes* (lots) of equal value were recorded and her five children drew for their lot. Thanks to their mother's forethought, they all remain good friends and neighbours.[1] This form of dividing property was more common among the large estate and landowning families on the island (Moll i Suau 1979).

Marriage

As both family and named Houses are composed of one or more households, perhaps a clearer idea of each can be drawn by looking at the formation and arrangements of households. A household is formed or reformed by marriage. Marriage is an emotional, economic, and social union acknowledged by a religious or civil contract. As Lison wrote: 'Each spouse occupies a key position due to a simultaneous membership of three families (his, hers, and their newly formed one). Through him, or her, the three are interlocked in a complicated structure of relationships, rights, obligations and tensions' (1983:158).

Today, two people finding one another mutually attractive and sharing some interests will develop those factors into a relationship which they may chose to formalise and perpetuate. Approval of their mutual choice of one another must be sanctioned by the girl's parents first, and later by the boy's parents. In the past, boys would talk to girls at the front windows of the house. A boy never stepped inside a girl's house until he had decided to court her formally. Then the boy would ask permission to see the girl's father. Once the father agreed, the boy could 'enter' the house to continue the courtship. After a while the boy's parents would call on the girl's parents to make sure there were no inconveniences to the marriage. These might include economic or social factors. Nowadays, in most families it is a foregone conclusion that there will be no objection. By the time the boy actually asks permission he is well known by the girl's parents and has spent much time inside their home.

Although arranged marriages were more common fifty years ago, especially among finca-owning families, even today young men and women learn early about marriageable and non-marriageable types. The social class differentiations that locals make among themselves are especially evident when it comes to choosing marriage partners. A business or landowning family will endeavor to send their children to 'good' schools in Palma, at least until they are eighteen. The children are encouraged to learn languages and travel. Their activities are closely supervised by their parents who create structures by which they will meet other young people who share the same 'opportunities', i.e., good schools, chaperoned travel, attractive apparel, new cars, potential property ownership, etc. If the children are not academically inclined they will be included in the business activities of their parents. Parents organise social encounters and family visits that will keep their children in known social settings. It is not by coincidence that the contractor's daughter married a Palma real estate agent or that his son married a contractor's daughter from Soller; yet both were very much the young people's chosen partners. Joan Bestard describes a similar pattern for the smaller Balearic island of Formentera: 'A social picture emerges in which each individual represents the role assigned him by his position as the member of a family of a certain social standing' (1986:136).

Young men who have left school at age fourteen or sixteen and work in the village as waiters, carpenters, builder's assistants, lorry or tractor drivers, or on the land, have less structured encounters with other young people and most likely marry someone from Deià or the neighbouring village of Soller. Marriage between two Deianencs was preferred as two people born in Deià to Deià-born parents know all about one another and their families. The young usually go in groups to the village cafés on the weekend and occasionally a group drive to Soller to a disco. Their social life is lived side by side with young foreigners and the activities they enjoy are the same: pop music, dancing, some drinking, and being out with one's friends in a noisy, social atmosphere. They meet people from outside Deià through friends and family who live in other villages. There are very few relationships that develop with young people from other villages that are not through some form of connection with other people in Deià: a cousin of a woman from Santa Maria who marries a Deià man, a colleague of someone from Deià who works in Palma or Soller, or the son of the stone mason who comes from Fornalutx to work in Deià.

Most Deianencs can conjure up a long-ago relationship between many families in other villages or towns so that the source of marriage partners that have some Deià ancestry is quite ample. Reanimation of old ties connects people who live in Soller or Fornalutx and brings young people from these neighbouring villages into regular contact with Deià. A common expression, *tots som parents* (we are all relations), indicates a shared identity and solidarity between families based on the ideal (but not always the reality) of centuries of village (or island) endogamy.

Prior to 1965 there were six Guardia Civil in Deià. Also, a number of men were brought from the mainland to do roadwork, and women from the plains of Mallorca came for three- to six-month periods to pick olives. Many of these people married Deià men and women and settled in the village. Marriage partners for those employed on the fincas or in trades were preferably from Deià. Families were quite large, with five to eight children, and many potential partners were available. Marriages between close relatives were frowned upon. A seventy-five-year-old man told me that 'anyone coming to my house to visit my sisters who was less than a third cousin was shown the door. We were sheep breeders and we saw what could happen to the offspring of close family'. How widely practiced this was is questionable as the records of inter-Deià marriages between 1843 and 1940 suggest that second and even first cousin marriages were not uncommon. There were first cousin marriages arranged to preserve estates that might otherwise have been portioned between siblings. Church records show that letters were sent to the Bishop of Palma to request Papal permission for a number of first cousin marriages, although none of those still living recalls ever seeing a reply.

Estate owners look carefully for suitable mates for their sons and daughters. In the past, parents negotiated the unions of their heirs with those of similar economic and social standing. Marriages between children of estate owners were definitely preferred. Historic records show that since the fourteenth century the development of small estates and the building of new ones has been associated with the marriage of estate owners' children. The owners of Son Rullan, Ca'n Fusimanya, *Son Beltran*, and *Ca'n Puigserver* were all relations. The sons of the owners of Son Bauça owned Sa Pedrissa, *Ca'n Simo*, *Son Bujosa*, and Son Marroig. Other family members owned Es Moli and Ca'n Quet. The heir to Son Canals married the heiress to the *Palace Sollerich* in Palma and sold his Deià finca, Son Canals, to his neighbour Joan of Son Moragues (Seguro i Salado 1979:23–46).

Stories of the distances traveled by Deià men to claim a Deià bride are numerous. Young men who went off to Cuba or South America would return to an arranged marriage to a girl who had land and houses in which the suitor, who had only a small percentage of his own family's lands to inherit, could invest his colony cash. In other cases, the couple would return to South America until such time as either of their parental lands or homes were to be distributed or they had sufficient capital to purchase a large house or lands of their own. Among the buyers of the numerous fincas that changed hands in the 1930s (after the fall of the Banco de Credito Balear in 1934), four of the purchasers were Deià men who had worked in what were referred to as 'the Americas'.

Older men were in a position to negotiate for the hand of a young girl. Land and cash were paid for youth. If a man's wife died it was quite acceptable, in fact recommended, that he remarry as soon as possible. Marrying one's deceased wife's sister or deceased husband's brother was not uncommon: there are three such marriages at present in Deià. This arrangement was recommended when small children were left motherless or fatherless. It was considered most fitting and beneficial for the children if the widowed parent could marry someone of the 'same blood' as the deceased. It also kept the inheritance between consanguines.

Girls of twenty sometimes married men of fifty with four or five children, some of whom were older than the girl herself. There are tales of girls who, forced to marry men older than their fathers, literally wished themselves to death within a few years of the marriage. There is one particular riddle that is often repeated which suggests the complexity of some of these arrangements. 'Two women look up the street at two approaching men. One woman says to the other: 'Here come our dear fathers, our mothers' husbands, our husbands and the fathers of our children.' How was this possible? Solution: 'Two widowers married one another's daughters and had children.' Another riddle points out the age difference between spouses: 'My father is my son-in-law.' In this case, the son married an older widow with a daughter and his widowed father married his step-daughter. When a widower was to marry a young girl, the boys her age would blow the conch shell the evening before the wedding. During the agricultural season up until 1950, widowers were married at 5:00 A.M. at a special mass while all other marriages were held at 7:00 A.M. mass. Marriages had to take place during the hours before sunrise so as not to interrupt the workday. Young people are often reminded of the simplicity of traditional weddings and receptions when only hot chocolate and *ensaimadas* (the local pastry) were shared with guests – in contrast to the large weddings, receptions, and honeymoon trips they take for granted today.

With fewer and fewer people working the land today, marriage prospects for some have become rather bleak while others, especially girls with some schooling, have set very high targets for themselves. Men over twenty-five who left school at fourteen to work on the land or in construction are finding it more and more difficult to find a girl from within the village or in neighbouring villages who is willing to settle for the lifestyle the land requires. Young people are no longer required to help in all the chores associated with agricultural life, and most want to learn a profession or train for a job that will provide them with a steady income, a five-day workweek, and the means and time to live a comfortable life.

Marriage aspirations have risen. Girls express their choices for a husband in the following order: (1) business owner, (2) company or bank director, (3) employee (of a bank, hotel, office, or company), (4) hotel employee (reception, waiter), (5) landowning farmer, (6) lorry driver or construction worker, (7) labourer, and finally (8) agricultural worker. The first three are conceived of as occupations that will allow one to live in the city, preferably Palma. Until the late 1970s, the city offered an 'escape' to those in the rural areas and suggested a 'better' way of life. A young woman's ideal was 'to be a *senyora*' (lady) which meant she could dress up every day (instead of just on weekends)[2] and go out to work in an office (clean work), go to the shops, or meet friends for coffee. They imagined that they would work only if they wanted to as their husbands would make good incomes.

The local young men prefer girls from Deià, Soller, Fornalutx (all northwest coast villages), the plains, or finally Valldemossa. They are not too concerned with what job the girl has as long as there is a possibility of two incomes since it will secure a better life for both of them.

Aspirations and choices change. Two twenty-five-year-old women who have recently married men from Palma have decided to make their homes in Deià. Neither of them actually wanted to live so far away from the village, and when the opportunity to live in the city arose they chose to live in Deià instead. The previous generation, now in their forties, wanted to make a definite break with the agricultural life of the 'peasant' and moved outside of Deià at marriage. For today's youth, with a choice of work situations and many amenities now available in Deià, the city no longer holds the attraction it once did. In fact, they believe that the increase in robberies, mugging, and other primarily drug-related crimes, has made the city a frightening place to live.

Whatever the economic circumstances, every couple needs a place to live when they marry. Most young people would prefer a home of their own, quite separate from their family houses. Girls prefer to live in fairly close proximity to their mothers or sisters. A photograph from 1950 shows a group of people standing in a doorway of a house on one of the little streets in Es Clot. I was told this was a picture of 'the neighbours'. In the photograph is a woman about sixty years old, her son and daughter (both in their thirties), her brother and his wife and two children (about ten and twelve), and her widowed sister. They lived in four households on two adjoining streets and everyone who knew them said they were from *Ca'n Deya.* Until the 1970s, family and neighbours were often synonymous. In the past, large houses were sectioned off to create separate households within the main family house or nearby houses were purchased (often with furnishings) by parents for their children's future marriages. Many houses had been left intact when their owners, seeking work abroad, migrated to France in the 1930s. Property values were very low and houses were temporarily left vacant as owners planned to return.

Marriage could be matrilocal, patrilocal, or neolocal. If the man's house was a business or farm he would bring his new wife into the parental house. If he was employed by others he was more likely to move into his wife's house. Moving into one's spouse's house needn't mean shared quarters as a marriage required some reorganisation of the existing household. A minimum of two rooms, to be used as a sitting room and a bedroom plus a kitchen (one's own fire), was considered a separate household. The furniture for the new household was provided by the couple with the aid of their parents. The parents of each would discuss the provisioning of the household and its furnishings. *La dot* (dowry) is commonly mentioned but the understanding of the term was very loose. Before the 1940s, in most peasant families a dowry consisted of an olive-wood table and a few chairs, a wooden chest, and a marital bed. Most people agree that the husband bought the marital bed but it became the property of the woman at marriage. In most cases, the girl's parents provided the largest amounts of money, goods, land, etc. The dowry (often an advance on the girl's share of her parental inheritance) could be promised to the husband and used for the purchase of property or to convert part of the maternal house. In some cases, the couples were given land in another part of the village where they could build a house which they would occupy after marriage.

On most farms and in businesses where the wife worked with her parents or in-laws the midday meal was taken together, but every new bride longed for her own kitchen. Kitchens were simple, consisting of a table, a few chairs, and a fireplace or small *fogó* (iron grill) which used charcoal for cooking. Most houses had indoor wells or nearby springs, and water would be brought into the kitchen for personal bathing. Those who had no family accommodation available rented a vacant house usually close to the girl's parents' house.

A couple's courtship usually lasted three to seven years, during which time they accumulated the goods necessary for their marriage. The girl made and embroidered all of the linens, while her female relatives crocheted a *vànova* (a lacy bedspread) for her marital bed. A second vànova (for a guest room) was usually provided by the man's family. I was told that the more embroidered linens a girl had, the higher her status among the other women. Today, with the earnings of both partners and the help of their parents, many more goods are purchased for the new household. The quantity and quality of furnishings and appliances increases as more goods are available in Mallorca. Often, as in other Western European countries today, when a couple send out a wedding invitation they include either a business card from the store where they have made their 'Wedding List' or they may even include the actual list, prices, and stores where the goods are on sale. A couple who married in December, 1984 included their bank account number – for deposit – in the invitation to their wedding. It seems they had purchased everything they wanted during their three-year courtship and were now asking their wedding guests to give them cash to reimburse them for their expenses! While both partners are working and living with their respective parents, all of their earnings can be directed toward their future household. Marriage today is an expensive proposition for all the participants, from the actual bride and groom and their immediate families to the invited guests. Gift giving and receiving are essential parts of the planning.

Unlike the conditions described by Robert Graves on his return to the village in 1946, when he laments the absence of any other foreigners in the village and comments on the number of empty furnished houses (O'Prey 1984:198), many of the couples that have married in recent years have had to find rented accommodations in Soller or another nearby village as none were available in Deià. Some couples have inheritance rights to houses occupied by relations or by long-term tenants and must either wait for the death of the occupants to claim their inheritance or become involved in expensive and often painful (for both owner and tenant) litigations. Those who have managed to stay in the village have had family-owned houses to move into or lands to build upon or been fortunate enough to find a rental accommodation. Godparents or other family are often a source of housing when one's parents are unable to help.

Households

There are 529 households listed in the 1991 census for Deià. Two hundred twenty-four households are inhabited year-round by 597 persons (348 are Mallorquin, 126 are Spanish, and 123 are foreign). Most households are corporate entities in that their members share in the activities that maintain the household and each member is provided for by that household. The household is a residential and productive unit. All of the household family members have a present and future investment in the household properties. Each is contributing his or her efforts toward the household maintenance and improvements, and all will share in the value of the property over time. The moveable property of the household, its tools of trade, animals, furnishings, vehicles, etc., are usually owned by the household members. The members of a single household seldom refer to any major purchase or belonging as 'mine'. When young people leave school and start a job, no matter what the circumstances of the house, most contribute some portion of their income to the household. They are told by their parents that everything they have or acquire comes from the household and therefore they too must contribute something toward that household. When a young person wants a cassette, radio, or music system, their parents insist on contributing, and if a television set or a car is purchased, it is a 'family purchase'. The household acts as a corporate unit on all such occasions and the parents remain the 'board of directors', maintaining some control over the younger members' actions by these economic ministrations.

Family households often share in the ownership of land and other property holdings. The arrangements within any household and between households are usually the result of arrangements arrived at in the Houses from which the members came. The household arrangements of a farming family over three generations can serve as an example of this. In Es Clot there are a number of households and lands which are known as Ca'n Deya. Matias, a farmer, his wife, and one daughter live in the largest of the households. This house is his, and was his father's and grandfather's natal home. Matias's widowed sister Francisca lives next door in a house that was sectioned off from the main house by her parents at her marriage. Matias stayed in the main part of the house and maintained the lands and the produce from the family properties with the aid of his sister and her new husband. Francisca's house was considered part of her share of the jointly owned family house but the lands were kept intact and she retained a percentage of their produce and future value. She and her husband contributed their labour to the maintenance of the family lands, and their basic consumption requirements were met by the produce of these family-owned lands. Their percentage of the olive oil produced from the family olive trees provided the exchange commodity they needed to barter for grains and other goods. They also helped her husband's parents during the olive harvest and could sell their share of the oil from both family properties for cash.

When Matias married he brought his wife Catalina from her natal home in Maria de la Salud (a wheat-growing village on the plains) to live at Ca'n Deya. The house was reorganised so that Matias and his wife would have more privacy, and Francisca and her husband no longer had their midday meal with Matias. The new wife, Catalina, was in charge of her own kitchen but also had to help her husband in the fields. When Catalina's daughters were born, Francisca returned during each confinement to do many of the chores the new mother was unable to do. Matias and Catalina had three daughters. Today, they are adult women. The youngest, Xesca (diminutive of Francisca), was the first married and was given a small cottage by her aunt Francisca, after whom she is named and who is also her godmother. The cottage and the land it sits upon is a portion of her share in the lands her father and aunt inherited from their parents and that she will someday inherit from them. She, her husband, and two children live with the aunt during the week and work on their cottage at weekends. The other two sisters opened a boutique, first in a front room of their aunt's house, and later in a building they had constructed on family-owned lands nearby. When the oldest sister married in 1985, they closed the boutique, converting it into her marital home by the addition of a few rooms. The middle sister, Catalina, is now the only one who remains in the parental home.

The aunt's husband was entitled to a share in the properties of his parents but as he died before them and there was no 'blood' (children) she received nothing at her in-laws' death. Neither Xesca's husband nor her sister's husband own or are likely to inherit any lands in the village; therefore, each of the new households, established on their marriages, are parts of the women's paternal House, Ca'n Deya. The three sisters have recently been given properties by a maiden aunt in their mother's natal village. They will hold onto these for occasional visits and as a form of savings much respected among land-working people.

Mallorquin women have always retained ownership of any property they owned at marriage and the right to dispose of it as they pleased without the consent of their husbands. This was one of the statutory laws (*Fueros* or *Dret Forals* – privileges or exemptions conceded to a province or city) given to the Balearic Islands and Catalonia by James I. In Mallorca women retain their rights over property and goods they had at the time of marriage. They also hold the right to acquire property and goods during marriage and to dispose of those goods and properties as they see fit. Until 1984, on mainland Spain a woman had to have her husband's consent or permission to buy or sell any goods or properties, whether they were hers before or acquired after marriage. Although the law has changed, many women still give their husbands full rights to act on their behalf. The way women use their personal autonomy seems to differ greatly according to social class and location. Rural 'peasant' women, at least in Mallorca, are very possessive of their rights to own, buy, and sell properties while properties and businesses owned by middle- and upper-class women both in the city and the country are disposed of by men.

The Ca'n Deya family household arrangements and the rearrangements that occur with the marriages, birth, and death of its members over two or three generations are typical of the divisions and subdivisions of houses and the cooperative endeavours that take place within a house and between households over time. The family, in this case composed of a widowed mother, her son, and daughter, becomes two households on the daughter's marriage, but the lands remain one. The new household works with the natal household during harvest and busy times and separately at other times. The son brings his wife into the house to help his elderly mother. When the daughters are born the households are once again drawn closer together with the aunt assuming many of the household chores, including cooking. The two households share the midday meal again as they did before Matias married. Matias and his sister help the daughters to establish a business and additional households. All the members that marry bring their spouses to sections of the paternal House, and all the residents and their households are referred to as from Ca'n Deya. The various portions of land and buildings advanced to the two married daughters from their parental estate will be valued with all the remaining properties at the parents' death. The value of each of their advances will be deducted from their third of the partiple inheritance. Partiple inheritance can be unbalanced by godparent's gifts, especially when the godparents have no children of their own (as in this case). With their maternal aunt's gift they now own property in their mother's natal village as well as in Deià.

The parents and the father's sister at Ca'n Deya still maintain the family property and require regular help from the daughters. The scope of farming activities has been greatly reduced as the family labour force moved into other income-making pursuits. Nevertheless, the family members continue to live in their separate households, sharing land and produce, borrowing, lending or giving cash, labour, services, and goods to one another. Most of the food the four households consume is produced by the parent household with help during harvests from the children and their husbands. The oldest daughter cares for her daughter and helps her family with farmwork. The middle daughter works part-time in the local hotel and helps with work in her sister's and parents' households. The youngest daughter helps her parents during the day and teaches English with her husband in a Palma language school in the evenings. The mother raises chickens, rabbits, and turkeys (especially for Christmas), which she sells to friends and neighbours, and does laundry for foreign visitors. The aunt helps with her nieces' children and caretakes the house of a Mallorquin family who reside most of the year in France.

All of the independent activities provide 'private income' for each household, but often it is these private incomes which combine to buy the father a moped or a small tractor for the fields or a new car for the girls. The family, houses, and land are all known as one entity, Ca'n Deya, and both the family and the village acknowledge this relationship in conversation.

We see in the example of Ca'n Deya that the households formed by its members change composition over time. For the purposes of analyses, Deià household arrangements can be separated into four main types: interdependent, dependent, semi-dependent, and independent. The level of cooperation within and between households is quite different. The

Ca'n Deya households are an example of interdependent households. Each household exchanges innumerable services, activities, and commodities with the others every day. The boundaries of individual ownership are blurred, although they do exist. There are a number of households that have similar interdependent arrangements which include: one grown-up child remaining in the family house with the parents to maintain lands, business, or house and bringing his or her spouse to join that House. The other siblings in this case marry 'out' to someone from another House or to someone from another village or town. When siblings who have married out return to Deià for visits, they are provided with separate quarters sectioned off from the main house or directly adjacent to it. The main element these household arrangements have in common are two and three generations living in close proximity to one another (in the same house or adjacent houses) and sharing the main productive responsibilities of the House. In the past, this was the most common household arrangement as most of the people were employed in agriculture, which required many hands to help in the seasonal activities. At present, there are a number of households that have maintained this type of interdependent arrangement for at least the past three or four generations. They include the few families who still operate fincas: the Ripoll family, owners of Son Bauça; the Payeras family, third-generation tenants at Son Bujosa; the Vives family, owners of Ca'n Puigserver. The oldest grocery store, *S'Estanc*, has been owned and operated by the same family for four generations.

Another form of interdependent households occurs when a large house is divided into flats. One child remains with the parents in the main flat and the other flats are occupied by brothers and sisters when they marry. Each flat is a corporate unit with its members pursuing separate occupations from that of the main House. However, the close proximity of the parents involves all the households in innumerable interchanges on a regular basis.

In a third form of the interdependent household, although separate households are formed at the marriage of each child, the males of each household are employed outside the house while the women – mother, daughters, and daughters-in-law – operate some joint business venture. This is the case with the 'old' bakery and two of the grocers. These households have gone through many stages of interdependence before arriving at their current arrangement.

The organisation and reorganisation of the House known as *Es Forn* (the bakery) is a typical example. When I first knew the House in 1960 the 'family' living on the main (ground) floor was composed of husband and wife and four children, the wife's sister, and their great aunt. The two upper flats were rented to foreigners. This was my 'House' and family for the first three years that I lived in Deià. The mother of the family is still referred to by all of us as 'Mama Mena' (her real name is Magdalena). Although we have lived in five different houses since that time, Es Forn remains our *familia familia* in Deià. Es Forn has been owned and occupied by the same family for three generations. It was divided into three flats in 1955. Prior to that time, the upper floor was a granary to store potatoes, onions, figs, hang melons, and keep other fruits and vegetables. The bedrooms of the four children were on the first floor. The ground floor had an entry hall, the family hearth area, and the parents' bedroom. The cellar had the bakery oven, work tables, and kitchen area on one side and stables and an outhouse on the other.

Until 1989, Magdalena's fifty-three-year-old son Pedro, his wife, their daughter, and the wife's father lived in the first floor flat. Since she became a widow Magdalena has shared the ground floor with one of her twin daughters, her husband, and their three children. When the second twin married, her sister's family and Magdalena were occupying the ground floor, her brother the first floor and the third floor flat was rented, so she had to find a rented accommodation in Soller. The upper flat became free in 1991 and Mama Mena, then eighty-four years old, moved into it. By this time, Pedro and his family moved into a new flat they built in a large nearby property left him by his father. His vacant flat was then redecorated for his sister who lives in Soller. She rents it out and stays with Magdalena when she is in Deià.

The business of the household has changed over the generations. Originally constructed as a bakery (the large stone oven is still in the lowest part of the house, hence the name Es Forn), the house later became the central telephone exchange, then a butcher's shop, a hairdressing salon, and a dressmaker's. After the death of the baker, his daughters (Magdalena and her sister Francisca) kept the bakery operating until it became too much for them. Then they took on the telephone exchange, and when electricity was connected they bought a refrigerator and brought meat from Palma to sell from their house. Magdalena's twin daughters (Catalina and Magdalena) converted the cellar into a hairdressing salon. The women of this family have maintained all of these businesses while the fathers, husbands, brothers, and sons worked outside the house at different jobs. The house has remained a three- to four-generational unit since it was built in 1908. Most of the members of the four households are known by the name of Es Forn (the bakery) except the father-in-law, who is from Soller and is given the respect of his trade – *Mestre Toni* (a master builder). The spouses of Pedro, Catalina, and Magdalena are from the neighbouring villages of Soller and Fornalutx and have become identified in the village idiom by the name of their in-laws' house, Es Forn.

Another type of interdependent household is that of the senyor and the tenants who run his estate. There are only a few estates that still have resident tenants and their families doing the work of the finca. In most instances, the produce from the finca does not suffice to maintain a family, so the tenant's children work at seasonal salaried jobs (waiters, gardeners, etc.) and the wife of the tenant works a few days a week for the landlords in Palma. There is also one small finca that was bought by a German academic and his wife in the name of their local friend. The friend and his wife maintain the house and lands, have built their own house nearby, and will one day be the full owners of this finca. This is a most workable arrangement for both parties as the German couple have no children and the Mallorquin family has been encouraged by their friends and benefactors to develop many common interests, especially music. In both of these examples the tenants and senyors share the costs and profits from the finca and, as in the past, the senyors maintain a commitment to sustain the finca in difficult times. These are the last remnants of the patron-client relationship so characteristic in Deià until the mid-twentieth century. However, in this case the tenant has equal power since the deed is in his name. This sort of arrangement depends on personal trust and honour, and this is one of the rare cases where it has worked.

The second type of household arrangement is that of dependent households. This occurs when the household of elderly parents or bilateral relatives, due to the illness or death of one of its members, becomes dependent on the care and maintenance provided by another household. This is quite different from the first arrangement as here the households have been quite separate over long periods and are forced by life circumstances to become dependent. Each household endeavours to cover its own expenses, which has been made possible through national socialised medicine and pension plans that provide medical coverage and an income for most of the retired people in the village. Despite infirmity, many elderly people prefer to stay in their own houses as long as possible. As a result, often a daughter or daughter-in-law must bring them food each day, clean their houses, do laundry and shopping, and be generally available to help them.

Until actually bedridden, most elderly persons are encouraged and much prefer to remain in their own house and be as independent as possible. A younger household will provide the care, energy, food, and any other goods or services needed and share these responsibilities with sibling households if such exist within the village. In one extreme case, a woman who lives with her eighty-five-year-old in-laws is also looking after her eighty-year-old parents in their house (on the other side of the village) and her ninety-three-year-old aunt in another house, as well as working in the husband's family grocery store.

When a person can no longer live alone it is common to move in with one's married children. Depending on the number of children, an elderly person can spend three, four, or six months with each child. When children are living outside of Deià they try to organise a system of sharing the burden of caring for a bedridden relative, or else special 'advantages' (usually an increased percentage of inheritance) are offered to one relative to encourage her to carry a larger share of the burden. Care is always provided by women: wives, mothers, daughters, grandchildren, or godchildren. Siblings and other relatives involved in this caring are fully aware of the future shares they have in their parental properties. Mothers voice a preference to be cared for by their daughters rather than their daughters-in-law. They say that when they must move from house to house they become like the statues of the Virgins of Fatima or that of Mary which circulated among the houses of the believers in the past.[3] Family members share the joy and the burdens of suffering in these cycles of caring for their infirm relations.

On rare occasions other circumstances arise that require unique strategies. A fifty-year-old woman who lived with and cared for her ninety-year-old mother was diagnosed as having a heart condition. She called a reunion of all her cousins and godchildren and asked if any of them would be able to care for her mother if anything happened to her. A cousin and his wife volunteered immediately and she was so moved that she had them generously thanked in her will. The woman recovered and her mother has since died but the cousins will remain in the daughter's will because they gave her support when she most needed it. The fact that they would have received a major part of both estates had the daughter died and they remained the only heir to the mother's estate is never mentioned. They continue to place flowers on the mother's grave each time they come to visit Deià. Some see this as an act of piety while others feel it is an exaggerated effort to convince their benefactress that their offer had been prompted by their depth of feeling for their aunt rather than for personal gain. Generosity is seldom seen as altruistic and people are quick to point out the benefits accrued through what is presented as self-sacrifice.

When a person has no immediate kin she must make arrangements with a neighbour or acquaintance to look after her when she is no longer able. A dependent arrangement between people who have neither propinquity nor friendship in common provokes speculation about the exchange that has been offered to prompt a person to help someone with whom she held no previous relationship. One family moved into the house of an aging bachelor to care for him during the last years of his life. The woman and her natal family had always referred to him as *conco* (uncle) more out of respect for his being the age of their parents than out of any actual tie of kinship. Although some people commented that this was a clever way for the family to acquire a home, the woman felt it was perfectly natural for her and her husband to assume the responsibility for this man she'd known all her life. She and her husband improved the house considerably while the man was alive and, at his death, they inherited his house. These arrangements can be viewed as strategies used by non-inheriting kin, but must also be seen from the standpoint of the recipient. His last years were made more comfortable and his House would be carried on after his death.

Another woman was asked to care for an aging woman who lived down in Es Clot. The old woman offered the younger woman a substantial sum to be paid on her death if she would look after her. The elderly woman's desire to remain in her own house filled with memories of loved ones and all the familiar objects of her past made the exchange worthwhile to her. However, few people took this into consideration when criticising the younger woman for having accepted what they considered a 'mercenary' arrangement. Any support given by other than kin is always suspect, and people are often heard asking, 'Why would non-kin assume such extra responsibilities if not for personal gain?' They say there is no such thing as 'a gift without ties'.

Another type of dependent household has emerged in the past few years. A young couple becomes financially dependent on their parent households due to pregnancy, marrying very young, unemployment, or military service. Since the costs of setting up an independent residence, whether rented or purchased, require regular employment and large expenditures for all concerned, these couples and their respective families are in a bind. With the movement of workers into the service sector and the division of larger houses into nuclear family-sized flats, family dwellings can no longer easily accommodate additional members. Similar circumstances might have occurred in the past, but extended family households could more easily accommodate the couple. Additional labourers were always useful in agricultural activities. Despite the difficulties, the girl's family will adapt their existing space to allow the couple to reside with them until their situation improves.

The third household arrangement can be referred to as semi-dependent. These are usually a number of separate, related households that help one another on a more or less flexible basis with activities ranging from operating a business to making preserves. Retired elders as well as younger family members from different households come together to engage in constructive pursuits that are intended to be pleasant and beneficial to all concerned. There is seldom any direct remuneration for this help. Rather, it is a means by which people with similar House names living in separate households maintain a sense of 'open house' or commensality. Family relationships are strengthened through this sort of reciprocity.

In both the interdependent and dependent household arrangements, no choice is involved. One is obliged to cooperate. Semi-dependent arrangements, however, are not based on moral obligations: they are the result of a desire for social and kin contact. All the households in this category would survive without this kind of family assistance. The unsolicited aid of supportive family members from other households lifts the morale of those who might otherwise feel isolated or burdened and maintains a social interchange between separate households. Girls who move to other villages at marriage always complain of the absence of these casual family visits. Older women who are widowed and childless are almost always willing to baby-sit and make great efforts to visit their local kin. They also go to evening mass with their contemporaries as often as possible to keep from feeling isolated. These are all social rather than dependent relationships. These are households that are interchanging with one or more other households in which at least one member in each is recognised by a common House name. The activities which they share give emotional, physical, or moral support to one another. The members involved in these interchanges may be men, women, or children. A mother might spend more time with one daughter than another or an aunt or uncle might help their niece or nephew more than their own children: the essence of this sort of arrangement is that it is optional.

In the greengrocers known as *Ca'n Burota* one might find the owner's mother and her maternal aunt sitting in the side room, knitting as their brother looks on. This might seem like a large family sitting room with everyone relaxing and chatting. Actually, the mother drops in almost every day to help her daughter fill the shelves or whatever needs doing. Her aunt and uncle usually join her a few times a week, and their maternal aunt of ninety-two usually manages one or two visits a week. There might be two or as many as four Margaritas, a Magdalena, Francisca, and Andrés visiting at any one time: all are known by the House name of Ca'n Burota. Each lives in a separate household but all share one another's social space whenever possible. They are all known in the village by their relation with their maternal grandmother's House, Ca'n Burota. Again, although their choice to meet at the niece's shop is beneficial to her economically, socially, and emotionally, it also adds to their overall family cohesion.

Other cases of semi-dependent households would be people who live in close proximity to one another but are not kin. In such relationships favours, goods, and services are exchanged, but again on a flexible basis and without obligation. Almost all the households in Deià are involved to one degree or another with other households in the village. The grocers, post office, tobacco store, and hairdressers' shops are located in the front rooms of people's houses. Although the individual members of any household have numerous daily encounters with members of other households, their principal productive and social activities usually revolve around the members of their own household, an independent corporate unit. Their interchange of activities with others is mostly voluntary. There are no formally structured neighbour relations in Deià like those described by Freeman for Valdemora or Ott for St. Engrace. Indeed, people make a point of denying that there is any structured pattern of reciprocity. However, one can detect various modes of reciprocity which are used over and over again by different people in similar circumstances: for example, when a favour has been done by someone (a light switch repaired, trees trimmed, or a gas bottle carried) the recipient may leave freshly cut flowers, fruit, or vegetables outside the helper's door a few days later (but never on the same day – pretending one gesture has no relation to the other).

The fourth type of household, the independent, is one that has no reliance on or involvement with any other household and would not have been possible prior to motorised transport. The majority of its endeavours are pursued as a separate entity. In the context of corporate-ness (a number of persons combined to form a single unit, a collective body represented as one entity) many households in each type are independent; that is, they can support themselves by the efforts of their own household without the assistance of another household. Few are independent of the social, political, or religious life of the village, which encourages mutual support, exchange, and reciprocity. The only households that make this category necessary are those who visit or stay in the village but make most of their purchases in Palma or Soller and have little, if any, contact with the village people. On the other hand, however occasional their village visits, their arrivals and departures will be noted and they will be recognised and identified in village conversation by their residence in a familiar named House. The Deianencs need to place each person in their village into some context or their sense of village as a continuity over time would be threatened.

The shared knowledge of those who perceive the village as a form of known space and time, of domestic groups and families, most of whom participate wholly or partially in similar social, economic, and religious activities, allows individuals to identify one another as members of known Houses that form 'the community'. The identification of one House with another over time generates a sense of community which the geographical idiom 'the village' articulates. Marriage brings together two people and two Houses to form a third household. Birth adds individuals to that household and members to the community. Age and illness reorganise households; death deprives a household of an individual and the community of a link in the long chain of connections by which it is formed. The concept of an enduring community over time is maintained by identifying progressive generations (and newcomers from outside the village) with a known House. By carrying the past into the present a sense of belonging to a community is engendered in its members, at least for those who understand the connections. As Zonabend found in Minot in France: 'To all appearances the village lives in a time that is continuous and homogeneous, a chronological time that is broken up into days, months and years.' However, in conversation she found time being expressed as 'multifaceted and broken up into separate slices'. So there rose up a time of daily living and a 'time of life', made up of an 'in the old days' and a 'today', a 'before' and a 'now', that cyclically became the same, fused together in a 'time of community' which plunged back into the origins of the group (1984:x). In Deià as in Minot, these variations blend into a stable vision of 'the village' – 'the community' – despite its contradictions, tensions, and changing members.

House Names As Metaphors for Social Relations

Deià is similar to other small communities in that each person living there knows about every other person and his or her ancestors. This is made clear when you ask one person for the name of another person and you are told: that is *Figuera* or *Carindo* or *Francisca de Ca'n Pera Joan.* Then I use one of these names to greet someone: *'Bon dia Carindo'* and I'm told, 'My name is not Carindo, my name is *Joan Ripoll Colom'.* After many inquires I discover that Carindo was the name of Joan's grandfather's House, and although Joan lives in a different house, he is known in the village by Carindo rather than by the name of the house he actually lives in. Now this may be just one form of a nickname as many writers of Spanish ethnographies suggest (Lison, Pitt-Rivers, Kenny, Iszaevich, et. al.), but in Deià, a person may have a nickname and also a House name. A House name used to describe a person acknowledges that person's relationship to other people in the village, and imparts a great deal of information about the past as well as the present social organisation of the village.

As Joan Bestard pointed out in his study of the neighbouring Balearic island of Formentera, 'people use a system of classification and identification much more complicated than a simple list of written names' (1986:33). A person can be referred to or spoken about with different names in different circumstances. Each person has at least one or two Christian names, two surnames, a diminutive, a nickname, and a House name. When people talk about one another, Christian names are always accompanied by descriptive names; e.g., a House name, a nickname, a profession, or some other attribute which distinguishes that person from all the others in the village who bear the same name. Since most first-born sons are named after their paternal grandfather and second sons after maternal grandfather and first-born daughters after paternal grandmothers and second ones after maternal grandmothers, the variety of names used in the village is somewhat limited, especially where there has been a good deal of village endogamy.

The conventions for the naming of a person have been shown 'to be central to the process by which social categories become integral elements in social action' (H. Geertz 1979:243). In Deià, the Christian name which all children are given at birth and with which they are welcomed into the community of God at baptism and the surname which recognises their parentage are only part of a person's social identity. Each person has at least one *malnom*, literally bad name or nickname, and is also recognised by a *renom,* renowned by a House name that places him or her within the social context known as 'the village'; e.g., *Miguel Coll Jaume* is the official name of Michael the son of Pedro Coll and Margarita Jaume (women and men retain their birth surnames throughout their lives). Surnames are composed of one's mother's and father's paternal cognomens. Miguel is also referred to as *Miguel Maleter,* Michael the porter, a nickname based on his first job lifting the heavy cases onto the daily mail coach to Palma. He is also known as *Miguel de Sa Fonda,* Michael from the inn, the House his parents and grandparents owned.

The House name identifies an individual in relation to a family (past or present) and functions as a surname in conversation. The actual cognomen is reserved for official papers and is often not used in the community. The twenty-two typical Deià surnames, which are used in innumerable combinations, present no lack of cognomen variation by which to identify people. However, House names and nicknames are far more informative. Young men commented that they were never referred to by their cognomen until they went to military service. After thirty years of relying on the *teléfonista* (the local switchboard operator) to connect them with *En Miguel Fornes* (Michael from the baker's house) or *Joanina Fidivella* (Joana the noodlemaker's daughter), the villagers were most disconcerted when automatic dialing phones were installed and they had to remember one another's surnames in order to find a telephone number in the book.

Children are given a Christian name at birth, usually based on the name of their grandparents. Additional children are named after saints or godparents. If a child dies, his or her name is given to the next child born to that family. In most villages throughout Spain, the names used in each village are those derived long ago from the saints most revered by that particular village. In Deià, the patron saint is Sant Joan (St. John). Joan and the feminine form Joana are among the most common names in the village. Other popular names in Deià are: Maria for the Virgin Mary, Lluch for the Virgin of Lluch, Francisco and Francisca for St. Francis of Assisi, Catalina for Santa Catalina, Tomas, Antonio and Antonia for St. Anthony, Pedro for St. Peter, Bartolomeu (Tomeu) for St. Bartholomew, Miguel for St. Michael, and Sebastian for St. Sebastian.

The Virgin of Lluch is a small figurine kept in the monastery at Lluch, which is on the north of the island. There is a legend that the figurine was found in a cave in the nearby mountains. It was brought into the church and a few days later it disappeared. It was found in the same cave as before and once more put in the church. When it disappeared and was found a third time in the same cave, the congregants promised to build a special chapel for it at the site of the cave. The yearly celebration of the figurine's return to its rightful place in the monastery is one of the few occasions shared by all the villages on the island. Many men and women pledge to make the annual pilgrimage to Lluch by foot if their prayers (for the improvement of a child's health or a happy marriage, etc.) during the previous year are answered. St. Anthony and St. Francis are the protectors of animals. Santa Catalina was a girl from the neighbouring village of Valldemossa who, it is said, 'escaped from the devil by hiding in the trunk of an olive tree'. St. Sebastian protected the village from the plague which devastated 40 per cent of the island's population in the eighteenth century. The passing of each year in a person's life is celebrated not on one's birthday but on one's saint's day. One's life on earth is a celebration of those who went before and those who will follow. Individual birthday celebrations have increased since foreigners began to invite their local friends to birthday parties.

Since at least grandparents, grandchildren, and probably a number of first cousins share the same name, innumerable diminutives and other adaptations have been developed. Each person, therefore, has a personal name albeit based on a shared generational name. Thus we find Francisco, Xisco, Xesc, and Paco all based on Francisco; Xesca and Paquita for Francisca; Toni and Tonita for Antonio/a; Cati and Tina, for Catalina; Tita or Marga for Margarita, and so forth. Sometimes the parents, or on occasion the Priest, will make the distinction by baptising a child with two Christian names, one recognising the grandparents and another from the name of the saint on whose day the baptism takes place. Thus, we have Catalina Maria, Maria Magdalena, Maria Rosa, or Joan Josep. A name like Maria del Carmen usually means that the girl's father or grandfather is a fisherman (St. Carmen is the guardian of the seas). It is very difficult to alter this naming procedure as both the registrar and the church in most areas of the country will not acknowledge non-Christian names. In order to register a birth and hold a baptism, the parents must therefore chose a proper name from the pantheon of saints.[4] The church's ideal of a community of God is reflected in the shared names of saints within the village.

A person is spoken to or about by using either the Christian name, its diminutive, or a nickname. The nickname is an individualising as well as a socialising device. It can be based on a distinguishing physical characteristic, idiosyncrasy, or action associated with a particular person or in some cases with one of their ancestors. A boy or girl is often nicknamed by a sibling or by their schoolmates. As Michael Kenny wrote: 'Nicknames help to personalise relationships but there are no fixed rules for applying or transmitting them. A nickname can be used as a form of social satire behind which lurks scorn and sometimes envy but it is not an insult except when used in the recipient's presence' (Kenny 1961:89). On the other hand, Gilmore (1982) felt that 'nicknames are emotionally charged, a form of verbal aggression and a displacement of competitive envy'. In contrast to these interpretations, I found that nicknames were used endearingly and tended to thus socialise unsociable differences between people (especially physical differences, but also social and sometimes behavioural or psychological ones). Instead of saying 'so-and-so is terribly tall or fat or ugly or dumb or mad', and implying that such a person is unlike the rest of the village, he can be called *el largo, el gordo, el feo, el tonto,* or *el loco* which makes all those characteristics part of the village. In Deià one would be more offended by the absence of a nickname than by having a negative one. A nickname recognises one as a member of the known village. The only time I have seen men react negatively to the use of nicknames is when they were used by a relative stranger. The listeners acted as though they had no idea whom the person was talking about, thereby making it clear that that person had no right to use local idiomatic descriptions as he was not a recognised member of their community.

The nickname has a social dimension, too. It is a sign of inclusion in the community when a nickname is coined and used by everyone (except the individual); those who understand the reference are identified as members of a group or community. Nicknames are not necessary for someone from another village or town who can be recognised by his or her Christian name – Alfredo, Esperanza, Roberto – or by his or her surname – Gimenez, Chicano, or Apestinguia. These are names from outside the village that will be mixed with local names and continue to identify future generations as descendants from someone from another town or village.

House names, by which people are known and referred to in the village idiom, can be registered names or village creations. Every house is registered by a name when it is built. Although the name may be selected by the owner, the villagers immediately associate the members of any new house with one of their family Houses and call the new house by that name, e.g., Joan built a new house and called it *Ca'n Torrente* (House by the Stream). The villagers refer to Joan, his wife, and children as *de Ca'n Rascas* (his grandfather's nickname and House name).[5] The House name may be based on the surname, profession, Christian name, nickname, or trade of the first occupant; the physical characteristics or location of the properties; or it can record some special occurrence in the life of the first occupants: *Son Dotze* (House of Twelve) was built with the money won in a card game where the winning number was twelve. Any kind of a reference can become a House name. Everyone in the village is associated with a named House and identified in the village idiom by their Christian and House name.

Unlike surnames, which are transmitted patrilineally, House names can be perpetuated by men, women, or adoptive members. One's House name links one with genealogically or economically related households. The village labels people as descendants or kin (in the widest sense) of a known family by a House name. Often the House name endures beyond the life of its members; it is usually carried on by new owners because it makes the transfer of deeds much easier. Most important for the village is the continuity that the House name embodies. Many foreigners who reside in the village were identified by a House name long before their Christian names were known. One's relationship to a named house may come via birth, marriage, employment, adoption, or purchase. The new owners or occupants of a known House are given a sort of 'fictive kinship' within the village idiom.

People are classified as members of a recognised domestic group (past or present) by the use of a House name. House names represent an acknowledgement of the attachment of each person in the village to someone else, either living or dead, and represent a continuity of people, land, and families – 'the community' over time. A House name does not refer to just a building and the ground it occupies; it is a metaphor for social relations that gives one a place within village life.

The meanings of family, household-domestic groups, and House names in Deià have been discussed in the previous sections. We have seen that the word for House is casa, which means not just a house but also the people associated with it and family. The Latin word 'familia' meant a fusion of kinship and coresidence, the root being servants of a household or a household of slaves headed by a patriarch who owned them. Today, 'family' need not imply residence as we have seen in the various forms of household organisation in Deià. A named House can be made up of a number of separate households (domestic groups). The term 'House' encompasses the smaller parts which are the various households that have developed from a core House. We have seen how one House may mean a related group of people, all with the same patronym; or a nuclear family; or a solidly structured and socially recognised organisation as in the estates of the past.

The names that people and Houses are known by present a social and economic history of the village. The largest estates that once formed the core of the village and gave employment to most of the people bear the surnames of their first owners. We have seen that each estate had a contracted tenant farmer and his family living on the premises in quarters sectioned off from the main house. *Missatges* were regularly employed workers and *jornalers* daily employees. The owner was referred to as *Es Senyor de Son Moragues*, the tenant as *l'amo de Son Moragues* and the employees were known by their Christian name and the estate name. A House built in the village by the tenant would be referred to by his Christian name followed by the name of the estate he managed: *Ca'n Lluch de Son Moragues, Ca'n Jordi de Son Canals.* This name and means of identification would be carried by the tenants and their children into further generations.

Until the 1960s, seating at church services was by Houses with the senyors in the front rows, the tenants behind them, and behind the tenants any other men who were employed by that estate. The benches they sat upon were donated by the estate owner and bore his House name. Women and girls sat in the back of the church on stools they carried from home. The stool cover, which had been embroidered while she was at school, bore the initials of her Christian name and her surnames. The wooden legs would have been a gift from her family for her communion after which she became a full member of the congregation and had her own place to sit.

Large estate owners contributed to the maintenance of the church and sent their employees to carry out repairs. The builders of a House had a permanent relationship to the owners until death. Not only would they be available to make minor or major repairs on the buildings, but it was always two of the builders of the large estates who volunteered to dig the grave for a deceased member of any of the households associated with that House. For the past twenty years, *Francisco Mosso* (whose House name comes from his great-grandfather who employed *mossos* – waiters – in his local bar) has always been the first person to be notified when someone dies. He was an apprentice builder in 1930 and accompanied his boss (*Mestre Valenti)* to the homes of deceased clients to set about preparing the body for burial. The builder would notify the priest who would announce the death by ringing the church bells (an even number of times for a man and uneven number for a woman).[6] He would also order the coffin from the carpenter. He would send two of his workers to dig the grave (or open the family plot), lower the coffin, and then close the grave with a new cement covering on which they carved the name and birthdate of the deceased.

Family tombs began to be marked with large marble stones during this century. Today, these tombstones with the patronymics of the parents of those buried there mark the family or House burial plot in which at least three generations are buried. Tombstones with photographs of the deceased became fashionable during the 1970s. This practice was brought over from France, where many of the local people had family members. It was restricted in 1977 when the village council took the cemetery over from the church and tried to establish some regularity among the graves. Despite the ruling, pictures continue to appear along with flowers ranging from fresh to plastic, and vases of every size and shape continue to distinguish one grave from another, reminding us that even on the grave the conflict between individual and collective representation is expressed.

One's connection with a House is also a citizen's only access to the political sphere. Participation in village decision making comes through being a member of a household, which makes one a *Vecino* (literally, a neighbour) and gives one legal rights in the village. New members of old Houses have ready-made support if they want to enter politics. At election time, people say candidates are voted for based on their House affiliation rather than party platforms.

This practice of grouping people together who share blood, marriage, or merely house occupancy or employment ties, brings history into the present. The first settlers in Deià were Cistercian monks and nobles who were given these lands by James I for their help in the conquest of the Moors and the creation of the kingdom of Mallorca in 1229. Anyone who came to live and work in Deià as a vassal, as well as any Moors who were captured and made chattels of these estates, was given the estate House name as a means of identification. This practice must have continued for centuries as new people came into the village and were incorporated into various finca households. Of the twenty-two most prevalent surnames in Deià, only five are not names of nobles who arrived with the conquest and after whom estates in Deià were named. Present-day usage of familiar House names to identify new residents certainly reflects these historical practices.

House names used by the village might be changed if someone in a future generation attains professional status, accomplishes some memorable action, or somehow identifies oneself as different from the House with which his or her family has been associated. Each generation identifies the most dominant personalities and activities of its period by the selective perpetuation of some House names, the alteration of others, and the reallocation of existing names to new domestic groups (i.e., newly married couples or foreigners). As Bourdieu wrote: 'The continuation of the name is not due to filiation, but as "symbolic capital" which each family is capable of maintaining or accumulating through the generations' (1984:68). Buying or occupying a named village house provides one with ready-made symbolic capital. For example, *Toni Quet* was the gardener at Es Moli. His father, Tomeu 'Quet', had been the manager of a large estate named Ca'n Quet, and he and his sons were all known by this estate name. Toni's nieces and nephews are also known by the name of the House that employed their paternal grandfather. Ca'n Quet was converted into a small hotel and restaurant in the 1950s. In 1968, a man named Paco came from Soller to manage it. It was not long before the village was talking about Paco of Ca'n Quet. Paco leased Ca'n Quet for seven years, and he, his wife, and children were incorporated into Deià life by giving them the name of the House with which they were now associated. Paco is no relation to Toni Quet but they both shared a connection to Ca'n Quet. The village has extended a fictive kinship to Paco and his family in order to identify them within the community made up of recognised Houses, families, and households.

There are few instances today of people living in the actual house with which they are associated. Most House names go back at least three or more generations. This system of identifying and associating each person in the village by House names that evoke tales of generations of associations, activities, and occupations maintains a sense of continuity despite the changing actors.

When the people living in a house are identified by the profession, name, or trade of one of the actual occupants, this usually indicates that it is the achievements of the living person which gives the name to the house, e.g., *Ca'l Metge* (the Doctor's House) or *Ca'l Bisbe* (the Bishop's House). Both the doctor and Bishop are respected public figures, and the name of the House they occupy (whether by purchase or lease) has been elevated to that of the present occupants' position and will be carried by the doctor's family and the Bishop's employees into future generations. By looking at changes in the House names used to label groups over time, one gains a sense of the accomplishments of individuals as judged by the village and the basis of social status in operation at any particular period.

Maria Coll was always known as *Maria de Casa Damunt*, the name of the estate her father and grandfather managed. Maria, who did not marry, became a dressmaker and developed a large local and foreign clientele. First foreigners and then locals started referring to her as *Maria la Modista* (Castilian for Maria the dressmaker). Had Maria married as well as becoming a dressmaker it is unlikely that her trade name would have replaced her House name. Had she had children it is virtually certain that at least the girls would have been known by the House name of Casa Damunt. Without husband, children, siblings, aunts, or uncles with whom she can share the Casa Damunt connection, Maria's inherited House name ends with her. The estate, once an important employer of Deià workers, now belongs to foreigners who have little contact with the village. It could be said that the village, by giving Maria a 'here and now' existence as Maria the dressmaker, has relieved her socially and idiomatically of the obligation to carry on the family name or its history, to marry, or to have children. In giving her a Castilian nickname, the village acknowledges that she serves mostly foreigners and also indicates that her new role and foreign-based success are part of a different value system (career rather than family). This is a clear example of how change is integrated into local vernacular.

Married women who combine dressmaking, hairdressing, or business with family duties are not usually acknowledged as dressmakers or hairdressers but rather as wives and mothers. More importance is given to the family-bound character of married women's lives. There seems to be a limitation on recognising married women's individuality, and all the metaphors used to describe them are related to reproduction and nurturing. The life cycle expectations for women are clearly articulated in references such as daughter of, wife of, mother of, and culminate with the use of Madonna or Doña, terms of respect reserved for women who have fulfilled the above roles.

A bachelor or spinster usually carries his or her parents' or grandparents' House name to the grave. When a woman marries and has children she can be buried in either her parents' tomb or her in-laws' tomb. The decision is often based not so much on familial altruism as on space and the quality of the tomb as status symbol. People say that if there is 'no blood connection through children' the two families remain separate, their names have not been joined.[7] Women retain their surnames when they marry and seldom use their husband's name even for official purposes. If there are no children in a marriage there is no new surname made up of each parent's patronym. The wife will usually be buried in her family plot and the husband in his, or they will both be buried in her family plot. Living near one's mother at marriage is the preferred practice in Deià: women's families more readily extend the term family, their living space, social space, and resting place to include sons-in-law.

The retention of one's House name after marriage is a common practice in Deià. Female children carry on their mother's House name and boys their father's. In marriages between one Deià-born person and another person recognised in the village idiom either by a unique surname or an occupation or trade, both partners retain their separate identifying names, but their children are most often known by the more socially significant of the two names. When one's spouse is from outside of Deià and that person was unknown in the village prior to the courtship and marriage, he or she and their children will carry the name of the House into which they marry.

For example, Toni 'Ferrer' (Antonio, the son of an ironmonger) married Magdalena 'Burota' (whose grandmother was born in Ca'n Burota). Both having been born in Deià, each carried his or her parental House name. They had a daughter who was born while they were living in France. They named her Antoinette (French for Antonia), after her grandfather and father Antonio. During their absence, they had a house built on land once known and used by the village as an enclosure for grazing sheep. Since their return, the entire family is known as *de sa tanca en mitge* (from the enclosure). Antoinette, her husband, and son are referred to by this House name, informing us that Antoinette married someone from outside of Deià. The names used by people to describe this household are indicative of the information that is transmitted through the use of House names: lineage, occupations, geographic and economic developments over time, endogamy, exogamy, etc.

To conclude: the House name indicates a person's heritage. Nicknames tell something about personality, physical characteristics, or other distinguishing elements. Most people have both a House name and a nickname. Although the surname acknowledges parentage, it is not the means by which people are grouped together in the village idiom.

A nickname is an individualising device which acknowledges a person's accomplishments or idiosyncrasies and momentarily separates him or her from the social matrix to which all people are connected. But it is a social device as well because it brings the individual into the local collectivity through an inside idiom only understood by members. Sometimes one's nickname is perpetuated into the next generation, in which case, House name and nickname are synonymous. If a nickname is perpetuated, it is in recognition of some special activity or personality that is of such significance that it has replaced the other name by which that person's House was known in the past.

Some foreign residents are acknowledged in the village idiom by House names and nicknames. Depending on which identification came first, the former may be the result of the latter or vice versa, but both symbolise the person's inclusion within the social relations of the village. A House name is a reference to a person and his or her connection to other people known to the village in the past or the present. Some House names can hold negative connotations. When a previous House name is not carried by a Deianenc into his new house and the children are identified only by the marital House name, it is usually because the marital House is better known or more esteemed at present. In some cases, the in-marrying person, male or female, becomes more identified with the marriage House (affines) than with their parental house. This suggests that personal, social, or economic differences between Houses affect the perpetuation of a House name. The use of House names stimulates an awareness of each House's place in the local hierarchy. A selective process subtly prunes away the names of less significant activities and personalities at any particular period and replaces them with more relevant names, so that the village idiom continues to be updated to reflect changing activities and values over time.

House names are the means by which 'the village' groups people together. Individuals are identified in relation to their present household or that of their ancestors. This recognises the 'symbolic capital' associated with House names and suggests some sort of bilateral lineage or descent group. Although the criteria for House names vary, the names are nevertheless a descriptive and selective device which acknowledges this generation's connection with previous generations. House names provide the basis by which individuals are associated with the collective and provide the means by which members of the village are defined. Once clearly defined as members, people perceive themselves and others as 'a community'.

NOTES

1. Ruth Behar in her book on *Santa Maria del Monte* has noted the contents of local family and council documents which detailed the condition and value of every item in a house to assure that disbursement of goods among heirs to even the smallest estates was correctly calculated (1987).

2. City dwellers dress up during the week and come to the village on weekends to relax and dress in casual 'country clothing', while the villagers dress up in their best 'city clothes' on a Sunday or fiesta.
3. Circulating statues of virgins is a common practice throughout Spain. See Christian 1972.
4. An article about the difficulties an official on the mainland encountered when trying to register his daughter's birth appeared in the national press. It seems that he and his wife had decided to give their daughter a name composed of letters from each of their names: Ramon and Elena, daughter Ramela. The registrar refused to issue a birth certificate until a religious name was prefixed to their creation. This happened often under Franco, but was meant to end with the new democratic constitution. Nevertheless, in small towns officials can still impose their own interpretations on any rules (Diario de Mallorca, 25 May 1988).
5. *Rascar* means to scratch. Joan's grandfather was a sheep-shearer and his nickname may have come from the effects of the fleece on his skin.
6. In a delightful play by Joan Mas (a well-known Deianenc), the death of a local man is announced by the uneven ringing of the church bells. It seems he had asked to be buried as a woman: only in death could he reveal his homosexuality. During the Franco era a homosexual was treated like a criminal. Pitt-Rivers wrote that there was no homosexuality in his village in the fifties. I'm sure this was not the case but I assume that he, as a gentlemen, could not say otherwise without jeopardising the safety of his informants. In the past, men with homosexual tendencies would try to marry in order to keep up the pretense of being like other men. Today, that is not necessary but people in a small village like Deià continue to make comments about any man who isn't married by the time he's forty. There are a few confirmed bachelors whose independence is not questioned and others who have married late to overcome any suggestion of homosexuality.
7. Campbell writes that: 'The honor of the family and its solidarity are symbolised in the idea of blood. In marriage a man and woman mix their blood to produce "one blood" which is the blood of their children. Relationships in the family are a participation in this common blood' (1976:144).

4. Tradition

Old Uses in New Conditions

The pattern of naming, the way people describe the village in terms of social and geographical space, and the use of House names as metaphors for social relations reflect the 'traditional' basis around which the modern village of Deià is organised. There is a historical content to so much of what one hears and sees today in Deià. Despite over a hundred years of contact with outsiders actually residing in the village, Deianencs still identify one another in an idiom based on traditional categories which are understood only by them. These categories have been extended to include some outsiders into the existing assortment of names and descriptions without altering the character of the idiom. In fact, character and vitality are added by 'others' who begin to participate in various aspects of local life.

These traditional practices, which are an effective means for preserving a sense of continuity, also create a convenient façade behind which all kinds of new and different relationships, beliefs, morals, and values are absorbed. People have learned to maintain tradition selectively. That which fits their needs is perpetuated and that which does not is forgotten or not mentioned. People hold on to what makes them feel secure. The past is ever present in the architecture, activities, and descriptive terminology used by the Deianencs, suggesting an accumulated experience and continued usage of that which has been handed down as belief or practice. But tradition is not inherited; it is a name given to something constantly being made. Whether it be in the form of rhetoric or ceremonies, tradition is a symbolic manipulation that hides behind history. Abner Cohen noted that 'societies undergoing rapid and therefore, destabilising processes of change often generate atavistically some apparently traditional forms, but impart to them meaning and implication appropriate to contemporary circumstances' (Cohen 1985:47).

The village maintains an ethos of a timeless paradise inhabited by related people and Houses and families, of shared space and familiar activities carried on within ancient walls. Yet most of the categories by which people are described have been reinterpreted to fit the constantly changing 'reality' of the society. Neighbours are not always those who live next door. Family include people living in other countries. House names are not only inherited but can be acquired by marriage, employment, or purchase. Spatial connotations and social activities are gender-specific despite social and economic developments. These are all safety devices which are kept 'in-check' while within each separate household all sorts of private, complex negotiations, conflicts, or struggles are taking place which could erode the smaller parts that make up the entity known as 'the village'. Just as House names disappear and are replaced by others which are deemed more relevant, families move away or split apart. Therefore, 'Society can no more be said to consist of families than a journey is made up of stopovers which break it down into discontinuous stages. They are at the same time its condition and its negation' (Lévi-Strauss 1956:285).

Family conflicts over property and official complaints between brothers and sisters or other heirs figure in village records since the fifteenth century.[1] However, the crisis of any one family cannot disrupt the 'traditional base' which has survived generations of adaptations. Anthony Cohen observed, 'Some patterns of symbolic action can be survivals from the past but they continue into the present, not because of inertia or conservatism but because they play important roles within the social setting. Indeed, some are revived from the past to serve in the same way. Other symbolic patterns called traditions are of recent origin and yet others are being continuously created for new, or for old purposes' (1974:7).[2] In Deià we find invented, assumed, and reinterpreted forms labelled traditions.

Individuals and families, fully aware of 'traditional' values and 'proper' codes of behaviour, have learned to project an acceptable image to protect themselves from too much attention. There are few matters that go unnoticed among close neighbours or family members. Nevertheless, what goes on inside a household is different than what is observed from the outside. There is a great deal of talk about people and what they have or have not done but very little action that would provoke confrontation harmful to village relations. Today, people in small groups will express anger about someone manipulating their irrigation water intakes but they will not actually challenge the 'culprit'. Traditionally, water rights were transferred with deeds of purchase, and this practice continues. An example from a document dated 1843 reads: 'Two bancals [terraces] with one and a half hours of water every second Wednesday of the year.' Another: 'small orchard with water rights each Monday of the year from 12 noon for one hour.' Owners must be on hand to be sure they get their water on the allotted day as it can be diverted above and not reach them. Most of the people in Es Clot have contracts specifying the number of hours of water per week to which they are entitled. The water is channelled off into many narrow canals that flow into each person's land. The canals are opened and closed by lifting a tile and putting it back in place when one's time is up but one often finds his water time being diverted by someone else. As anyone can have access to the opening and closing of anyone else's canal, it is impossible to obtain sufficient proof to identify 'the culprit'.

People may discuss the number of new cars a family has acquired and speculate about the source of the funds, but they will rarely confront the persons with direct inquiries. Rumours about money hidden in caves since the Civil War or the person responsible for the disappearance of a deceased woman's jewels are passed on from one area of the village to another. As Peter Lienhardt pointed out, 'rumour is an indirect regulating force, anxiety justifying, ambiguous communication of ideas, perspectives, public or private opinions' (1975:196). It is a convenient outlet for anger, frustration, jealousy, envy, and hostilities in general. Rumour defines the moral community, those who share the values in question. Social sanctions serve to maintain the status quo but also offer an ideal camouflage behind which independent domestic groups can continue acquiring and increasing their material and personal interests.[3] By maintaining the ethos of a 'traditional' community, individual differences can be masked.

As a Deianenc, one learns that 'you do what you have to do and then you let others discover what you have done and do or say what they like about it'. It is terribly important to seem unconcerned about problems and to make decisions and carry them out inside the household before the outside is allowed to gain information or obstruct your actions.[4] If neighbours are too well informed about your private household matters, it puts you in their debt. If you do not avoid them information will create an intimacy which people usually try to confine to their household. As in the card game played in many parts of Spain called *Truc* (trick or lie), you never put all your cards on the table at one go. Games, like life, are played in pairs – two, four, or six – and you communicate with your partner through signals that, you hope, none of the others understand. The object of the game is to deceive your opponents. Caught off guard, they will need time to organise their retaliation, which will give you time to plan your next action. By not showing all your cards at one time you can delay the action of the other players. Those playing the game know the rules, and the challenge is to outsmart your opponent, even if only momentarily. Once an action is completed, it doesn't matter if others are in accord or not. Playing card games is a powerful testing ground to get to know one's peers and their means of defense in gamesmanship.

If you ask for advice outside of your house, too many people will have too many ideas and you'll never get anything decided or accomplished. Public agreement about anything is a sign of weakness. Some people will feign agreement with what is being said and, then, as soon as the person leaves the group will begin to criticise him and his plans. A man has to keep up appearances and protect his interests by dropping by the bar at least once a day. If he is on hand to participate in discussions, he remains informed about village activities and assures his part in forthcoming events. A man asserts his 'individualism' by disagreement and shows his independence of mind and familiarity with the subject by provoking discussion. However, on major issues – politics or village development – each person will confer privately with many others before committing himself to a decision. The people to whom one turns for these more important decisions are often the village leaders in politics or business. Leaders have been drawn from the same small number of families for the past century. The new direction of politics after the death of Franco has not altered the source of leaders. Old families have just assumed the new roles under new political party names.

Most people seem afraid to contradict or disagree too loudly. The less involved they are in legal and political matters, the safer they feel. Some say that 'really all Spaniards are anarchists. Under Franco we were controlled and with the Socialists we've got too many choices'. During Franco's regime, if people wanted something done or changed they would group together as a body of *vecinos* (residents) protecting any one person by identifying themselves as a group. Now with 'social democracy', many people think a body for action is unnecessary, that each person has a right to express an opinion. Yet few step forward. In local politics, elected politicians are setting themselves up as the 'voice of the people', both those who voted for them and against them.

One man who is especially cynical about the difficulties of living in a village community told me the following story: 'When the people of Deià wanted a church they couldn't decide where to build it. They agreed to untether a goat, let it walk freely through the village, and when and where it chose to rest would be the site of the church. As goats like mountains it found Es Puig and there it rested. Anyone who allows their decisions to be made by goats deserves the consequences [in this case the long walk up to the church].' The word for a male goat, *cabró,* is used to belittle a man (by associating him with cowards, goats, and females).[5] The man who told the story feels just as much 'a goat' (helpless) as his fellow villagers. He has spoken out in the past to no avail and feels that his opinions fall only on deaf ears, so they are expressed only to sympathetic family and friends. Men (those who are politically active as well as those who no longer actively participate) are forever turning their palms upwards and dropping their chins when discussing controversial issues. They are implying and sometimes saying, 'That is the way things are. What can we do?'

When most of the men were involved in contraband activities, they learned not to talk about essential matters but to fill their public exchanges with issues of general interest and non-controversial subjects, i.e., the price of fertiliser, a kilo of lemons, olives, or whatever was being sold at that time of year. This reticence to discuss anything of personal importance in public continues today. A theme that occupies much of public discussion is the state of one's own or someone else's health. People dramatically describe symptoms and generously share similar but more gruesome details of illnesses, medications, accidents, or operations. Health, something everyone experiences and has little control over, becomes the major issue while personal politics and finances are kept secret. The most important things are seldom discussed outside of one's House. Silence conveys importance more than words.

Many men like to play the stereotypical role of *macho* in the public bar and street groupings. They compete to dominate the discussions, shout and gesticulate. A man never lights a cigarette or a cigar without having offered the pack to everyone at his table, and when drinks are ordered there is mock competition for the right to pay for that round.

Workers compete with bosses and young men with older ones. The channels of respect and hierarchy are challenged in this game disguised as generosity. When woman are nearby some men can be heard boasting that they don't go to church or that the bachelor's life is the good life. Yet these very men are seen at church at least on Christmas eve, Easter Sunday, village fiestas, and at all village funerals. At home they are surrounded by wife and children with whom they share warm, caring relationships. The few men who carry this macho role into their homes and exert excessive control over their wives and children are seen as bullies rather than respected men. Brute force is respected in the work place but not in the home. On the few occasions when someone's wife has been unfaithful, the man is pitied not scorned. On the other hand, when a man goes with another's wife, it is the woman, not the man, who is blamed. Villagers say, 'It was not his fault he married such a silly woman! If a woman offers herself, a man would be daft to refuse her, as long as they were not caught'. The woman is the temptress, the husband and lover only 'victims'.

During the forty years of Franco's dictatorship, joking privately about the Catholic Church or politics was an outlet for expressing the forbidden. Under Franco, the mayor was appointed by the Governor of Palma. No one wanted the position because it took up too much time from 'real work' and the remuneration was minimal. Criticism, which is levelled on many subjects in private conversations, was not heard in the case of the mayor because it was clear that the person in office was there out of obligation rather than choice and could not be held responsible for decisions that affected the village. As long as the mayor was a member of a village family he aroused little antipathy. Since democracy has been introduced, the main topics for joking continue to be the Church, politics, and the personalities that direct these activities locally or nationally. Boasting and joking are important social expressions that make light of shared values. When the mayor is in the local café he is expected to act like the other locals. If he takes on airs or imposes his status there, he is seen as acting incorrectly. *S'Encruia* (an oil lamp), a local newsletter published for a short time in the late 1970s, regularly included cartoons about the first democratically elected mayor (a young man from mainland Spain who had married a woman from a local family). In one cartoon, he is depicted holding a semaphore, suggesting he show the red light when he wants to be greeted in his role as mayor and the green light when he can be greeted as any other neighbour and villager. People who have lived in the same culture all of their lives are meant to understand these subtle differences: when to speak up and when to remain silent, when to be one of the locals and when to assert status, when to be a macho male and when to be a sharing partner.

Politics is viewed with suspicion whatever the content, since it is seen to disrupt harmonious social relations by causing the members to make decisions on issues on which they might otherwise not have to comment. Local men and women who have entered the political sphere as councillors have been given new nicknames which reflect their changed role in the village. These nicknames are based on international political figures such as 'Na Tatcher' (after Margaret Thatcher for a councillor named Margarita). People know one another's political affiliations almost as well as their family ties. Since political parties have been regenerated, connections between the village and Palma-based party political leaders have been increasing. In early 1986, the incumbent mayor of Deià, a member of the conservative Popular Party (PP), resigned due to business commitments. Although there was another PP candidate, the mayor sent a letter around to all the households suggesting that they consider supporting the assistant mayor (from the liberal socialist party, PSOE) who had been acting on his behalf since the previous year. A few PP members contacted the representatives in Palma, who came up to Deià and openly campaigned for the PP candidate, personally visiting many village voters.

Local village leaders all over the island now have party support networks from outside. Prior to the national elections of 22 June 1986, meetings were held in the village by all of the competing parties: PRD (Democratic Reform Party), CP (Popular Coalition), PSOE (Spanish Socialist Workers Party), GOP (Ecology Party), and PCE (Spanish Communist Party). The meeting held by the party of the incumbent mayor, by this time changed to the Popular Alliance (AP), a coalition of the smaller conservative groups PP and MP (Mallorquin Popular Party), attracted the largest number of village men. These local meetings acknowledging national party affiliations have given Deià voters a sense of importance despite their small numbers. Deià cast 78 votes for AP, 64 for PRD, and 44 for PSOE. It would have been extraordinary if Deià ever elected a liberal mayor as it has always had an extremely conservative vote. Nevertheless, the more liberal party leaders in Palma made the effort to be sure their interests were represented, and the token socialist councillor can continue 'knocking his head against the stone wall' set up by his opponents.

The village mayor had greater autonomy and power under the national socialist government than ever before. He combined the old *enchufe* system (based on connections through family or wealth) with socialist bureaucracy to confuse issues and act independently. He could draw on government funding for village improvements as well as on local money and power to support and instigate projects which were used to provide favours for supporters as well as personal gain. In 1988 the Deià municipal council (elected in 1986) passed a bill which states that only four of the eight councillors need be in attendance to convene a meeting and make decisions about village affairs. This meant that meetings could be arranged at any time and that the one socialist councillor (who resides outside of Deià during the week) need not be present.

The pressures of social acceptance and the knowledge of one's obligations as a member of a household, family, church, and the village can be demanding. Great effort must be exerted to balance the conflicting interests of these various commitments in order to comply with social expectations. Joking or boasting that you don't have to conform to such 'nonsense' reflects the insecurity that many people feel in public situations where they are subject to constant scrutiny by their contemporaries (Du Boulay 1979:22). The most effective social behaviour is that which allows a person to participate, without commitment, in joking and storytelling while avoiding discussion of any really important subjects. The highest compliment to one's behaviour is to be told that he or she has *seny.* Seny is sense or wisdom and includes prudence, discretion, judgement, sanity, and soundness of mind. Few people receive such compliments. In fact, the word is used to describe those qualities which most people lack but should strive to attain.[6]

The values of the community are evident when someone drinks too much or behaves noisily or aggressively in public. Everyone says that 'the only people who behave like that are unmarried men who have not followed the usual pattern of courtship, marriage, and family'. A person who behaves poorly on repeated occasions demonstrates to everyone else the result of life without the safeguards of a supportive kin group. The two village men who can be seen inebriated nightly at the bars are tolerated as long as they do not bring harm to themselves or others.[7] They are the subject of many jokes, and people often comment that there could be more like these two if it were not for the protection of kin. A 'complete' person has a spouse or, alternatively, lives with a mother, father, aunt, uncle, sister, brother or child. Widows, widowers, and men or women who have not married but remained at home to nurse their parents may live alone, but they are recognised as the heirs of their households and members of larger kin networks.

The House names by which people are known have been shown to preserve for this generation information about personalities and activities previously practised in the village. There are also many expressions that point out that a person's bad reputation is carried on by members of his family well after his death: *Herba mala mai mort, ni bestiar vol menjarla* (Bad herbs never die and not even animals want to eat them). The Civil War brought out hostilities that had been festering for years between friends, neighbours, or brothers and left scars that will never heal. There were two brothers who fell out at this time and their respective families did not speak to one another while their fathers were alive. They say it is even less likely that they will speak now that their fathers are dead. Children are sometimes referred to as *mel vella* (old honey). This is a *double entente*, since it can refer to their being 'from an old family' or that they carry the past mistakes of that family into the present. Those who survived with their families intact appreciate the vulnerability of relationships within a House and between Houses.

Social and political life in Deià today is based on the adaptation of old uses in new conditions and by using old models for new purposes. The conservatism we saw in the historical relations between landlords and workers still pervades modern life. A preference for the old and established over the new and untried is seen in social relations, public behaviour, and attitudes as well as in political life. But this is not a blind adherence to the past. Deianencs, more than any other residents in the village, have been able to adjust to and benefit from the changing composition of their village as well as to the new materialistic and social values introduced from outside and highly desired by those inside. By adapting old institutions, references to the past, and ritual idioms to meet the needs of the twentieth century, a 'fictive' continuity is maintained among those who identify themselves as Deianencs.

Joan Bestard in his book, *Casas y Familia* (based on Formentera, one of the Balearic Islands), describes a similar social continuity based on place and kin. 'The island as a locality converts to a community – the substance of the native man (or woman) and the place are the same. Everything that comes from the village is different from all else that comes from outside' (1986:118).' The people of Formentera call themselves 'pagés' (peasants) as a means of collective affirmation and a mode of social communication which ignores the differences between the forms of life of the past and those brought in by tourism. By identifying themselves as peasants, they maintain the stability of their value system and affirm their own tradition and its continuity with the present.

You Are What You Have

During seven centuries many Deianencs worked as peasants whose lives were controlled by the decisions others made for them: the monks, the leaders in Valldemossa, city landlords, the national government (represented in this century by the Guardia Civil who lived in the village), and the local church and village councils which were made up of the landlords, tenants, and the village priest. The greatest power and authority was wielded by those men who held ownership or control over land. Every man, woman, and child became aware very early in life that to get ahead one had to strive for two ends: to form and maintain one's own household, and to find the means to acquire land of one's own. People were brought up to believe, 'You are what you have'.

It was clear from the beginning that their were 'classes' of people and 'a rough general agreement as to who was superior socially to whom'. However, the class system relating to the traditional structure of the village was not the same system as that relating to the outside world of modern national urban society (Pitt-Rivers 1961:2). Landlords who inherited or purchased land were senyors treated with reserve and respect. Don and Doña preceded a landlord's Christian name and the formal *vos* or *voste* (formal 'you') was always employed. On some estates in Deià, when the senyors came from Palma to visit, their staff was waiting at the entrance when they arrived. The novel *Bearn* by the Mallorquin writer Villalonga is a literary record of the class differences that existed during the nineteenth century. The senyora returns to the finca after a four-year absence. The entire staff is there to greet her coach as though she had left just the previous day. The actions and authority of senyors was beyond question or criticism.

L'amo was the share cropper or tenant farmer who managed both the landlord's lands and the labourers who worked those lands. His wife made the food for the workers but they ate separately. The workers were ranked according to the permanence or seasonality of their employment: *majoral* – person next in line to l'amo in charge of a finca; *missatge* – a full time salaried employee; *parell major i minor* – person in charge of the pairs of plow animals; *roter* – men who worked the lands high up on the mountains for an agreed price per kilo of the grain, charcoal, or lime their work produced; *pastors* – shepherds who worked for their keep; and, at the bottom of the social ladder, *els porques* – men who cleared up after everyone else and looked after the turkeys, pigs, and goats. Workers were fed and housed on the fincas and the tenant farmer kept strict order.

They were told that they could not eat before reciting the rosary. The only one allowed to abstain from prayer was the *parell*, who cut the bread (which was the mainstay of all their meals) while the others prayed.

If one did not have the good fortune to be born a senyor, he could strive to be a tenant farmer. Tenants were members of the village and some had managed to acquire control over the lands of more than one estate. By managing someone else's lands or a number of different owners' lands, one could accumulate the means to buy one's own lands and develop a following of workers on whom to rely for labour and support of one's interests. Tenants were middlemen or brokers without whom most of the work in the municipality could not be carried on. In a letter to a friend Robert Graves reveals the power wielded by his friend Gelat who 'managed six fincas, employed forty men, held the water rights to two of the main fountains, had the first lorry, taxi and coach in Deià and became the Republican Mayor for a short time before the Civil War began' (O'Prey 1984:214).

With the landlords in Palma, tenants held leases and supervised local properties. They were the local representatives of those who owned the major part of the village. They held the fate of the workers in their power as they were the ones who decided who would work where and when. Tenants were in a position to hire and fire, negotiate prices of goods produced in the village, transport and sell those goods to the city, and sell water rights. Standing between owners and workers, the tenant controlled access to the resources and the productive force necessary to tap those resources. It was the tenant farmers during and after the Civil War who were able to divert enough olive oil and grain to sell on the black market, invest their profits in contraband, and come out a few years after the war as rich men. Tenants held a political force within the village and between village and town. This power was most evident in the organisation of contraband networks.

Contraband companies were formed by a number of tenants who would put up large sums of money to make purchases. When the goods were to arrive, usually by sea, the word would be spread through the village, and helpers (workers) would appear in various locations to transport goods to the selling points. Profits were distributed in relation to the contributions made. The main investors got the largest proceeds and the workers, who helped in the transport over the mountains, were paid in cash. A number of workers would combine their gains and invest them in the next shipments. It was like investing in stocks, 'sometimes you'd win and sometimes you'd lose'. They say there were actually very few losses. If goods could not be sold, they could be distributed among the contributors. Everyone who might make problems was included in the process: Guardia Civil, police, women who lived on the fincas through which the goods passed. They all received a share for participating or turning a blind eye. A man's identity as a worker was greatly enhanced if he had a role in the complex contraband network where economic and entrepreneurial opportunity gave him a sense of contributing to the betterment of his condition and to the process of change in his life situation.

'As in Malta, a rural middle class gradually emerged from the tenants – leaseholders and supervisors of large estates – who formed an intermediary category between landowners and peasants. This new class derived its power from its control of the links between the main social strata, between the regions and between town and country. Its strategic position enabled it to attract a following of peasants who depended upon the members of this middle class for access to land and protection. Their local power base also enabled them to perform important services for the urban elite' (Boissevain 1974:7). In Deià they were influential in helping the early foreigners to find houses to rent and properties to buy.

Although contraband activities and the means to acquire small parcels of land began to relax some of the class distinctions, one main difference remained. Those people to whom one could not respond in any way except 'yes' were not equals. You could not refuse to do whatever a senyor asked of you or even what a tenant asked, since he was the senyor's spokesman and the source of your livelihood. If one of them broke their word or did not carry through on a promise, there was nothing one could do or say. In the contraband networks, if a man did not get what he felt was his just share he could say or do nothing about it.

The habit of always saying 'yes' to senyors was projected onto the first foreigners. Until quite recently, it was a dominant characteristic of Mallorquin tradesmen and workers to say 'Si, senyor' to any request from a foreigner. Often the person was far too busy to complete the task, but nevertheless he would never refuse. Pedro Muntaner, a local historian, has described the Mallorquin character as 'accommodating and self-contained, with an inbuilt prudence that avoids any risks. They see an ally in time itself and to put an idea into practice or to take a decision is often a matter of lengthy consideration. The answer to "when" is normally next week, month or next year. This doesn't mean that Mallorquins are allergic to work (in fact Mallorquins are very industrious), but they are skeptical of new projects that threaten to alter their daily routine'. Although such generalisations cannot hold true of an entire people, they do give some idea of the contrasts people from northern Europe find when they come to live on the islands. It is very difficult to get a firm answer on when a job will be finished, and once it is begun one is obligated to wait. After weeks or months, if one inquires if the person is ever going to appear, he will inevitably reply, 'demà' (tomorrow). This attitude creates relationships of obligations and serves to maintain a potential income source for the tradesmen and an ongoing 'saga' for all concerned. If the foreigner loses patience and issues an ultimatum, 'If you are not there tomorrow, I will hire someone else', the tradesman will appear the following day and begin the job but then not return to complete it for days or weeks. In all events, no new workers will take on someone else's half-finished job. One can request a bill for work done or purchases made and receive it three months later. This, of course, keeps one trading with the same people because one can not consider changing shops or workmen if one has an outstanding account with them. These drawn-out trading arrangements keep channels of communication open and bring about continued contact.

Landlords and tenants are subject to one another's manipulations and do not always receive the respect they might feel they deserve. One tenant farmer said that his landlord had offered to take a shipment of oranges to Palma one day. The tenant never got his share of the money. Friends told him that the landlord had gambled away the proceeds that were meant for him. The tenant could not afford to jeopardise his residence and livelihood by telling the landlord how upset he was or even asking for an explanation. The landlord never said a word about it. On the other hand, a tenant who held rights to a number of estates and controlled a large work force could make demands on landlords that they had to meet if they wanted their lands maintained.

This awareness of class differences has had an enduring effect on the use of the Mallorquin language and the attitudes held toward people that were, and in some cases still are, perceived as superior. Until the 1980s, the language was associated with a backward, rural population in contrast to Castilian which represented urbanity, education, culture, and nation. Today, when Mallorquí is an accepted regional dialectal variant of Catalan and is taught in all of the state schools, there are still some people who fear that Mallorquí is a language which marks one out as a peasant and that only the continued teaching and use of Castilian will allow the people of the Balearic Islands to be considered part of the more cosmopolitan world. Although a minority view, this fear is evidenced by the way older people defer linguistically to those persons who have had experience working and living in the city. The diagnosis of the doctor (who is from mainland Spain) will always be repeated in Castilian in the midst of an otherwise completely Mallorquin conversation, even when the terminology is familiar enough for the speaker to translate it. A certain severity and importance is added by interjecting the Castilian. The Pensioners' Association recently had to elect a new secretary. Their main problem was to find someone who could speak 'the language of the city'. Although, Mallorquí is spoken in most city establishments, local people feel intimidated when dealing with bureaucrats. When I began my research, the older people kept saying that what they had to say wasn't important, that I should talk to such and such a person who was a historian or teacher. The devaluation of their language, which is the source of their experience and their means of representation, causes them to underestimate the value of their knowledge.

Most Mallorquins who went into professions from 1920 until 1985 use Castilian in most of their formal dealings and have relegated Mallorquí to their intimate family language. Some have brought up their children speaking Castilian. In the 1980s Catalan (and Mallorquí) became the official languages of the Balearic Parliament, and public use of the language is widespread. Foreigners and Spaniards from the mainland have to ask officials if they speak Spanish. Official forms and street signs are in two languages and most bureaucrats address other Spaniards in Catalan. There is an ongoing, heated debate in newspapers and books concerning the similarities and differences in Mallorquí and Catalan with which one could easily fill another volume.[8]

It was definitely clear to me, from the moment I began to struggle to be understood in Mallorquí rather than converse more fluently in Castilian, that the village people began to reveal personalities and humour and vitality which never came through when they spoke Castilian. When we travelled or worked together they told stories and unselfconsciously related invaluable information about themselves, their lives, and their attitudes. By learning Mallorquí I showed that it mattered to me, which made the local residents much more open. There were a few people who preferred not to converse with me in Mallorquí and continued to speak Spanish. They were accustomed to speaking Spanish to outsiders, officials, and foreigners, and said it was difficult to change. This suggests an exclusive attitude toward their language and makes one feel that one is trespassing in a private domain. However, one woman speaks Castilian with her husband (although he understands Mallorquí) and suggests that their relationship has been formed over thirty years in Castilian and would not be the same in another language.

Before large numbers of foreigners came to Deià people were dependent on local experience. After work or school, church attendance took up three or four hours a night with vespers, meetings, choir practice, and cleaning and decorating for mass. It was not well looked at for anyone to be absent. The church, social sanctions, and gossip provided effective social control. As Boissevain noted for Malta, 'Catholicism with its range of benevolent patron saints intermediate between God and favour seeking, dependent humans provided an ideological world view which closely parallelled the realities of village life' (1969:81).

Estate owners provided the examples of pious persons regularly attending mass with an entourage of family and servants as well as contributing the material means by which the church was enhanced and maintained. The landlords and their families were perceived by the villagers as their representatives before God.[9] Owners and tenant farmers were asked to become the godparents of children born to their workers. Fiestas and other communal activities sponsored by landowners allowed the villagers to celebrate their benefactors' generosity, as well as acknowledging their own contribution to the social and economic survival of the village.

By the 1930s, landowners who had inherited their lands began to lose prestige as the workers gained more independence. While workers were *a la miseria* (living in misery), they had heeded respectful titles and differences between the classes were more marked. Robert Graves preferred to ignore these differences when he recorded his impression of Mallorquin society in the 1930s:

> No social distinction is acknowledged in Mallorca between the peasants, professional classes and merchants. Everyone is a gentleman or a gentlewoman because all consider themselves bound by the same high standard of politeness and rectitude implied in the adjective formal. Informal though I am by nature, I try to pass as a 'caballero muy formal' doing nothing in public to shock my neighbours' susceptibilities. As I always remind friends who write to me 'for information about your island': It is not my island, but theirs. (1965:29)

Although his attire was tattered and torn and his espadrilles threadbare, Graves maintained a 'gentlemanly' relationship with the locals for fifty years. As village men carried his casket from his house to the cemetery the day he died, they commented that it would be the last time 'Senyor Gravés' would pass along this route they had seen him walk everyday since they were boys. This 'caballero muy formal' had maintained a class awareness that had begun to change during the 1930s. As the fincas were bought by outsiders or tenants or villagers who had made money abroad, the title of senyor was less esteemed. The Civil War saw peasants fighting their oppressors only to be defeated and subject once again to oligarchic domination and a fascist state. Graves had not changed his style nor his manners in the forty-seven years he lived in Deià. The material prosperity that followed World War II had managed to convert his 'ideal community' into a social setting where any one could be the equal of any other not only through 'politeness and rectitude' but through modernisation. By the early 1960s, work in the service industry and increased incomes from tourism began to filter into the village.The marked social and economic differences that were part of the past lived on only in House names, nicknames, surnames, and memories.

Brandes noted the importance of ritual ties in the Spain of 1975: 'Catholic law provides considerable flexibility in the choice of sponsors for ritual occasions allowing individuals to manipulate ritual sponsorship for the furtherance of social ends by validating existing social ties or establishing new ones' (1975). In Deià at this time the choice of godparents began to change from senyors to one's peasant family and friends. Social mobility or recognition was less likely to be gained through patron-client relations with landless senyors. Since the eighties, the choice of a brother and sister of the new parents as godparents reaffirmed kinship ties with close family who had moved out of Deià and those still in the village.

The political and economic progress of recent years has begun to redirect some of the power held by the privileged. However, awareness of traditional hierarchal relationships is still apparent in most aspects of official and social activities. The large number of unfamiliar people at the funeral of an American priest who recently died in Deià were described as *'senyors de fora vila'* (gentlefolk from outside the village). Although he made Deià his home six months each year during the past twenty years and often conducted the Sunday mass in the village church, he was described as a 'gentleman's priest'. The comportment of Graves and the priest was such that the villagers were always reminded of their status as educated outsiders. This was sometimes to their advantage and other times provoked resentment. The modern village has endeavoured to reinterpret these social categories so that the material differences in wealth and education are not ignored but hold far less importance than in the past. Today, the influx of a number of wealthy German, American,

French, Swiss, and British investors who have bought homes and retired to Deià has reawakened the awareness of class differences. The main criteria for a gentleman or gentlewoman remains the same: one who is not seen to work for a living and has smooth hands and the means to pay others to do all that is required. Despite their economic security, the local Deianencs feel they still have to work very hard for what they have and for the future. The work ethic has not changed even with improved living conditions.

The Wealth of the Mountains

Olives have often been called the wealth of the mountains. Although clearly no longer the most abundant of the crops produced in the area, the diverse uses of the olive and its oil provided wealth and a way of life until the 1960s. The olives were and are an accompaniment to most meals and the oil is used to cook and dress foods. It formerly provided light and heat (the pulp is still used in combination with wood in stoves and chimneys), was used medicinally on burns, infections, and other skin ailments, and was prescribed for stomach complaints. Olive oil was used in the church for the chrism of confirmation and for baptisms. The residues were used to make soaps. Oil was an exchange commodity that could be traded for wheat, flour, and milk products from the centre of the island.

An olive harvest does not guarantee profit. Each year the quality of the fruit differs and until the pressing begins one is never sure of the results. Certain areas are more valued than others for the growing of olives. People say that the best olives are produced on trees that are the farthest away from houses which cause humidity. Those trees completely exposed to the circulation of the air are considered to be superior. Many of the collection areas are high up the mountainsides; those that grow near the sea are the least valued. One year a litre of oil will be made from 3½ kilos of olives, another year it might take 4 or 5 kilos. *Una trullada* (a pressing) requires 300 kilos of olives and makes from 70 to 80 litres of olive oil. In 1982 it cost the producers 1,200 pesetas a trullada, which produced 80 litres. The government paid 10 pesetas per litre to the press owners (to encourage them to press for others besides themselves). With 800 pesetas (of 1,200 pesetas) paid by the government, the pressing only cost the producer 400 pesetas for 80 litres. This oil could be sold back to the press for 150 to 180 pesetas per litre or sold to the public for about

250 pesetas a litre. The producers calculated that collection, transport, processing, etc., cost them about a 100 pesetas a litre so they counted a 50 to 80 peseta profit on each litre of oil. If producers could collect a sufficient amount without having to employ anyone outside their own family, this was a good year for them.

Until the 1980s, despite the difficulties and the unpredictability of the crops, many people in Deià were involved in activities dealing with olives and their products during much of each year. They picked the green olives from September to November, putting some in brine for home use the following year and selling the rest. The *blava* (blue black) olives were picked and pressed into oil from All Saints' Day (at the beginning of November) until the feast of St. Joseph (mid-March) and some were put into brine. Later in the year the men turn the soil, prune the trees, and add grafts for the next season. When at least seven months of each year was involved with the collecting and processing of a lucrative multi-use product, it is understandable that olives were considered to be thc wealth and the way of life of Deià.

The camaraderie during the collection of olives was spontaneous and humourous, as though the preoccupations of village and home life were left behind and everyone was on holiday. Outside, the gaily coloured clothes, hats, and scarves worn by the women and children presented a strong contrast to the more somber tones of clothing and body movements used in the village. They sang as they walked the two or three kilometres to the different fincas. There were dances on Saturday nights during the olive season in Deià. The local men and women met women and men from the plains and other villages on the island, and many marriages followed these seasonal encounters. Some of the men – those who did not marry girls they met during these seasonal visits – say the priest would hold a special mass on Sunday evening for all the young people to make sure that they had an opportunity to confess 'before they accumulated too many *pecats* (sins)'. These remarks not only imply that the morals of those from other parts of the island were not up to Deià standards but that Deianencs were not to be blamed for the lapses caused by these outsiders.

Olive collecting is one of the activities which best highlights the attitudes and role relations of men and women. When I began to pick olives, I was told to 'handle them carefully because *olives son dones*, olives are women. If the young green ones are handled too harshly they are scarred, if they are picked too soon they are bitter. The overripe ones fall to the ground without any help and the best ones need a bit of persuasion to fall. They are those which have remained on the tree and ripened last'. The olive oil produced in 1986 was found to be higher than usual in acidity. I was told that the early sun in March, April, and May ripened them too quickly. People say that young women are (green) inexperienced, vulnerable, easily offended, and slow to forgive. Unmarried women who have been given too much freedom are easy catches (overripe and bitter), but women who are still watched over by their families need persuasion and are the most desirable.[10]

Although working together toward the common end of collecting as many crates of olives as is possible, men and women have clearly defined roles in the olive harvest. Men's work emphasises a visible contribution and hard physical labour while women's work stresses flexibility of skills, tasks, and time. The men climb up the trees and knock the olives to the ground with a long cane pole. On the narrow Mallorquin terraces ground cloths have never been very practical, so the women and children spend most of their day bent to the ground collecting olives by the handful (sometimes with the aid of an '*ungla*' a metal fingernail which fits around the index finger and speeds up the work).[11] They fill small round baskets which are emptied into larger canisters. The men will carry the heavy crates full of olives to the pick-up site and return to collect the next one that has been filled. The olive harvest illustrates not only the complementarity of women and men's work, but also the adaptability of women. Just as in the village, women observe a fairly gender- and age-specific, regularly patterned spatial orientation during the year (see Chapter 2), and the men go back and forth to work and the cafés; in the fields, the women spend their days within the olive groves while their husbands climb above the trees or move in and out of the groves. Men do the climbing and the heavy work, women do the complementary collecting. As olive harvests show, women are expected to be competent at household work and, when necessary, enter into the role of husband's helper.

There seems to be some idea that work cannot be pleasurable or it would not be work. 'Work is for the means to other ends.' Work maintains life but it does not give it meaning. Work is the labour one does for someone else for a wage or some commensurate exchange, e.g., tenant farmers work for percentages of produce, and live-in help receive room and board and a small wage. Owning land or paying rent has its risks but gives one a sense of being 'in charge'. The planning and carrying out of work on one's own land or farm is a personal choice not subject to the directions of fellow villagers who have been given superior roles by landowners. If a household has enough land to support themselves or if they run a successful business, their attitudes toward work will be more positive, but if agriculture or business requires selling one's own produce or goods then one is always working to meet the demands of the market. Everyone agrees that leisure is pleasurable because one does what he or she wants to do (within culturally defined limits). Older men say that they worked so hard all week that to attend church on Sunday was a form of leisure. Today, they say, people pursue physically demanding leisure activities to consume excess energy built up during a week spent in sedentary occupations.

Pleasure is derived from what people do for themselves, their families, friends, and community. Everyone in Deià has always had to care for their home, the graves of their deceased relatives, land, crops, animals, orchards, or whatever else they have been able to accumulate during their lifetimes. When everyone was employed on the fincas, on Sundays men helped one another to build their houses. Anyone not asked to help carry beams over the mountains from Soller felt left out.[12]

Women helped their neighbours to whitewash their houses and in numerous other activities. They cooked and served food at fiestas while their men entered competitions of fishing, shooting, or cards. They cleaned the church for fiestas while the men repaired benches, lights, etc. None of these activities has ever been referred to as work. There was never any calculation of time spent or wage paid. These were reciprocal exchanges that recognised long-term relationships. Men are said to have the strength and stamina to do more physically taxing jobs: cutting wood, pruning trees, hauling heavy sacks of produce, or using agricultural equipment. Women's jobs include anything to do with the house, either her own or another's. Cleaning, washing, cooking, arranging, and organising are all women's 'territory'. The men tell a story about a man who was late for a funeral. A friend went to his house to see what was detaining him. The man was sitting at the kitchen table with his head resting on his folded arms. His friend asked him what was the matter and he answered 'My wife has gone to the city and I don't know where she keeps my Sunday clothes'. The purpose of telling this story is not to make fun of the man; it is to emphasise the control women exercise over the domestic side of men's lives. Women most often select the furnishings for their houses and often pay for them, letting the men arrange for delivery and installation. Women are quite adept at encouraging men to make major decisions while actually doing so themselves. Every action has its coordinate and the flow of life depends greatly on this cooperation between men and women.

Work is defined as man's work or woman's work according to the situation. As Masur noted for Andalucia, 'How work is defined and evaluated is directly related to who is expected to perform it and under what circumstances it is performed' (1984:25). If there are only daughters in a farming family, the girls will learn to do the heavier outside jobs to help their fathers. Men who do not marry or widowers who have no kin to care for their houses and belongings must learn to cook, clean, and wash clothes for themselves. People might joke about a widow who is 'like a man' or a man who is 'like a woman', but they also respect the person for being able to do things themselves instead of becoming dependent on others. A widower is far less experienced in coping with domestic chores than widows. Women learn to do male chores – cut wood, make fires, and carry heavy loads – and expect widowers to adapt to changing circumstances as well.

When today's elderly men and women were younger, most worked for themselves, managed a farm, or were employees. The men learned to work in rhythm with the changing seasons, not against them. Heavy work days were balanced by rainy days spent around the fireplace. Sometimes, because of impending rains, olives and almonds needed to be collected rapidly, but this active period was followed by long dull periods around the table peeling off the pods and shelling the almonds. Women helped on the land when they were needed and they maintained the hearth and home at other times. 'Women's work does not necessarily refer to wage work, so it is necessary to consider typical tasks performed by women to see the expectations of flexibility, complementarity between the sexes, and the relative value placed on female work' (ibid.:27). Women's experience gave them the confidence to put their time and effort into the activities each knew best, so that the earth could bring forth the fruits of their labour and this produce could be converted into cash for the maintenance of home and family. They had other activities to complete if the weather was harsh. Every house had embroidered linens, crocheted bed covers, knitted sweaters, and clothes sewn by the women.

For men and women the endless cycle of clearing, plowing, planting, protecting, harvesting, drying, storing, clearing, etc., was celebrated by the seasonal festivals. Their work was symbolised by their homes, their family and the meaningful events that marked out each year: marriages, births, baptisms, communions, and saints' days. A successful season's work was evidenced by an attic or cellar full of *sobrasadas* (local sausages), garlic, potatoes; sacks full of rice, flour, noodles, sugar; barrels full of olives, oil, and wine.

Tomeu, who is eighty years old, would go with his father to buy supplies in Palma when he was a boy. During the harvests, usually in late September and again in June (before the village fiestas on St. John's Day), they would need three or four additional mules to transport all the supplies people ordered. The trip took them eight hours each way. He said the goods were bought by the sack or shared between two households. A woman whose husband had been a tenant for a number of smaller landowners told me she had a difficult time trying to spend a *duro* (a five peseta piece). With her attic full of sacks of everything she would need to feed her family and animals during the winter, her material needs were satisfied. 'We all wanted enough not to have to worry. When you had enough there was little cause for envy or greed.'

Life was not easy in the past and not everyone was as content as the woman above. When the men discuss their experiences working in agriculture, they use the expression, '*qui oli menja (o mesura) els dits se n'unta*' (whoever manages or measures the oil has slippery fingers). They believe that one who manages the money of others cannot avoid the temptation of using some of it for one's own purposes. For this reason, they strive to have some land of their own as a protection against the 'slippery fingers' of others.

Low wages from agriculture over the past twenty years has been offset by 'occupational pluralism'. Men who work in offices, in construction, as waiters, bartenders, or mechanics, and even tenant farmers combine these jobs with gardening or caretaking of absentee homeowners' properties, tending orchards, market gardening,or doing odd jobs for older people who can no longer prune their trees or weed their fields. Women are working outside of their homes in other people's houses, in hotels, restaurants or their own businesses. Their children are cared for by their mothers or aunts or sent to a nursery. Family enterprise and exchange networks continue to be the preferred mode of socio-economic relations and reflect the easy adaptation of 'traditional' structures to meet present day needs and demands.

Today, time is measured in economic terms. Most young people prefer jobs that offer a monthly salary and fixed hours. This leaves them time to pick olives and almonds for household use, if they are so inclined, to have free days to go to the beach or shopping in Palma and a holiday of at least a week or more to visit other parts of the world. The wealth of the mountains is no longer based on the the olive but on the landscape and image of the past so admired by the visitors who come to experience a short stay in paradise. The maintenance of paradise requires the services of locals and has begun to offer them the time to enjoy the fruits of their labour.

Ideals and Experience

As men and women move in and out of activities and spaces which are culturally defined as special, sacred, public, or private, their sense of personal identity is developed. While abiding by the customs of their forefathers people receive an established pattern often labelled 'tradition' on which they base their daily actions, values, and expectations. Activities are classed in accord with the existing value system which is morally justified by the home community. But when traditions are 'bricolage', made to fit the present needs of the society, there are bound to be differences in interpretations by those of each generation. If these 'traditions' are organising features, there is going to be a different experience of morality for men and women of different ages.

An eighty-three-year-old widow had been unwell for a week. On Sunday, feeling much better, she decided to go to the restaurant next door to her house for lunch. She had worked at this restaurant until she was seventy-five. The owners were delighted to see her and invited her to be their guest for lunch. When she told one of her contemporaries about her outing, the woman responded by shouting at her, 'You went into the restaurant alone, you shameless whore' (*puta de poca vergonya*). For women of their age, external moral sanctions are obviously still important. The most conservative women are those widows who live alone and have not been able to grow old in an extended family setting where elders partake in the daily experience of the next two generations.

The younger generation is more lenient with one another. Each time one ventures out a bit, if there is no comment, then another can go a bit further. Little by little the behavioural norms expand. After one or two generations, it has already become very difficult to determine any absolute standards by which actual behaviour should be measured. If one is able to 'perform' the 'expectations' of their gender, which also change between generations, then whatever else she or he manages to do may go unnoticed or be condoned. As Herzfeld points out, 'Moral and aesthetic values are negotiated through social performances' (1986).

Appearances cover many actions that could easily be disruptive if they were practised openly. Now that both husband and wife work, some couples share many of the household chores from bedmaking to child minding. Often, as they get older and work less arduously, men become more involved inside their homes; they help to whitewash, move furniture from room to room, lay the table, cut the bread, and clear up. Cooking meats and fish over an open fire or grill has become a man's specialty. Rules pertaining to male/female roles and activities hardly concern most people within their own homes, but when they are outside in more public situations, conforming to standard role models is common practice. Experience teaches men and women how to behave around different kinds of people. Men learn which other men have inflexible attitudes and women soon know which women they should try to please and which they should avoid. Not everyone can get along with everyone else so it is best to know your adversaries and your friends.

In some households the father is still honoured in a manner reminiscent of the past. He sits at the head of the table, is served first, and has the ultimate word in discussions. However, in many other homes children participate more freely in discussions and there is less formality at the table. Although the men tend to sit back and let the family get on with their lives inside the house, it is the man's work schedule and preferences that dictate the actions of the rest of the family. Neither wife nor children will openly contradict his authority when visitors are about, but decisions about expenditures and family activities usually involve the entire family. Nevertheless, it is most often the woman who directs and maintains most of the inner workings of the domestic group and transmits the desired image of that household to the outside via her actions and encounters.

A widow who remarried at age fifty-five (after twenty years of widowhood) was ostracised by her grown children who felt she was dishonouring their father.[13] Over time they altered their opinions and learned to accept the new husband. It is difficult to employ the term honour today, as it is seldom used by locals. However, men and women over forty have internalised these values that were once such an effective means of social control and cannot completely ignore criticism. The fear of *que diran* (what will they say) still concerns most, but it doesn't stop younger people from enjoying themselves: they feel they have learned how to play the game and not get caught. Being talked about makes some young men and women feel important.

Today, one's reputation is no longer based on hard work or being honourable or shameless but much more on material success. The effect of what the village says about one is offset by personal and economic independence. Instead of fearing criticism, people now see it as envy. In fact, people hesitate to criticise others too strongly or publicly because they all know that there is something in their own lives that could be criticised in return. As material acquisition increases, people become more private about household or economic affairs and give others little opportunity to criticise. The underlying controls on people's behaviour have become much more family centered.

A woman's self-image is dependent on her family's well being. Her strength lies in her control over her own domestic space so that, when youngsters come in from school or older children and husbands come in from work, they always find her 'in charge'. When women go out to work they endeavour to maintain control over their home by preparing the midday meal the night before, staying up late in the evening to wash and iron children's clothing, and leaving the house in order. A well-kept house has all beds made and everything in its place before a woman goes to work or to the shops each morning. The younger married women who are managing their own businesses say they sometimes feel as though they may have lost 'control' over their homes and children as full-time occupation gives them so little time to keep up with domestic chores. However, they are finding that increased income allows them to employ other women to help with the housekeeping jobs that were perceived by previous generations as 'a wife's pride'. Based on their experience of coming to terms with new and different roles for women in their society, these women encourage other women of their age group to work outside the home; the self-image of women under thirty-five is showing evidence of a turn from domestic fulfillment to financial and educational advancement.

Boys have always been allowed a wide range of behaviour under the heading of 'growing up'. They can drink too much at fiestas and go out with many girls, but when it comes time to work and think about a 'serious' relationship they are expected to be sober and faithful. Girls can go to most village activities with other girls their age, and at the annual street dance held on St. John's Day they can be seen dancing with one another or in groups of boys and girls of the same age. The rest of the year they are expected to be studious, help at home, or work in the village during the week.

Until ten years ago, the first twenty years of a girl's life was spent in preparation for marriage. She would begin to embroider in school and have a collection of sheets and pillowcases, table cloths and napkins ready for her future marriage. While the morning classes at the two girls' schools in Deià were devoted to studying, in the afternoon the girls from the teacher's school joined those at the convent school and they all did 'handicrafts' together while the nuns told them Bible stories. Until the 1970s, there were still a few old women dressed in traditional black seen spinning wool into yarn in the front entrances of their houses along the main street of the village. Many songs make symbolic references to women's roles as the basis of society and their continuance and maintenance of the social order. The Balearic national anthem, *La Balanguera*, is about the women who '*fila, fila, fila, filera*'. *Fila* is the act of making thread of wool, linen, silk, or cotton. Generation after generation of women weave the thread that forms the fabric of life. *Filiacion* is the connection between children and their parents.

Among the older generations, the conservatism of the local men and women seems to have maintained certain restrictions on women's behaviour. While unmarried girls now move freely in and out of public bars and drive their own cars to dances and discos in other towns, once married, women seem to adapt quickly to the patterns of their mothers. A young wife soon learns that her own household takes up a great deal of her time. Marriage and one's own house are seen as stabilising factors in one's life. The couple have one another and a future to work toward. Their work has a direction and their social life and expenditures begin to alter. After they are married, in place of going out with other engaged couples and single friends on the weekends, they spend more time at home, at his or her parents' houses, and attending to family matters. Girls spend more time with their mothers and neighbours. Unmarried friends are neglected and the peer support that one relied on while single begins to be replaced by family sources.

The sign of a 'happy marriage' until about ten years ago was that each partner gained at least five kilos during the first year and the woman remained full and round after having her first child. A woman of sixty told me how a man of her age had upset her daughter when he told the girl (who was very proud of her tall, slim silhouette): 'You will never be like your mother.' The woman traced out her full form with her hand and said, 'the men of our generation liked women to be voluptuous'. Recent emphasis on proper foods, fat and cholesterol control, and keeping fit has altered the 'body shapes' preferred by younger people. The assessment of a marriage today is less dependent on weight gain than on future prospects of a financial and material nature.

The sense of accomplishment that women are able to develop by managing their own home (with occasional help from their mothers and mothers-in-law) and spending most of their time with other women whose experience is readily available, often reintegrates them into the 'traditional' conservatism of previous generations. The security that one experiences in the company of other women who can advise, discuss, and help one, draws the younger women into a value system that supports their transition from girls to women, wives to mothers. The cycle that begins when a girl is born and reaches its fruition when she becomes a grandmother has reached its middle stage. The child adored and pampered by her parents and grandparents, the young girl given freedoms to pursue her pleasures before choosing her future work and mate, has re-entered the social order which she must help to reproduce.

The tensions between women's and men's worlds become more evident at this stage of their relationship. Some men complain that women feel that their 'obligation as a wife' is completed when they have had one or two children. From that time onward, the woman is very much in control of the bed and her 'conjugal obligation' becomes one more 'exchange commodity' with which she can negotiate the expansion of her domestic sphere. With access to contraceptives women are less concerned with unwanted pregnancies, but for those who continue to use the rhythm method (prescribed by the Catholic Church) the fear of pregnancy is a deterrent to sexual activity. Women offer other explanations for this reduction in sexual activity within their marriages; these include breakdown in communication, the husband's preferring the company of other men (hunting, fishing, or in the café), and his showing little or no interest in the woman's activities, child rearing, or home improvements. If the satisfactions these women gain from homemaking and child care are not shared by their husbands, the women feel unappreciated. Women who have gone to university or work outside their homes have discovered other forms of autonomy and seem to find more pleasure and compatibility within their marriages.

Food, its growth, purchase,and preparation, once occupied a great deal of most women's time and was a focal point for conversation. Women did most of the transforming of food from one state to another. They picked and pickled the olives, picked and bottled the tomatoes, and planted vegetables and herbs in their small gardens which were later consumed at their tables. They made fruit into jams and preserves, beat oil into egg yolks to make mayonnaise, and boiled, fried, roasted or grilled meats into savoury dishes. If a woman did not live too far outside the village she would go to the shops each day to buy fresh produce and bread. When iceboxes were replaced by electric refrigerators, the variety of meat available in the village increased greatly but women bought only 100 to 150 grams of meat for a family meal. When I began to keep house in the village there were always ten or twelve women in the tiny corner shop. There were more or less fresh vegetables to chose from according to the season of the year. Each woman would buy 100 grams of rice, beans, or pasta, a few vegetables and other items. The weighing and dispatching of each tiny quantity involved the rolling of the edges of torn newspaper into perfect little packages which were gently placed within the basket that each woman carried over her arm. What seemed to me to be a very long time for each customer proved too short for them as they continued to chatter among themselves long after being served. It was evident that the corner shop dispatched as much gossip and local information as foodstuffs. If one wanted meat she had to remember to order it in advance from the butcher, who slaughtered once a week, or be left with a few scrappy bones.

The local grocers say that today, with vegetables available year-round, women still prefer fruits and vegetables that are grown on the island 'because they know they taste better and are certainly fresher' than from the mainland. They also buy only the best quality sliced ham and other prepared meats. The shops have learned not to bother stocking lesser quality goods except during the three busiest months of summer when tourists look more at price than at quality. The local shops allow the women to select their own goods, and fruits and vegetables are well picked over by the day's end.[14] There is no longer a butcher in the village and only frozen meat and fish are available, so many women go to supermarkets in Palma every few weeks to stock up. For fiestas and special occasions they will buy a whole animal from a known farm and share it among their kin. For Easter, when every household makes *empanadas* (lamb meat pies), parents and two or more siblings will buy a lamb and divide it among themselves. All of this contrasts with the purchasing of goods twenty years ago when a household bought only the barest minimum from stores and grew or raised all their needs at home. The traditional rice and bread-based dishes are still preferred by most men and women, but the younger generation has become accustomed to beefsteak and chips. A nuclear family household will consume approximately 400 grams of meat at the midday meal each day. With more married women working each year, the time spent in food preparation is much reduced, although there are still many grandmothers who continue to prepare food for their married children and grandchildren each day.

In the past every household held a *matança* (a pig slaughter to make sausages for the house). The work of men and women was clearly delineated. A man trained in butchering (by his father or other male) cut the animal's throat and bled it into a pot. A woman would swirl the blood in the pot around with her hand to break up any lumps. The men completed the scraping, cleaning, and butchering and carried the meat inside the house, keeping meat for the *sobrasada* (paprika sausage) separate from any that might have blood on it – blood would cause the sobrasada to spoil. Blood-tainted meat is used to make the *botifarra* or blood sausage. The women were responsible for the cleaning of the entrails, which is a three-stage washing process that begins with vinegar and salt, then clear water, and finally oranges and lemons cut up, squeezed, and mixed with the intestines, which are then hung to dry. They also did the mixing and spicing of the meats that were ground and fed into the intestines from a hand-turned grinding machine and became the sobrasadas and botifarras produced from the pork. Each House had its own way of spicing, but the other aspects were fairly similar between houses.

Contrary to Pitt-Rivers's observation that 'no taboos step in to prevent women from scraping or men from making sausages' (1971:85), *matançes* maintains the clearest example of 'taboos' associated with gender roles that I was to encounter. Just as the meat that goes into making sobrasadas must be free from any spot of blood or it will spoil, the women involved in matançes must also be 'free from blood'. A menstruating woman cannot participate in any of the activities that involve touching the meat since it is believed that the preservation process will not be effective and the sausages will spoil. A woman's hands are said to be hot at these times and it is this heat that causes the meat to spoil. The various women that have explained this to me over the years have expressed their own doubts about its validity but have been convinced by experience that whenever a woman prevaricated and participated in the handling of the meat, 'it always spoiled'. The negative effect of menstruating women on food processing activities that require things to take form, grow, or keep for some time (i.e., mixing mayonnaise, planting of vegetables, bottling preserves, etc.) is generally accepted as valid today. Women say that when they do not heed these taboos, seeds do not grow, preserves do not keep, and these failures only serve to reinforce the prohibition. Things that should last should not be undertaken at these times as menstruation, it is believed, inhibits growth or duration.[15]

Today, an older woman's ideal is to be at home in her own house where she has everything in perfect order, her family well-nurtured and handsomely turned out, and time left to visit with other women. But many young women do not share this vision of their future. The reality they observe surrounding their mothers' lives suggests to them 'an inequality of stress in family dynamics'. The demands of keeping an orderly house, shopping for and feeding a family, washing, ironing, and caring for elderly kin do not seem particularly idyllic. A mother (no matter what her age) is subject to unmarried children's demands. I have seen a thirty-five-year-old bachelor arrive home at midday, sit down, and bang on the table for his meal while his widowed mother was busy caring for elderly relatives. In another instance, an eighteen-year-old girl burst into her mother's shop (which was full of customers) and demanded to know if her shirt had been washed and pressed for her afternoon excursion.

Those women and mothers, who have succeeded in establishing control over their domestic spheres by making all their family dependent on their care and services, pay dearly if this is the source for their apparent self-confidence. They find it rewarding to cater to their families' needs and caprices as long as required, but by doing so, they put themselves in a position to be exploited. Women under fifty are trying to create a balance of responsibilities among the members of their household, but altering the habits of family members who have been brought up to be dependent on their mothers to provide care and services throughout their lives is a difficult task. The women accept these long-term responsibilities because they assume that when children are married and their husbands retire there will be far less for them to do and more leisure time in the company of loved ones. Unfortunately, men die younger than women and after twenty or forty years of coping with excessive work, a widow is faced with ten or more years of caring for remaining kin or living on her own. If a woman's life situation is altered (she goes out to work, is widowed, or as a widow remarries), she may be able to restrict the time and services she offers loved ones. However, in most instances, her responsibilities increase.

Most women under fifty-five work both outside and in their homes. In some cases, women are the primary support for their households. Women work in the hotels, go out to clean other people's houses, or take in laundry. They combine business or caretaking, cleaning, and cooking for others with their family chores. Middle-aged Deià women say that they are 'well off' because even though many of them work they have time to come home to prepare a hot midday meal. They compare themselves to the women on the plains who still must go out to work in the fields with their husbands, sons or fathers, and eat cold food during the week having time only on Sunday to prepare a 'proper meal'. A woman who can offer a friend a piece of homemade cake when she stops by is expressing the luxury of time she has at home to be able to make these extra treats.

Women today hold the jobs that keep the village alive. They run the bakery, the three groceries, the post office, the bank, two boutiques, and the pharmacy. Their husbands hold separate jobs or bring in supplies, make deliveries and work alongside their wives in their small businesses. Two of the six city councillors, the administrative secretary and two assistants at the City Hall, the school teachers, the president of the church council, the managers and three out of five hotel receptionists are all women. Two of the cafés are run by men with their wives in the background cooking. One café is owned by a man but is run by two girls, and the fourth employs only men. The two beach cafés are run by husbands and wives, their sons and daughters and affines. Although most of the cafés and restaurants are known by men's names – Christian's, Jaime's, Paco's, Lluch's, Ca'n Pep Mosso's et al. – all of their wives are involved in the everyday running of the business.

Schools that were previously single sex are now coeducational and girls and boys grow up with similar learning and social experiences. Today, a girl's free time is more often spent with other young people. During the week she can meet friends at the café, listen to pop music, watch television at home, or go to Soller to see friends. On the weekends there is shopping in Palma and in the summer, days in the sun and sea. Unlike some of their mothers and certainly all of their grandmothers, girls today wear bikinis, swim, surf, and sail. Almost all of their weekend activities include the boys of the village, and be it on the beach during the day or at the disco late into the night, young people of Deià are together. Girls and boys of seventeen spend most of their year studying and practising for their driver's test. Some pass within days of their eighteenth birthday. After that, a boy may drive himself, his cousins, or friends to and from the secondary school they all attend in Soller. The girls expand their social horizons and occasionally venture off to Soller or Palma discotheques or other tourist centres to partake of the less familiar and more exciting life of the island.

Young men and women who have finished school and begun to work are able to do and have many things that their parents never dreamed of at their ages. Before they are formally engaged they spend a major portion of their earnings on clothing, entertainment, and transport. Once they become engaged, all their money is saved toward their future home. *Festejar*, a word that can mean to court, to make love, to feas,t and to celebrate, expresses the expectations that a recognised engagement can hold. It is used by older people to describe a formal relationship, yet also provokes blushes from girls and smirks from boys. It is interesting to see the different uses of the term festejar. An old man will be accused of being a *festejador* (a gallant flatterer) if he is seen talking to a young woman. A married man seen talking to another woman more than once will be asked if he is *festejant* (courting). Flattery and sarcasm, once the domain of men, are practiced today by young women who feel free to joke with or criticise the men of their father and grandfather's generation as well as their peers.

Early ethnographies on political and social life in different parts of Spain showed women to be left out of public life and confined by gender stereotypes to private spaces. Today, this description might apply to women over fifty, but certainly in Deià we see young women in every sphere. Unlike their mothers and grandmothers who strived to attain ideal models and moral evaluations, women today seek to establish goals that are in keeping with their real life experiences and differences.

Faith and Reflection

The previous sections revealed the realities behind the ethos of paradise that has been so successfully maintained in Deià. The concepts of family, neighbour, space, class, what is defined as work, behavioural norms as well as rules pertaining to gender have all been adapted to the demands of modern society. Religion and ritual have also been adapted to meet the needs of contemporary life. Religious observance of seasonal rituals has always been an important part of Deià life. Ritual confirms and strengthens social identity and a people's sense of social location. It is an important means through which they experience community. When rituals are altered, as they were with Vatican I and II, what effect does this have on the role of ritual and community identity over time? In this section we will look at how Deianencs have responded to the changing values of the Catholic Church during the past decades. The modification of traditions under Vatican II was intended to help the Church adapt to the needs of a changing society. I will suggest here that Deianencs used the Church's modifications of tradition to select religious rituals that would support their claim to local identity in contrast to the increasing number of outsiders who reside in the village.

First, some information about the changes brought in by Vatican II. Catechism as a form of instruction in the essentials of Christian doctrine once used for the basic education of children in the faith is now taught in a different way than in the past. The current teaching hopes to develop faith and reflection on one's life, rather than a mechanical repetition of formulas. Personal confession is no longer a prerequisite of the acceptance of the Eucharist. The priest and congregation join together in asking for forgiveness. One can chose to commune or not. With Vatican II, the church was trying to develop an interest in attending mass as part of the central and expressive side of life, as part of a community and not as a routine obligation (Boletin 1976).

Today, the Church, Christ, and the people are to be presented as a unity. Communion with God is possible without much more effort than an occasional walk up to Es Puig. To most people the Church continues to offer a support system from which strength can be drawn and equilibrium established in a life that is often fraught with problems. Although not everyone goes to church, most people say they need belief to contain, express, and understand their negative feelings. As one woman said, 'Believing and living by those beliefs, teaching our children to be generous and considerate, are all part of life that makes it easier to live and clears the way for better days'. Many people will admit to not fully understanding the workings of the Church nor to having a clear idea of the motivations that lead them to observe the rites and obligations pursued. However, there is a general agreement that these are things you do, that have always been done, and until someone returns from the world beyond and says that it is all in vain, most people will continue to make the effort to comply to the Catholic teachings as they understand them.

A woman of seventy-five trying to explain her faith told me that going to church had become very difficult for some people during the second Republic (1931 to 1936). The Church was linked to an oppressive establishment and there was hostility toward the clergy. She said, 'We did not know what to do. If one did not acknowledge God and the Virgin, they would not look after us. They needed to know we cared so we went to church despite our misgivings about the priest. We were like children who continue to seek advice and guidance from their parents after leaving home'. She then moved into the present 'we experience anger, hostility or envy. We can release these feelings in church, in confession. By accepting the Eucharist we allow our lives to move beyond these thoughts to a unity with God and all people'. Such a system of belief acknowledges both the imperfection of human existence and the circumstances that so often keep one's life on earth from ever attaining perfection.

Although women are assigned a role of nominal inferiority in the Catholic Church, they are actually far more involved in the religious life of the village than the men. The beatas, the title given to the devout women who attend nightly mass and hold strong attachments to the rituals of religious life, continue to carry out the traditional practices that most other people have abandoned. They care for the graves of their deceased relatives and make regular contributions for the remembrance of the dead. They look to the priest as their intermediary to Christ. The current priest does not fulfill the image they hold of the domineering curate of their childhood who always reminded them of their duties to church and home and the perils that lay beyond those confines.

The priest feels that the older generation have internalised their religion, but that since young people are not obliged to attend, they are being lost to the Church. He encourages any activities that will bring the young into pleasurable contact with the Church. He insists on prospective godparents attending classes on Catholic life before allowing them to participate in baptismal ceremonies. He rightly assumes that few young people asked to be godparents today realise their responsibilities, as moral and religious tutors as well as guardians and protectors to their godchild.

Many see the priest as condescending and judgemental. When godparents were senyors, there was never any doubt about their knowledge of their obligations. The parents and grandparents of these young people and future godparents feel he is too demanding on the young and that, like their parents, they will assume their responsibilities when the time comes. Parents feel their children get enough religious education growing up in a village where 'religion is all around them'.

The power of local class or wealth was once closely tied to that of the Church. The priest was dependent on the wealthy for repairs and upkeep. The priest and senyors were the moral, social, and economic leaders of the community. The current general spread of wealth has altered power relations. The priest is seen as a usurper of power who, instead of being a mediator between his congregation and the trinity as prescribed in Vatican II, continues to assume a domineering position which no longer gains believers.

In a society where Catholicism continues to be part of people's lives, we encounter diverse interpretations of the doctrines promulgated by the established Roman Catholic Church. Most people feel a necessity to perform the ritual of going to church and know the verses by memory. By attending mass at least once a week they feel they are fulfilling their Christian duty, as well as soothing their souls. However, life is seldom lived according to the beliefs professed inside the church. Men continue to be corrupt or ruthless, many girls are not virgins at marriage, abortions are possible under certain circumstances, families have only one or two children (contraceptives for men and women are sold without prescription), and divorce and remarriage are common occurrences while the Church adamantly defends its stand against all of these practices. Reality allows people to make these decisions about their own lives without the fear of hell and damnation.

When men and women tell us they do abide by the Church's teachings and see no contradictions between their actions as individuals and their acceptance of their faith, one realises that there is a great deal of elasticity between belief and action. One women used the example of the multitude of virgins all over Spain to explain that although women were not all alike, they were all accepted by God. 'You see, there is really only one Virgin Mother but many representations are necessary to reflect all the different experiences of the women who believe in her.' The Virgin Mary still represents the perfect state of womanhood, but no one imagines attaining such a state.

The variety of ritual response today can be seen in the celebration of fiestas that were once the central focus of local religious and social life. In 1986, on the morning of Corpus Christi, over 60 percent of the village had no idea what the day commemorated. Only some of the men and most of the women over sixty-five could describe the procession which followed the mass and the sense of community with God the day was meant to celebrate.

On St. John's Day, the fiesta for the patron saint of the village, the entire village was in the church, the mayor and councillors occupying the first two rows in the front and eight priests (four of whom were sons of Deià) in attendance. The usual choir of twelve women was enhanced by a number of Franciscan nuns who had come especially from Palma, and a Palma brass band was playing outside the church as everyone arrived. The ritual acknowledgment of the village as a community before God, protected and dedicated to the remembrance of Sant Joan, allowed each and every member to recognise their affiliation with the precepts and teachings of Catholicism and those saints who gave their lives so that the community could endure.

Small children and many local young men and women were dressed in local folk costumes as had been the custom for many years. After the mass, the mayor, holding his official staff of office, held an official reception for the village on Es Porxo. The Franciscan nuns, whose convent had been established in Deià in 1866, were made *Hijas Predilectas de la villa de Deià* (Favourite Daughters).The Mother Superior from Palma graciously accepted the tribute. Everyone agreed that the nuns had contributed to the ethos of the traditional village and, despite shortened skirts and the removal of head scarves, they maintained the dedication inherent in their commitment to the Church and the community that it included. In his dedication speech the mayor said:

> The community of Deià nuns has demonstrated, above all, their religious vocation, their humble and simple life, with total dedication and saintly ministries. Always connected to the life of the village, the nuns have continuously furthered the activities that were celebrated in Deià's past. Their exemplary life and their impartial devotion to others, has always been admired and appreciated by the people of Deià. It is this appreciation that is being expressed by the City Hall on behalf of all the community in this ceremony.

Just one week later the nuns gave notice of their forthcoming departure from Deià. They said they recognised their connection to the past of Deià but felt they were able to make little contribution to its present life. They only looked after a few old people whose houses needed tidying now and again, gave a few injections to diabetics, and kept the church in order. As one departing nun said, 'Spirits were not their only concerns, they needed a purpose as well. There were needier people in Palma'. The departure of the nuns forced the village to reassess its relationship to the Church and the kinds of services they had come to expect from the self-sacrificing religious women, who had provided care for the aged and infirm, a nursery for babies, and a preschool program that cared for children from dawn to dusk during harvest times. All of these services would now have to be organised by individuals or by the City Hall.

Another important seasonal celebration is the Epiphany, referred to in Spain as *los Reyes Magos* (The Three Magi). Once again everyone lines the roads, waiting for the torch-bearing pagés to lead the three kings and their bundles of gifts into the church. Village men (18–35 year-olds) dressed as the three Magi distribute the gifts that parents have bought for their children. In recent years, the ostentation and bad taste of some of these gifts provoked criticism. It seemed a bit ludicrous to give a two-wheeled bicycle to a child who was not old enough to walk. Everyone seemed to be competing to give the biggest and most costly gifts to their children. This excessive public display was quite out of character for villagers who had tried for generations to present a public image of conformity to prevent the hostilities and envy that a public show of excess would provoke. Although people repeat the refrain, 'One is meant to have neither too much nor too little', these displays made it clear that this was a rather unrealistic attitude in these times of material prosperity.

People say, 'A full sack can't bend and an empty sack won't stand'. All excess is frowned upon, but what was once considered excess is extending to include goods that fit into no familiar categories. When everyone was involved in similar economic, social, and religious activities the social pressures to conform were effective, but with the move into the service industry and increased incomes people began to assert their differences through the acquisition of material goods. Improvements to one's home, new cars, expensive clothes for special occasions, and the choice of how and when to celebrate and spend money or time were hard-earned prerogatives.

Younger people do not feel obliged to contribute to the church fund to repair the roof or help support the church with either their time or money, nor to abide by the priest's suggestions that they attend classes before they marry or before their children have their first communions. They want to make their own decisions, organise their own activities, and make religious ritual more attractive for themselves and their children. Today, social life once associated with sacred events has become more secular and matter-of-fact. Every weekend is a social event rather than the periodicity associated with church festivals. Behind the performance of church attendance, personal choices are being made about religious participation and moral issues. However, the effect of continued public performance of religious ritual has been to reanimate a collective consciousness among the people who share this religious heritage. Religious festivals such as the annual St. John's Day mass, Christmas eve mass and the Epiphany have become social encounters for the people who identify as Deianencs. The sacred has become more secular and social and is attracting the young as well as holding onto the old.

The traditional practices of naming, of grouping people together by Houses, and the maintenance of the image of the village as not just a place but a 'traditional' people in a 'traditional' setting have become effective measures behind which the technology, values, and activities of the outside world can be incorporated into local life. We have seen that the social and moral stereotype for a man or woman in Deià has become a composite of these selected 'traditional' values. Many people feel they no longer have to conform to conservative values and idealistic images; they want to chose their own priorities, express their success when they feel like it, be generous or frugal as they please.

Social Democracy, Vatican II, increased incomes, and many years' experience of dealing with outsiders have given people a sense of independence both individually and in collective terms. Rather than fragmenting the village, this individual and personal development is reforming and fortifying the fabric of society by maintaining the basic structures on which the conception of the village has evolved: the House, family, shared heritage, traditions, and rituals. Although the meaning and composition of these structures has changed over time, the 'image' of people participating in culturally defined activities continues to provide a foundation for the Deianencs' concept of 'their village'.

The Struggle for Coherence in a Changing World

Old men say, 'We lose our senses but the young do not find them. The young do not pick them up'. Some of the over-sixty-fives feel that their married children who have moved to other parts of the island are interested only in their own lives and have no time for their parents. They feel their children have different values and no respect for their parents' experiences. Their children have made lives for themselves, married and formed families during the years when there were few opportunities to work in Deià. They come to Deià for occasional Sunday visits and the village fiesta, but their social life has developed around their affines in the place they have brought up their children. From the children's point of view, returning to Deià only occasionally can be somewhat intimidating. They have not kept up with inside events and feel out of touch with Deià life. People regard them more closely and either ask a lot of questions or show no interest at all in life away from Deià. They seem to be looking for some reassurance from the returnees that life anywhere else can't be as interesting, good, and safe as inside Deià.

When extended families worked and lived together (in any of the various arrangements described in Chapter 3) it was quite common for parents to transfer ownership of their house or lands to their children and retain usufruct until they died. Now, in keeping with the changing perspectives between generations, parents will not cede ownership under any circumstances. They say that every generation has different interests, and one cannot be boss in someone else's house. A number of fincas have fallen into disrepair while the heirs wait for an elderly parent to die. In the interim, half the house may collapse. The properties of the parents will be shared among the siblings. To repair an estate at this point would benefit only the heir to the finca. Furthermore, the heir cannot begin restorations until the property is legally his or hers.

There have been instances of married children selling their parents' house while the parents were alive. The sale would be made with the stipulation that the purchaser could not have access to the house until both parents were dead. Although this serves as a means of raising money in difficult situations, in the long term the sellers lose out as the price of property in Deià has increased continuously since 1965. In 1973 a man bought his neighbour's house for 300,000 pesetas (£1,500) on the agreement that the elderly parents in residence could remain there until they died. Ten years later, the purchaser needed money to buy another property. He sold the house to a friend, who was also willing to wait to take occupancy, for 3,000,000 pesetas (£15,000). The old couple died in 1988 and the house was worth at least 6,000,000 pesetas (£30,000). The children have no claim on it as they collected their money years ago.

When we bought land in 1960, we wanted to register it in the name of our daughter who had recently been born in the village. The lawyer we went to in Palma said that was very unwise because one day our daughter could put us out of our house if she wanted to. I must admit, I found that a rather unthinkable prospect. However, I have found that older people in Deià are quite worried that their children will sell their houses out from under them while they are still alive, and the lawyer's advice to us had been based on years of experience in such matters.

Although relatives often think they are doing the best thing for an aging aunt or uncle by taking them into their home, an aged person puts a great deal of importance on the items collected over a lifetime and finds it extremely difficult to settle into another's home. Older women who have moved in with family members are often disoriented by the absence of their belongings. Men say they feel idle, refraining from doing odd jobs for fear of interfering with a son or daughter-in-law's wishes.

A woman told me that one day, many years ago, a neighbour came to see her husband when he was out and explained to her that his son was threatening to put him out of his own house if he didn't return six hundred *duros* (3,000 pesetas: sums were calculated in duros – five peseta pieces – until recently) which he had lent him sometime before. The woman was so upset that she gave the man the money without waiting to ask her husband. When her husband returned he agreed she had done the right thing and suggested she should tell the man that instead of worrying about paying them back, he could give them some terraces he had on the mountainside.[16] The man was delighted and so were they. As long as older people can remain in their own houses they feel they have some dignity. Moving into another's house places them in debt and that is what they have avoided all their lives. On almost every occasion that people have been nursed in the homes of their children or in hospital, they have insisted on being returned to their own house to die.

The Pensioners' Association recently bought a building they wanted to convert into a residence for the aged. The derelict house, which was almost destroyed by fire in 1986, belonged to an eighty-year-old man who had lived there happily without electricity, water, or gas for most of his life. He cooked in the chimney in the dilapidated area that had once been a kitchen, and the rest of the house was filled with the debris he collected from people's rubbish bins each night. As far as the villagers were concerned, Sebastian was a decent man who had somehow never kept up with the times. His idiosyncrasies had long ago ceased to be noticed – they were like part of the landscape. Left to himself, he cared for his animals, picked his fruit, and sold it to anyone who would have it. He would walk up the Clot road with his burlap bag filled with lemons, oranges, cherries, or plums slung over his shoulder. He often brought us fruit. He would heave himself down with a sigh, and after having some water or juice (he did not drink alcohol) he would tell me what he had in his bag. We would then discuss the prices in the local shops, haggle a bit on the final price, and if I felt like making marmalade or jam and agreed to buy the whole bag, he was very pleased.

Being the last son of Ca'n Boi, once the village 'bankers', he was rumoured to have more money than most people in the village, but no one, not even he, knew where it all was. A few years ago, an American resident befriended him and after innumerable visits and chats, he convinced Sebastian to sell him another house he had inherited by bringing him a wicker basket filled with cash (two hundred thousand one-thousand peseta notes). Cash seemed to be the magic potion.

After the fire Sebastian was quite ready to go back to his ruin, but the people who had helped to fight the fire feared for his safety and offered him a place in their homes. He wouldn't hear of it and said he would sleep under his trees until things cooled down. During the next few days many people went to see that he was all right and took him food and blankets. By week's end, the Pensioners' Association was holding a general meeting to decide how they would go about raising the money to rebuild the ruin that Boi had sold to them for 2,000,000 pesetas.[17] In return, they promised to build him a small house with bedroom, bathroom, and kitchen just behind the ruin. The fresh, new, clean little house was ready within a few weeks, but Boi didn't really adapt to it and he spent many nights under the stars next to the hut where he kept his chickens. The pensioners thought they were improving Sebastian's living conditions, but from his point of view he had lost the only home he had ever known. He had merely kept it as it had been when his parents were alive fifty years ago. Out of kindness, the Pensioners' Association had done exactly what they feared their children might do to them someday.

Just three months later, Boi was hospitalised with a heart attack and died intestate. His body was returned to Deià and was buried in a communal grave in the municipal cemetery. The costs of his hospitalisation and funeral were covered by 300,000 pesetas found in his house at the time of the fire. The rest of his money and his extensive lands in Deià will probably be claimed by the government, if and when the various deeds and accounts are discovered. Someone remarked that Don Pedro (who had been the village priest from 1941 to 1972) would have gone to the clinic and told Sebastian that they might not be able to bring his body back to Deià and give him a proper burial unless he signed everything over to the church. Don Pedro was said to have often threatened old people on the verge of death with the fear of dying without having the last rites. His unction and care was guaranteed in exchange for their goods and property being willed to the church.[18] Although everyone agreed the Pensioners' Association could make better use of the money than the government, no one would consider approaching a dying man with such a proposal. 'Only a priest would do such a thing,' they said.

The entire mode of working, earning, saving, borrowing, and spending has altered so radically during the past ten years that one must refer to those earlier times to comprehend the way that incomes, values, and attitudes have evolved. Recent studies suggest that human evolutionary processes have taken place in dramatic surges and jumps rather than the previously held idea of slow progressive stages (Gould 1982). Such is the case with the process of change in Deià. People who are over eighty say they have seen more changes in the last ten years than in all the previous years of their lifetimes.

Prior to the Civil War, if a man needed money to get through a difficult winter, he could make a small loan from the Boi brothers or exchange a small bit of land with a friend or get an advance on his produce from one of the four village shopkeepers. They would handle the sale of his goods in return for future sales. Some years after the war, the banks began to encourage tenants and master builders to overdraw their accounts when they needed extra cash to pay suppliers or labourers.

These were seen as short-term 'carry overs' that earned the bank 15 to 20 percent interest and stimulated the builder or farmer to continue expanding despite temporary cash shortages. All of these arrangements were made on a face-to-face basis. All the locals knew each other, and bankers were direct acquaintances or related to someone to whom the borrower was well known. The people who attempted to borrow money were those whose reputations spoke for them.

Under Franco, pensions, unemployment compensation, medical insurance, and job security were introduced. It is now possible for older people to retire without becoming burdens on their families. Medical services are available to them and their pensions give them capital to maintain the basic costs of their life. Some are even able to contribute to their children's well being. The ability to borrow funds to acquire housing has become a reality. In the 1960s to 1970s young couples, thinking about moving to the city, were attracted to the long-term mortgages offered by builders of high-rise apartments in Palma. But in Deià the idea of buying anything on credit was still frowned on. People had deferred forms of payment and established networks through which their products were transported to market; the only accepted form of borrowing was against these small future earnings.

The first vehicles in the village were used for the mail, taxi services, and deliveries. Lorries were bought by the storeowners who took Deià produce to Palma and returned with goods to sell. Money was immediately invested in land, houses, transport, etc. People tell the story of a couple who ran the water generator. They had been in Deià for many years. They had no children and worked for years to save 10,000 pesetas to buy a house. By the time they had the 10,000, the cheapest house they could find was 15,000 pesetas. When they had the 15,000, houses were selling for 20,000 pesetas. They never did buy a house. People say, 'they spent their lives caretaking other people's houses and paying rent when they could have bought a piece of land for five thousand that would have given them food to eat and served as collateral for anything else they wanted to buy later'.

In 1920 a Deianenc family bought a house for l,500 pesetas (approximately £30) with the earnings derived from five months carbon-making in the forests on the Teix. Today, the new houses built by young Deià couples above the park on Carrer de Sant Joan are valued at 26,000,000 to 30,000,000 pesetas (£130,000 to £150,000). The combined incomes of husband and wife, plus the help of their families, make such purchases possible, and short-term mortgages are becoming more common with young men and women now involved in full-time employment.

Since 1975, young people have opened businesses or been employed in activities that provide long-needed services in Deià: hotels, bakery, bank, butcher, pharmacy, and grocers. They are earning salaries or making profits which give them surplus funds never experienced by previous generations. Their parents, too, are earning predictable amounts each month, affording them the opportunity to give more to their children as well as to have everything they themselves need and want. Parents and grandparents already have their own apartments, houses, cars, televisions, appliances, etc. Grandparents are in a position to be able to use their pensions and savings to go on excursions with others of their own age.

In many areas of the Mediterranean, increased economic opportunities brought in by tourism have lead to modernisation, 'the process by which an underdeveloped region changes in response to inputs (ideologies, behavioural codes, commodities, and institutional models) from already established industrial centres rather than to development of local potential'. In these areas, financial proceeds from migration and tourism have been used, not to further development, but to further modernisation. They are used to purchase consumer goods produced outside the area that consumes them, thus increasing the dependence on industrial areas (Schneider, Schneider, and Hansen 1972:43). In Deià, although the catalysts might have been foreign investment and tourist demand, there has been a concerted effort to change from within, to draw on local potential and develop better local infrastructures to accommodate the changes. Modernisation has occurred but is purposely masked behind traditional architecture and social values.

Deià's tourists have been somewhat different than those who have been flown in hoards to other parts of Spain on package tours organised and executed by foreigners in foreign lands. The first foreigners to visit Deià were drawn into the existing hierarchic system, which distinguished those who served from those they served. They were able to share in some aspects of community activities and developed relationships with their neighbours and friends, but with the arrival of more and more foreigners, newcomers would seek information from other foreigners whose contact with their local neighbours diminished. They could get by without learning the language of the village or even Castilian. Foreigners formed their own social networks. No longer relying on the local people to help them settle into Deià life, the foreigners began to be seen as a separate group.

Deià housed two separate communities, each concerned with its own problems. Coincident with this change of relations, the incomes of local people were increasing. Deianencs began to acquire consumer goods and modern technology which they incorporated into their lives. The material differences between Deianencs and foreigners are relatively minor as compared with twenty years ago. Some Deianencs have come to value material goods as the symbol of their new status and prosperity, and it is commonplace to hear both women and men discussing the prices of new acquisitions or conspicuously displaying the labels that now identify everything from designer clothes to Mazda and BMW cars.

Some Deianencs have had a great deal more power than others realise in making the decisions that have brought about village development and the resulting modernisation. Indeed, many people blame the local politicians, who have the decision-making power about where and by whom houses can be built, for any negative changes that have occurred. Yet what seems negative to some has been quite beneficial to others, who remain in the background supporting those who publicly represent them. Most recent changes have been met by passive resistance, with one or two people speaking up and most everyone else sitting back and saying: 'Patience. We will see, perhaps it will bring good.'

Foreigners who have come to Deià over the years found it to be the paradise they were seeking and set out to 'experience the tranquillity of nature and rustic living'. They were able to buy old houses and their contents and put time and money into preserving these 'ruins' of the Mallorquin past. In 1934 Robert Graves wrote a letter in which he described a jacket Laura Riding was having made 'from a sky blue hand woven silk, very ancient, that was the dust cover for the Madonna in the Es Moli chapel'. Old items were given new meanings.

While most Deianencs were putting hard work, time, and earnings into trying to modernise their lives and houses, foreign owners were 'buying up the past' as enthusiastically as the Deianencs were putting it aside. The very 'symbols' of the material past the foreigners have chosen are the ones rejected by the locals. Mallorquins all over the island have replaced stone floors with tile floors. Heavy olivewood tables and chairs have become 'old fashioned' and been replaced with matching veneer tables, chairs, and dresser sets. As Bourdieu wrote: 'The house is the principle locus for the objectification of the generative schemes; and through the intermediary of the divisions and hierarchies it sets up between things, persons and practices, this tangible classifying system continuously inculcates and reinforces the taxonomic principles underlying all the arbitrary provisions of the culture' (1977:89). The similarity between goods selected by individuals continues to reflect a collective representation, and this is reiterated by the new goods selected to replace old ones.

The house has become the symbol of the 'new tradition'. Couples who started out their married lives in the 1980s chose to return to the rustic materials their parents had rejected. They renovated old houses or bought land and built houses in areas that were once considered 'outside the village'. They modernised the interiors by opening previously closed spaces, taking away partitions, literally divesting their lives and homes of the old restrictions their parents and grandparents lived by. But they combined old furniture, bedcovers, and miscellaneous objects from the past within the open spaces, making a statement about the way they see their lives changing. Old things no longer represent dominance, oppression, or subservience but rather hold a sense of identity with a cultural heritage from which they have developed. Nostalgia for articles from the past expresses an awareness of the rapid changes that have occurred.

In the brief span of twenty-five years, the villagers have gone from the rejection of old symbols of distinctiveness and their replacement by new 'modern' ones to the reintroduction of those old symbols as a means of holding onto a past they felt was slipping away. Young men and women are taking a renewed interest in church activities; there are classes for folk music and folk dance offered in the village. 'Traditional' activities are the focus of most of the group social activities that occur, and everyone wants to be included. One acknowledges membership in the village through participation in these activities. Fear of sin and purgatory are no longer the stimulus behind religious activity. Today, it is the social aspects of religious ritual which have become the accepted means by which Deianencs express the very clear separation between insiders and outsiders.

The solid stone houses still present an image of continuity within the village while inside those walls family members partake of modern conveniences and more fluid spaces. The local population, which once lived very much inward-looking, thinking, and acting, has begun to draw ideas and practices from the outside. Moreover, they have learned to bring the changes inside their homes and families without disrupting the social order. The present generation of Deianencs who did not turn away from the village to find material security outside but remained after they married to bring up their children in the village have managed to revitalise the life of the village. The older people see their efforts realised in their grandchildren who are staying on at school much longer and have transport, leisure, and time to enjoy being young and carefree. All ages are combined to support the transitions, so that the ethos of the 'traditional community' need not be altered as it moves into the future.

NOTES

1. According to the Mallorquin historian and noble Pedro Muntaner, inter-aristocratic litigation went on for centuries, usually for motives concerning inheritance. Yet, while they were filing their complaints, they were carrying on their usual social and familial relations. 'Nobles smiled while they duelled. The strength of blood ties obliged that complaints be heard by a tribunal and not at home' (interview, Diario de Mallorca, 22 June 1986).
2. This terminology is used by Hobsbawm and Ranger in *The Invention of Tradition*, 1983.
3. An interesting example of this sort of reasoning is humourously portrayed in the film, *Victor, Victoria*. Robert Preston suggests that Julie Andrews present herself for an audition dressed as a male who impersonates women. He plans to introduce her as a Czechoslovakian prince and transvestite. She says: 'No one will believe I'm a prince.' 'That is the whole point,' he says. 'While they are sorting out your blue blood, no one will question that you are not a male.'
4. Campbell (1964) describes a similar sort of secrecy among the Sarakatsan.
5. Campbell found that in Greece among the Sarakatsan shepherds, 'sheep and goats, men and women, are important and related oppositions with a moral reference.... Women and goats are conceptually opposed to men and sheep. Women through the particular sensuality of their nature are inherently more likely to have relations with the Devil; and goats were originally the animals of the Devil which Christ captured and tamed for the service of men'. Hirschon (1988) makes similar associations, as do Brandes (1975) and Gilmore (1987) for Spain.
6. Hansen describes *seny* in Catalonia as political acumen.
7. There is seldom a time that one or the other is not being reprimanded for riding his motorbike while drunk, and it is quite common to see them bruised or in plaster.
8. Debates concerning Catalan and Mallorquí are ongoing. Francisco Borjas Moll's Catalan-Balearic-Valencian dictionary gives a proper discussion of the issues.
9. Prior to independence from Valldemossa, in Deià and other villages where there was no resident priest, the senyors would hold mass on the fincas, each of which had its own chapel.
10. The sexual symbolism inherent in these descriptions could be developed further, e.g., men knock (discharge) the olives from the tree onto the ground where the women collect them in round-topped baskets, etc.
11. See Masur for details of Andalucian olive harvests where ground cloths are used.
12. In December of 1752 fire destroyed most of the village church. The story of how everyone in the village cooperated in the reconstruction is still retold to

each new generation. The men were said to have carried large stones and women clay pots filled with water each time they walked up to mass, which, according to the story, occurred every day. Once all the materials were in place, the work was completed by builders in 1760 (Segura i Salado 1979).

13. Married children's objections to a widowed parent's interest in another widowed person are often based on their fear of loss of inheritance if the parent were to remarry.
14. New hygiene rules imposed since Spain's entrance into the common market in 1986 will alter customary habits considerably. Small shops have been forced to restrict the handling of goods to employees. Large markets have overcome this problem by wrapping everything in cellophane. People have already begun to make weekly visits to the Hypermarket in Palma where they can continue to select by 'touch and squeeze' methods.
15. Menstrual blood is viewed as contaminating in many societies. Some see this as a means of controlling and containing women by putting checks and limitations on their involvement in certain activities (J.K. Brown and V. Kerns, eds. 1985).
16. The husband's strategy is calculated to embarrass the borrower for having put the woman in a compromising position. She has acted without her husband's advice on a matter that concerns them both. The borrower is shamed into agreeing to her repayment request for fear of provoking problems for her. I have noticed that women will attribute questionable decisions to their fathers or husbands to free themselves from any responsibility in controversial matters; i.e., why one went to nun's rather than teacher's school; why land was bought or sold or inheritance queried. One can draw on the dominance of male or female according to the circumstances in question.
17. The *Associación del Tercer Edad* (The Association of the Third Age, which I refer to as the Pensioners' Association) was given 2,000,000 pesetas by the City Hall in 1985.
18. Apparently, a widow with no kin was persuaded to will her house to the City Hall in exchange for a 'proper burial'. The proceeds from the sale of that house provided the 2,000,000 pesetas used to buy Ca'n Boi.

A view from the road into the village of Deià.

The cala (cove) of Deià.

Deià village and the hamlet of Llucalcari.

Fishermen's huts and Cala Deià.

The toast to mark the first stage of matançes.

Baking empanadas in the outdoor oven for Easter.

Village women and children gathered to watch folk dancers.

The simple grave of Robert Graves in the Deià cemetery.

Resident foreigners at a local café.

Young locals and foreigners in one of the cafés.

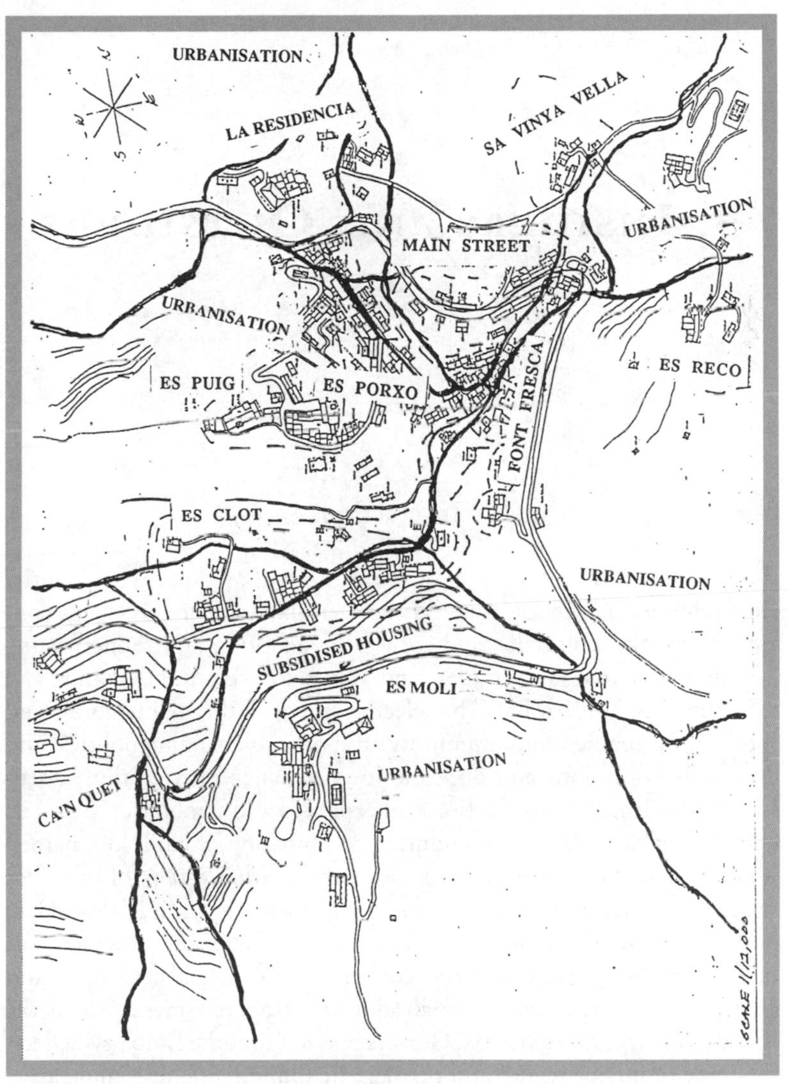

The plan of the village of Deià.

5. Insiders and Outsiders

Interaction

*I*n the previous four chapters we have seen that those who identify themselves as Deianencs-Insiders have been able to maintain village continuity visually, culturally, and socially by adapting and reinterpreting 'traditional' activities, attitudes, and values to meet the demands and aspirations of modern life. The selective use of traditional relations and symbols has marked the community's response to changing political and economic conditions and opportunities. Reliance on tradition reveals history as a legitimator of action and expresses and symbolises the social cohesion of the village as an enduring combination of land, kin, named Houses, shared occupations, and coexistence with a variety of outsiders who have always been part of local life. Being a foreigner in Mallorca had positive connotations for over a century, and we have seen how the visits of famous foreigners have been converted into legends. Chopin and George Sand, Archduke Luis Salvador and Robert Graves helped the islands to attract more visitors. Graves's poem 'From the Embassy' reflects the sense of independence and privilege he found living in Mallorca:

I, an ambassador of Otherwhere
To the unfederated states of Here and There
Enjoy (as the phrase is)
Extra-territorial privileges.
With heres and theres I seldom come to blows

Or need, as once, to sandbag all my windows.
And though the Otherwhereish currency
cannot be quoted yet officially,
I meet less hindrance now with the exchange
Nor is my garb, even, considered strange;
And shy enquiries for literature
Come in every post, and side door. [1953]

This chapter will look at those who are included within the term Estrangers-Outsiders (foreigners, persons from other countries): how they are seen by the local Deianencs and how they perceive themselves and others who are clustered together under this heading. The problem of definition lies in trying to discern the subtle distinctions made in conversation and action which indicate the conceptual basis for the terminology being used. The actual terms insider and outsider are not often used. First of all, most conversation goes on within the home or in the shops and cafés with people who know 'almost everything' about one another. In such instances, the person being discussed is referred to by a familiar nickname or a House name. It is only when absolutely nothing is known about a person, or when discussing foreigners as a group, that the speaker will use the term estranger. Estranger is a generic term while forms of address such as senyor or Don, House names, nicknames, or Christian names imply recognition and inclusion in village vernacular.

Insider-Outsider is a binary opposition which allows a group to define itself, establish an image, an identity, or community in contrast to another with whom it shares physical space. It is not necessary to explain belonging to one who belongs. Anthony Cohen describes what it means to belong:

> Those nebulous threads running through the life of a culture which are felt, experienced, understood, but almost never explicitly expressed. They provide a subterranean level of meaning which is not readily accessible to the cultural outsider. (1982:11)

Those who include themselves and others in the category of insiders understand what this category means although they might be hard-pressed to explain it clearly. In Spanish and Catalan there are two different terms for outsiders: estrangers and forasters. Each implies a distance from the centre or inside. Forasters are Spaniards who were born outside of the village, outside of the island, or outside of the mainland in what were once other Spanish territories. A foraster shares a national heritage and the rights and obligations of a citizen of the Spanish State. All

Spaniards are allowed to become *empadronados* (registered voters) wherever they make their home within the country and there are many who have made their homes in Deià. When the term estranger is used it refers to a stranger, a foreigner, someone from outside of Spain. An estranger-foreigner-outsider has no such official status. A foreigner is not a Spanish citizen. She or he may be interested in the political life of the village, but one's 'political actions' will take place through discreet social relationships of friendship, neighbourhood, or patronage. Many locals stated that estrangers are more welcome than forasters. Estrangers are either completely disinterested in local affairs or can add constructive suggestions and prestige while forasters (especially Catalans) can be quite intrusive in local affairs and provoke controversies that might otherwise be avoided.

Exclusion of foreigners from politics may be of objective importance: their informal roles are too important to allow them to become confused by direct involvement in political competition. By remaining outside, one can influence politics, interpret, challenge, represent, interfere, or coerce. Robert Graves's value to the village was his foreigness and his international reputation. He attracted innumerable other foreigners to visit or reside in the village, and a visit from him to the Civil Governor of the Balearic Islands on behalf of the village could bring instant results to a problem the village council had dealt with unsuccessfully for months. Equally, the German contractor who buys old houses, employs dozens of local men to convert them into private dwellings and hotel complexes which employ forty local people, and brings international guests and buyers from Germany commands more power as an outsider than almost any local person.

Outsiders is a category which can only be defined by its opposite, insiders. If, as I have tried to show in the previous chapters, insiders are those who share 'traditional' knowledge, common values, and a concept of the village as an enduring social space made up of kin, known histories, landmarks, and Houses, then outsiders must refer to all those who do not share these qualities. However, after a hundred years of coexistence, the division is not so clear; foreigners have been integrated into village life, and foreign names appear on the local birth register and on tombstones in the cemetery. It is more a question of degrees of insideness and outsideness. If we imagine a continuum with Deianencs on the far left and outsiders on the far right, we can place people along this continuum and come closer to understanding the complex nature of social relations in Deià.

Different groups of people hold distinct concepts of the social space they call the village, but all share a common concern for the continuance of the entity known as Deià. Deianencs are aware that their culture is a composite of generations of interaction with many outside groups rather than exclusively local or national. They express pride in their own unique characteristics and values, which include coexistence with outsiders, in contrast to other villages and their characteristics. A Deianenc conceives of the world from the inside looking out. The inside is made up of the families, Houses, rituals, beliefs, space, and time with which each person associates every other person. According to the number of shared associations, one is closer or farther away from the complete Deianenc. A complete outsider would be one who shared none of the above associations.

The British writer Laurie Lee (1975) described the Spaniard as 'someone who believes himself superior, both in culture and morality to any other people in the world, and believes this so strenuously he neither boasts nor hates but welcomes strangers with a chivalrous warmth based on compassion for their benign shortcomings'. This is probably true on a short-term basis but, when foreigners become residents, chivalrous warmth turns to ambivalence. In Deià, most locals have a sense of compassion for foreigners who live alone, have no religion or property. However, long-term relationships between local and foreign residents, like those between locals, are built on shared interests and individual characteristics. One is not expected to get along with everyone and Deianencs are fully aware that they may not see eye to eye with one another, let alone with outsiders.

Deianencs and Foreigners: A Historical Perspective

Those foreigners who travelled through and the few who settled in Deià during the nineteenth century were strangers in the full sense of the word: unknown, unfamiliar, alien. Islanders, especially those in coastal villages like Deià, had always been in a vulnerable position, easily accessible to outsiders by sea and with no adequate means of defense. The island history and regularly recounted legends had led them to be wary of strangers and to assume that strangers brought oppression, conquest, or, only occasionally, gifts. Locals had a number of preconceived notions about strangers. Strangers were to be feared as aggressors but at the same time welcomed as potential benefactors. Since one could not predict the outcome, a welcoming attitude was recommended. Cordiality structured an otherwise ambiguous relationship. Hospitality to a stranger expressed a relationship of unequal parties. The home dweller was opening her door to one who did not have a home in that place. The guest may have been wealthy and propertied but as the guest in another's house was temporarily subject to the host. The local practice of extending hospitality to strangers is described by the Archduke Luis Salvador, who came to the island in 1867:

> All foreigners, even if completely unknown, are treated as welcome guests and the Mallorquins do not tire of giving attention. I do not exaggerate when I state that any foreigner can travel the totality of the island without putting his foot in an inn, as he will find the same cordial hospitality and welcome in the luxurious finca of a great person of Spain as he will in the poor hut of a peasant in the mountains. (1959:245, author's translation from Spanish)

According to the Archduke, at the time of his visit the Valldemossins and the Deianencs 'considered it a matter of honor to give gifts and show a guest the beauties of their island and especially those of the village they lived in' (ibid.). The people felt that each person's behaviour reflected the entire village's response to the stranger. The guest's perception of the village was also a reflection of its people.[1]

The Archduke and the many well-known people who visited him became models for social behaviour. Santiago Rusiñol described the Deianencs' perception of foreigners at the end of the nineteenth century:

> The times have changed a great deal from those days when the sight of a man oddly dressed or behaving queerly would cause a commotion amongst the villagers of Deià. So many of those once called strange have passed through Deià in every imaginable dress that the people have reached the point where if someone arrives and does not distinguish himself by some exotic action or dress, he is considered of no importance and no one pays the least attention to him. (1958:141)

This early experience with a certain type of foreigner allowed Deià to become a haven for individualists and eccentrics. They were seen as eccentrics by the local people because they were so different from themselves. Individualists were those who saw themselves as different from their parent societies and were seeking to discover a 'paradise' where they could fulfill their dreams of poetry and prose, or express their inner visions on canvas. They all shared the idea that enlightenment must lie beyond their own homes and could be found only through travel to 'exotic' places.[2] A stranger who settled into a place remained an outsider because he was not subject to the local norms. However, he was no longer a stranger or unknown guest. The host's responsibility to provide hospitality as a means of keeping up appearances or to control, coerce, or manipulate the guest was no longer necessary. Different strategies, expectations, and values surround one who is always there. As they become valued by the few insiders with whom they most closely interact, these outsiders are protected and defended from those they do not know so well. The outsider is represented to insiders by his or her association with one of their members, whether these be powerful men or peasants. Outsiders gained information about houses for sale or rent from their first local acquaintances: the taxi driver, the pension owner, the barman, or the grocer. Contact networks increased to include professionals, landlords, neighbours, builders, cleaning women and their families.

As experience with foreigners increased, strangers were converted to neighbours, potential patrons, clients, benefactors, or friends. These foreigners no longer had to be controlled or feared, as in the host-guest relationship, but to be endured as other outsiders had been in the past. Old models used in new situations allowed an adaptation to changing social conditions. Continued contact into the twentieth century led locals to predict foreign requirements and to carry on social and commercial transactions with greater ease. Increased associations and communications brought change and mutual obligations.

The fact that the Mallorquins had a history of welcoming strangers served the interests of both outsiders and insiders. The foreigners found the paradise they were seeking and gained access to the space, lifestyle, goods, information, and services they required. The hosts were involved in these acquisitions and in many of the activities organised by the new residents. There was reciprocity between people of various levels of social and economic standing. The existing social structure, which included hierarchical relationships as a normal part of life, could easily accommodate these gentlemanly types. They were like the senyors to whom the locals were accustomed to proffering services. In fact their continued presence reinforced an existing social system.[3]

Within Deià history we have seen that different groups have been considered outsiders at various stages of local development: monks, nobles, landlords, tax collectors, city owners, tenant managers. The sort of people who were able to travel to this area in the past were also outsiders of clearly leisured classes. Since the earliest travellers passed through Deià, foreigners were automatically placed into the category of senyors, landowners, or educated, well-mannered, well-dressed men with 'smooth hands' (the local definition of a gentleman is one who does no manual labour).[4] Peasants who worked the land were able to conceive of themselves as a group in contrast to senyorial groups who held control over land and livelihood. Throughout centuries of 'silence'[5] a feeling of powerlessness to alter their situation and a fatalistic acceptance of their lot brought Deià peasants together. They formed closely knit circles that contrasted with those who controlled their livelihoods. Including foreigners as senyors required no compositional changes in familiar social groupings and thus did not alter the status quo.

Forms of Address

Forms of address or reference indicate the villagers' perceptions of each person and in some cases that person's relationship past and present to other people or places known to the village. In listing the modes of reference used for the many foreigners in the village today, i.e., the titles Senyor or Senyora, House names, nicknames, Christian names and diminutives, one encounters a marked difference in the forms used at various periods during the past fifty years. These differences in forms of address present a clear picture of the changing concepts of insiders and outsiders and the relationships of foreigners to village social organisation over this period. Through forms of address we can see the subtle means by which villagers transmit information about people both to one another and to future generations.

All of the men and some of the women who arrived between 1929 and approximately 1970 were addressed as Senyor or Senyora (gentlefolk): i.e., Sr. Gravés (1929), Sr. Lehman (1928), Sr. Ross (1952), Sr. Bil (1953), Sra. Isabella (1954). The use of the surname reflects the early years of contact and a more formally structured relationship, while the use of the Christian name after the title seems to have begun sometime after the Civil War and indicates less formal interaction between locals and foreigners on many levels (domestic, social, economic). Foreign women were more difficult to categorise than the men as most local experience had been with men.[6] Married women and children were referred to by their relationship to a man (husband, father, or partner) rather than by their own names: the wife of Sr. Bimel or the daughter of Sr. Bil.

According to a book written by Gaspar Sabater, a local schoolteacher at the time of Robert Graves and Laura Riding's stay in the village (between 1929 and 1936), a man's status could be affected by the actions of the woman in his life. He wrote: 'To Deianencs Laura was the Senyora and Graves the servant. She gave the orders and Robert did all the shopping, delivered messages and ran errands. When someone came to the house and asked for "El Senyor" Laura always answered, "I am the Senyora what do you want?" The villager's impression of Graves, the man, was incomplete until he returned with another woman and three children' (1986:73).

If Sabater is correct, this implies that the title of Senyor showed respect for the person's social position but was not synonymous with manliness (*machismo*). Although Graves was addressed as Senyor, his machismo was in question until he was no longer bossed by a woman and had become a husband and a father, the familiar defining categories for men in this society. Mallorquin women are often assertive at home but they know how to feign submission or at least passiveness in front of their husband's male visitors to protect his public image as head of the household. Seligman described a similar 'image' in France, 'statements about male authority and female subordination abound. Songs proverbs and sayings all create an image far removed from actual practice' (1983:155). It is these subtle strategies used by locals to maintain an image of 'traditional' roles and values that are seldom understood by foreign residents and outsiders in general.

Referring to a person as a senyor or senyora has a double meaning. If a local man is referred to as a senyor, the speaker is suggesting that he is not working, is lazy, or is living off another's earnings.[7] Identifying foreigners as senyors aligned them with that level of the society which was both revered and resented. Local workers felt obliged to enhance the foreigners' status with a title which recognised that their relationship was unequal. A clear status difference between locals and foreigners established both the locals' willingness to serve and their right to receive payment in exchange for those services.

Deference to superiors was well ingrained. Peasants referring to someone as a senyor implied that the person was an outsider to them while at the same time placed him within another status group who regarded peasants as outsiders. In all cases, foreigners identified as senyors and senyoras who made their homes in Deià were made to feel from the beginning that they were recognised as participants within an existing status group because of their similarity to that group. Being associated with senyors allowed foreigners to have much more freedom in their activities than if they had been included within peasant status and subject to its social controls.

As foreigners began to purchase named Houses they were drawn into the existing social hierarchy by another means. We have seen how local people identify one another through House names. Deianencs are recognised by House names throughout their lives. I have shown that House names can be metaphors for social relations connecting everyone in the village to other people past and present. Personal, social, and economic differences between Houses affect the perpetuation of a House name. The continued use of House names stimulates an awareness of a local hierarchical order and each House's place in that order. The continuation of a House name is 'symbolic capital' which each family is capable of maintaining or accumulating through the generations (Bourdieu 1984).

By purchasing named Houses foreigners gained the symbolic capital that their House had accumulated. The name of the House one bought allowed the village to place the buyer in a social and economic place in village reckoning. This insertion of outsiders within the village's social space could be considered a kind of fictive kinship. At the same time, foreigners – outsiders – were made to feel that through their acquisitions and restorations of neglected and abandoned properties they were accepted as part of the community. They saw themselves as 'preservers of the past' at a time when locals were unable to care for it themselves.

Throughout the period from 1929 to 1970, the houses left vacant in Deià by those who emigrated to France, Palma, and other developing mainland and island areas were available for purchase. Foreigners were able to settle in Deià during this period because the low cost of living was such that they could combine their interests in writing or painting with a style of life unaffordable in their home countries.

When Robert Graves was looking for a place to settle down with Laura Riding, he asked Gertrude Stein to recommend a peaceful place to resettle and she replied: 'Go to Mallorca, it is paradise if you can stand it' (Seymour-Smith 1984:190). The early foreign residents found their ideal of paradise in Deià and in the local people who moved so gracefully over the terraced landscape. This idyllic setting epitomised the contrast to Western materialist society that most came to escape. Foreigners wanted to own their piece of paradise, and this was possible in Deià for just a few hundred pounds.

Despite Gertrude Stein's description of the Mallorquin people as 'a foolish host of decayed pirates with an awful language', Graves found that the locals were welcoming and made an effort to understand the outsiders' efforts to communicate. French and Spanish (Castilian) were the most commonly used languages during this period.[8] Many of the people who were involved in innkeeping in the village had spent some time in similar enterprises in France. Their expertise in dealing with outsiders in a professional, formal, and amicable manner was extremely helpful to those foreigners who arrived during this period; it was through these persons that foreigners gained access to information about local activities and houses for rent or sale.

As more foreigners arrived and rented or bought a house, the new owner was given the identity of the House. It was not long before the oral history of shared kinship and genealogical connections associated with local people was extended to include foreign occupants of local houses. The 'traditional village' had been formed by members of various households with familiar House names and continued to exist as long as those Houses continued to exist. Foreigners who occupied any familiar House carried the name of an old House into the present. This perpetuated a fictive continuity with the past. It was through the occupancy of a village House that foreigners entered into relationships with local people and helped to keep the village alive.

Just as some local people's House names change over time in relation to the relevance of the activities of the occupants, so outsiders' actions began to alter public images and their House names were changed to fit the new situations. The teacher and the doctor, employed by the state to work in the village, were at first known by affixing their profession to the name of the house each rented (e.g., *el metge de Ca'n Lluch* – the doctor who lives in Lluch's House), but after a few years the house dropped its previous name and became *Ca'l Metge* (the Doctor's House) and the same occurred in the case of the teacher *Ca'n Mestre* (the Teacher's House).

Ca'n Bi is a large house in the area known as Es Clot. The local family who lived there and married into other local Houses was known by the name of its family House. Today, there are no members left of the family once associated with that House. Referring to a man today as *el senyor de Ca'n Bi* (the gentleman from Ca'n Bi) informs the villagers that the person being referred to is a foreign gentleman who arrived before 1975 and bought a house which is part of village history. The villagers first recognition of him was through the name of the house. In this instance, the house was bought in 1965 by an Englishman and his wife who spent three to six months there each year. Their son Toby lived in the house for many years while his parents were in Britain, and people began to refer to Ca'n Bi as *Ca'n Tobi* (Toby's House). Toby's presence in the village over an extended period had changed the image of his House. When his parents visit they are still referred to as 'el senyors de Ca'n Bi'. While the reference to the parents maintains an image of past social relations in Deià, the new reference acknowledges social change and the relevance of the occupants to current village activities. In the 1960s Ca'n Bi was a recognised House within the village. By 1975 there were no longer any local people connected through that House. Old people could associate the description of Toby's parents with the house named Ca'n Bi, but the rest of the village chose to update the information transmitted through House names. In contrast, Robert Graves and Laura Riding named the house they built in the 1930s *Canelluñ,*[9] but it has always been referred to in the village as *Ca'n Gravés* (the House of Senyor Graves). These are further examples of what I referred to in Chapter 4 as 'selective tradition' – the mixing of traditional and modern symbols and terms. House names reflect the social organisation of the village at particular periods. Ca'n Gravés continues to be associated with Graves's children and grandchildren and will undoubtedly be retained as long as foreign visitors continue to ask to see the house where Robert Graves lived.

After 1970, some of those who bought or rented houses were identified by their House name, and if they had exaggerated characteristics (e.g., big nose, long legs, odd behaviour, etc.), nicknames were invented for them. Nicknaming is an individualising device and defines a person and a particular relationship to the village (see Chapter 3). The nickname can be satirical, mocking, or degrading but it nevertheless identifies the bearer as one encompassed in the village idiom. An American artist who painted his large abstract paintings under the bridge where his neighbour kept his pigs was called *el porque* (the pigkeeper); *el indiot* (the turkey) was the nickname given to a man with a beaky nose. An expressionless man was dubbed *el mort* (the dead man), and *yo quiero* (I want) was an Englishman who spoke very little Spanish, and while building his own small house appeared daily at one of the local builders' houses saying '*yo quiero* this or that'.[10]

The rapid tourist development throughout the island altered the status differences that were once so important. Emigration from Deià to the cities and newly developing resorts during the 1960s, along with social security, regular wages, and controlled working hours, allowed young people from villages to cross the economic gap that previously existed between those who worked in agriculture and all others. Young people referred to one another and foreign acquaintances by Christian names and most foreign adults introduced themselves by their Christian names. These names became more familiar through village usage and reflected the more relaxed relationships between locals and foreigners.

We have seen that foreign visitors to Deià in the 1960s and 1970s were somewhat different from the hoards of tourists who went to the other parts of the island and mainland Spain on package tours organised and executed by tourist companies in foreign lands. Mass tourism had little contact with local communities while foreigners who came to Deià were drawn into the existing social system. Foreigners were able to share in some local activities and developed relationships with neighbours and friends.

Increased tourism altered the social relations of foreigners and locals in Deià, too. As a greater number of foreigners came to Deià, they relied on other foreigners for information about the village, and they had less contact with the locals, which made it more difficult for the locals to individualise each newcomer. Foreigners could no longer be easily slotted into a single category of gentlefolk. The title of Senyor seems to have been used less and less after 1975. This was the period of political reconstruction of the nation. Travellers were now referred to as tourists; no longer full of 'wanderlust' or the search for unknown truths in other places, they were just ordinary hard-working people temporarily on 'holiday' (Smith 1978).

By 1980 over a quarter of the houses in the village were owned by foreigners. There were a dozen foreign children in the local schools and a few foreigners buried in the cemetery. Most of the parents knew little or no Spanish while the children learned quickly and moved around the village, becoming regular participants in most community activities. Their parents tended to mix with other foreigners and, except through their children, were not known by the village. A typical example is Tommy, who came to the village when he was four. His parents had bought a house some years before. When the marriage had problems, his mother decided to leave England and live full-time in Deià. Tommy attended the local nursery school and his name soon became well known in the village. When his friends went to play at his house they said they were going to *Ca'n Tomis* (Tommy's House) because he was the person that gave that house recognition in the village. Older people still associated foreigners with the named House they occupied, but the local schoolchildren identified the house and the parents of their schoolmates by their Christian names. This dual reference to houses by different generations reflects the waning significance of the past for the young and an increasing awareness of changing relationships within the village.

Foreigners who built new houses were identified by nationality and by the name of the general location or area where their house was built, e.g., *el Ingles de Sa Heretat* (an Englishmen from an area outside the village known as 'the Inheritance') or *el Alemany de S'Empaltada* (the German from a mountainside development on the edge of the village known as 'the limb grafted onto the olive tree'). Both are the 'old' names of these areas before they were developed. By using these old names the people that live there, both local and foreign, are indiscriminately grouped together as part of the village. However, those who understand the idiom recognise the distinctions made through the use of nationality or Christian name.

New House names are not readily absorbed into the village idiom. Over time, one's Christian or surname or children's name or a nickname may replace one's House name depending upon one's relationship to people in the village, the regularity of visits or residence, the person's personality, and the time one remains in the village. The family member who mixes most around the village is often the one whose name is used to identify family, House, and kin (e.g., Tommy). The regular use of Christian names is a sign of the decreasing concern with status differences and the changing relationships between locals and outsiders.

The social and economic changes going on in both the local arena and the outside areas from which people move into the village have been recorded in the different forms of address and reference used over this period. Foreigners have been given a kind of fictive kinship by including them in the village idiom. Even today, some newcomers are enfolded within the village through the inclusion of their child's name or the location of their house in the village idiom. However, because they do not understand the reciprocal rules of inclusion which imply participation, they remain outsiders.

Class and status consciousness of the past has been replaced by insider-outsider dichotomies today. These are clearly visible in family and household arrangements, habits of dress, activities and spatial connotations, as well as in Christian names. Common names unite the past and present generations of Deianencs (Joan, Xesc, Catalina, Francisca) while unique names indicate outside influences (Alfredo, Vanessa, Tali, Tana, Mya, Amy, Sean). As noted earlier, while Deianencs observe a fairly gender- and age-specific, regularly patterned spatial orientation where certain spaces and times are special and require appropriate behaviour and attire, foreigners move in and out of shops, cafés, houses, restaurants and occasionally the church or cemetery at any time and seem to make little or no distinction between weekday and weekend space, activities, dress, or behaviour (Chapter 2).

The increased awareness of symbolic boundaries between insiders and outsiders seems to be the outcome of increased numbers of foreigners and the breakdown in modes of communication and adaptation between foreigners and locals. The presence of this ever enlarging group has begun to threaten the fabric of social relations, the meanings and values of local culture. One or two eccentrics added entertainment, distraction and increased economic activities, which could be included in village life; two hundred strangers is another experience altogether.

In the face of the 'other', the local identity, the sense of being a Deianenc had to be asserted. In so doing, internal pressures were directed outward and a sense of oneness reinforced. The Deianencs could no longer accept being either silent or invisible.[11] Today, foreigners tend to be drawn into foreign groupings rather than being absorbed as individuals into local activities. Each group begins to close in on itself. The growing number of foreign residents leads locals to categorise foreigners in generally amorphous terms as outsiders.[12] Foreigners, on the other hand, no longer see themselves as a collectivity, but rather as many distinct foreign groupings, each concerned with its own interests and problems and less and less involved with one another.

The people identified as outsiders today are far less amenable to definition than in the past. A large number of clearly different sorts: long-term residents/newcomers, those with capital for investment/those on limited incomes, the educated/the uneducated, trained artists/amateurs, retired/employed, and old/young of different nationalities have been lumped together as outsiders. The Deianencs, despite their differences, associate as insiders and distinguish themselves from this large number of diverse people by grouping the varying clusters together as outsiders, although at times some will be distinguished from others based on the circumstances of a given situation. Those who fit most into the category of outsiders are those who do not participate in the life of the village that they occupy.

Long-term foreign residents see themselves more closely aligned to Deianencs than with the foreigners who have come to the village since the 1980s. They feel that after decades of shared experience both locals and foreigners are being forced to question allegiances and take sides. Deianencs assert that only they know what 'the village' is and what it needs; residence in the same social space does not give everyone the same right to comment on the use of that space. They no longer feel an obligation to welcome the unknown stranger, be hospitable, or project an image of their village that is not of their own making. On the contrary, unable to control the influx of outsiders who are competing for the same limited resources, they want to assert their birthright to the village they see slipping away from them. Therefore, they identify as outsiders any who lack reciprocal relationships with locals, effective status, or collective consciousness derived from participating in Deianenc society.

According to the 1991 census, only 32 percent of the population of Deià was born in the village; 26 percent was born in other villages of Mallorca and in the city of Palma; 21.5 percent was born on the mainland; 20.5 percent are foreigners. The Palma figure is not completely accurate in that there was a short period when births that took place in the hospital in Palma were registered as born in Palma when, according to the locals, such births should have been attributed to Deià. Nine of those born in Palma have foreign parents and the number of foreign children born or brought up from an early age in Deià is increasing annually. This means that many estrangers and forasters identify with insiders on many more levels than they do with the other foreigners with whom they share the generic classification of outsiders.

Foreigners and Deianencs: A Historical Perspective

Local commentaries, history, and discussion suggest three main stages in the arrival of foreign settlers in Deià: (1) 1867 to 1940; (2) 1940 to 1975; (3) 1975 to the present. Each division encompasses major political, economic, and social stages in the development of the Spanish nation and its relations to world events. These dates do not indicate tight boundaries but rather markers that include the events that made various impacts on the lives of those within the village and the many foreigners who chose to live their over the past century. Stage I includes the period of the late nineteenth-century Grand Tour, World War I, the Spanish First and Second Republics, and the Spanish Civil War. Stage II includes World War II and the post-war development of European and American economies and the development of a tourist industry. Stage III begins with Post-Franco Social Democracy, the entry of Spain into the European Community, and carries on to the present.

The people that arrived during each of these periods were motivated by the effects of the above-mentioned events on their home countries and on their individual lives. The people who arrived during the first and second stages may be distinguished from those of the third by the display or absence of various characteristics: idiosyncratic behaviour, an idealisation of nature over culture, literary or artistic aspirations, economic independence or necessity, interest in foreign languages and cultures, and a concern for reconciling individual freedom with social justice. These traits were reflected in their permanence of residence and their social and economic investment in the village. Their involvement in local life was recognised by the village through various references: senyor or senyora, House names, nicknames, and Christian names.

In keeping with the local attitude toward strangers, foreigners who arrived in Deià during the first two stages were incorporated into the social system at one level or another, encouraged to participate in local activities, given a local identity through status or House purchase, and often requested to intervene with authorities on behalf of the village. These foreigners represented the 'feared' outside and were 'tamed' by inclusion into existing social categories which allowed the locals to see them as interesting, useful, unobtrusive, and yet contained. Outsiders did not live by local norms and values, but as long as they did not interfere in local politics (unless requested) their idiosyncrasies, excesses, and mere presence were tolerated by locals. Certainly during the Franco dictatorship, officials such as the mayor, the Guardia Civil, and the priest kept a keen watch for political interference, blasphemers, 'fornicators', anarchists, and the like.

Deià, removed from the competition, the pressures and sounds of large towns and cities, was an ideal place to develop the creative lifestyle many foreigners were seeking. Over the years they succeeded in pursuing individual aspirations and met others with whom they shared many of these ideals. They did not all get along with one another, but there was plenty of space and time for different activities and encounters, for individual and social pursuits. The foreign colony developed into a small community within the local community where differences were taken for granted and each developed his or her own points of reference.

After 1975, most of the foreigners that began to buy houses and settle in Deià had different backgrounds, attitudes, and values than those who had resided there for years. By the 1980s, with changes in the economic and political climate within the village, house prices had increased and higher incomes were needed to purchase village houses. The long-term foreigners feared that these new people and values would be destructive to the paradise they had so long enjoyed. They felt they had formed long and meaningful relationships with local villagers. What they had not considered was that the circumstances and desires of the local villagers would alter during this period of change.

Different social, political, economic, religious, and moral conditions offered locals new opportunities to modernise their lifestyles, while foreigners struggled to maintain the sense of simplicity and timelessness they found so attractive.

In the chapter 'Conceptions of Space' it was shown that foreigners seem to describe the village from outside: a socially distanced personal view of landscape and architecture from which they derive emotional, physical, intellectual and spiritual benefit. For many long-term foreigners, Deià seems to exist only as they perceive it – a paradise for their pleasure and creativity, an exotic landscape and congenial people designed to inspire, test, or soothe one's soul. This community is perceived in different terms from those used by Deianencs who describe the village as a known physical and geographical space within which personal associations, collective identities, and histories are experienced with others who share this knowledge.

According to Anthony Cohen, 'Community seems to imply simultaneously both similarity and difference. The word expresses a relational idea; the opposition of one community to others or to other social entities'. The perceptions of the village held by local Deianencs are those of the village from the inside looking out (families, Houses, shared activities and values), and those of the foreigners from the outside looking in (landscape, beauty, peacefulness). However, both see themselves as part of a community known as Deià. Community is not a reality in itself but a conscious construct of the varying interpretations that are held by those who live there.

Foreigners identified with the setting, which reflected their perceptions of beauty and of the integrated existence of humans with nature; they adopted some of the peasant garments as their everyday apparel; they purchased, restored, and maintained the culture's artefacts as their means of showing respect to the local people. Although there has been no pretense at assimilation, foreigners feel they share common concerns with their local neighbours. Prestations (exchanges of varying kinds including favours, home produce, consumer goods, or transport) and counter-prestations go on between them all the time. Over the years and through their relationships with foreigners in the village, the local people have been able to reassess their association with their village land from that which bound them to a life of toil and fatigue to a valued possession, exchange item, and symbol of their heritage. Local dreams and visions of a future, in which their everyday needs would be satisfied and a better life for their children provided, have been realised.

In the previous section, I suggested that the changing forms of address and reference used for outsiders reflect the changing attitudes and social relationships that have evolved in Deià during the past century. However, the regular use of the term outsiders does not indicate these subtle differences. It became evident that the term outsider encompassed a wide variety of people: long-term and short-term foreign visitors and residents, artists, writers, senyors, homeowners, parents, Spanish professionals, and tourists. Some long-term visitors and residents resented being part of such a general category of people. Although foreigners, they felt that they had more in common with Deianencs who identified themselves as insiders than with the increased number of foreigners who had settled in Deià since the 1980s. A review of the development of the foreign colony over the past century will suggest some reasons for this sense of difference and the problems these different perspectives impose on the definition of the term outsiders.

1867 to 1940

The Archduke Luis Salvador of Austria may be responsible for the beginnings of the art colony that has been associated with Deià since as early as 1870, the year in which the first volume of *Die Balearen* was made available to the German reading public. Over the years he invited many of the leading figures in the arts to be his guests at Miramar, one of the many Deià properties he bought. He acquired most of the large estates along the coast from Valldemossa to Deià, had paths cut into previously inaccessible parts of the forests, and had minarets built at spots he found beautiful. He found a large working population willing to do any task he needed done, and for a pittance. The relationships that developed had to be based on both his value system and theirs. The Archduke's employees expected him to assume the role that all landowners did at that time, that of patron, and he was obliged to take on their values in this sense of patronage. He was invited to participate in life cycle rituals, and was said to have advanced goods and money in times of difficulties. At the same time, he imposed his values on them. He wanted no trees cut down on any of the land he bought nor any hunting to occur; he wanted everything to remain as 'natural' as when he had found it. His cultural heritage and mode of living began to affect the religious, social, and economic lives of some of the local Deianencs and Valldemossins as soon as he purchased his first property, Miramar.

For a start, he created an immense household and work force that included a young student from Deià named Antonio Vives, who was educated at his expense and travelled with him, serving as his secretary for forty years. There are innumerable stories about his 'love' affairs with young village women and men, but there is no concrete evidence that he actually fathered any children (a number of his employees' children, however, bear a striking resemblance to him).[13] The Archduke's estates were inherited by local Valldemossins and Deianencs, and the effect of these inheritances on the social structure, especially that of Valldemossa, was extreme. He left almost all of his properties to local people who had been his employees or the children of these employees (which only served to increase the gossip about his personal relationships with his workers). Almost overnight agricultural tenants became owners of vast estates with all the accompanying responsibilities and obligations. The residence of the Archduke is visited today by hundreds of tourists who for a small fee can go inside his main house, Son Marroig, where they are shown the archaeological artefacts, drawings, original maps, manuscripts, and other paraphernalia collected by this nineteenth-century gentleman.[14]

By 1868 the number of foreign residents on the island had risen from 98 (in 1860) to 140. Few of these visitors got to Deià. The Archduke noted in his diaries in 1882 that 'the road from Palma to Valldemossa, Deià and Soller is not yet finished but can be used by day visitors to get as far as Miramar'. Until the highway was completed in 1901, the travellers who found their way to Deià were few and adventurous. They had to wander outside the city areas developed to cater to their needs and often experienced discomfort in pursuing their curiosity to meet the 'real island inhabitants'.

The peasants were used to identifying their social superiors by differences in attire, behaviour, and manners. A guidebook from 1888 notes that, 'one of Deià's chief characteristics is its collection of strange and eccentric foreigners' (Wood). Strangers had a demeanor which bespoke worldly experience. Even the most humble carried a pad to sketch what they saw or kept notes while the locals admired these abilities.

The local experience with foreigners was already well established when Robert Graves decided to settle in Deià. He lived there with Laura Riding from 1929 to 1936, left when the Civil War broke out, and returned with Beryl Pritchard Hodges and two children just as the Second World War was coming to an end in 1946.

During his first stay, he and Riding endeavoured to create their ideal of a 'perfect community': organising social life for artists and writers and their local friends in Deià, and publishing a literary magazine. Graves tried to define and limit the membership in 'their community' and this was to set a pattern for foreign social relations in Deià until his death. There were always some 'in' the Graves group and others who were excluded or wished not to join in their activities. Graves attracted many visitors to Deià. Since so much of Deià social life went on around Graves and his activities, most foreigners tried to maintain amicable relations with him but he did not always make this easy. He helped some to meet local people, find a place to live, and become part of both local and foreign activities. Others he ignored or rejected (for no apparent reason), excluding them from the social activities he organised and speaking poorly of them to his foreign and local friends.

A falling-out between Graves and some member of the foreign colony occurred every few years. At these times, he would assume his role of patron. He would 'call in' the favours he'd done for friends and ask for their support. The basis of his claims against people was so tied up with his own personal, 'poetic' way of seeing things that his friends merely humoured him rather than taking sides.[15] If he walked into the café and one was sitting with the 'current enemy' he would look around for another group of friends to sit with or leave the café. On one's next meeting with him he would query how one could have sat with so-and-so. His good friends were expected to share his opinions so that he not only excluded some people from his group but also exerted a great deal of social control over those he included in his 'ideal community'. He wanted to feel that his friends were on his side under any circumstances, and it was often this irrational commitment that brought about the disputes that took place over the years.

From the first group of English and American writers organised around himself and Laura Riding in 1929, Graves evolved a network of friends, colleagues, admirers, and the inevitable hangers-on and enemies. According to him, the focus of all of his relationships was his search for 'poetic truths'. This often took the form of intense friendships which required his friends to adapt to his ideas and value system or fall 'out of grace'.

Tom Matthews, an American writer in Deià at this time, has recorded his experiences in a book originally entitled *Jacks or Better* (1953) and reissued as *Under the Spell* (1989). He relates how very difficult it was to enter the Graves-Riding 'group', but on being accepted (as he was) one was taken under Riding's tutelage, spending many hours of each day occupied with the group's activities. Riding would arrive at Matthews's house at six in the morning and offer her unsolicited help in reading and editing his manuscript.

In 1935 Graves wrote to his friend W.B. Yeats: 'We are both very watchful in our relations, whether with literature or in neighbour-ship; never casual and least of all here in Mallorca where we live permanently in hard-working privacy. With the many foreigners who visit the island we have, as a rule, nothing to do – unless they are friends of ours who come here purposely to see us' (O'Prey:236, 251). Graves tended to form rather instant likes or dislikes for people depending on the circumstances of their meeting.

The Graves-Riding entourage could be clearly described as a group. There were the two self-appointed leaders who stated their goals clearly and selected the members in accord with that criteria. The symbolic patterns of behaviour that were implicit in their special style of life performed many organisational functions. One had to be economically independent, unfettered by responsibilities other than to creative and intelligent pursuits, amenable to interference and guidance, yet able to set limits which indicated personal commitment and self-awareness. Discourse was esoteric and automatically excluded anyone who was not part of the clique.

In Graves's biography Seymour-Smith writes that 'the sense of happiness in Deià, though, was felt most strongly by those visitors who were not writers, those whom Laura did not consider as suitable for her ideal community. There were parties and dancing on the patio of Canelluñ, visits to the cafés, card playing and joking conversations … but the life in Deià was one of strong contrasts; Laura light, good humoured, full of fun (usually with non-intelligentsia) or strained, erasable authoritarian….' (1982:236).

The authoritarian manner of Laura Riding and the dominant role she and Graves played in social relationships must have made life extremely pressured for those who were included in their 'ideal community', but to be excluded could be equally frustrating. Graves and Riding could 'open doors' for young writers, for they were colourful and highly educated and involved in the 'world' of literature. Graves had access to the only motor vehicle in Deià through his friend Gelat; he organised excursions to the city; he knew local people and could help one to find accommodation, housekeepers, gardeners, blacksmiths, or carpenters. He could give introductions to bank managers and moneychangers and could be generous when others were less well off. He was the energy behind almost all the cultural and social activities open to a foreigner in Deià at that time. Despite the drawbacks, he and Riding were friends worth having.

When the owner of the estate on which Graves's house was built announced in 1932 that he was selling a large portion of the land to a local German resident who had plans to build a hotel, Graves and Riding decided that the best thing they could do to protect their privacy was to 'boldly get the land ourselves and as Deya has no hotel and is bound to have one, put up one ourselves in a corner of the land far enough removed from our house not to matter' (from an undated, unpublished letter to T.E. Lawrence now in a private collection). The road which joined cala Deià and the main Valldemossa-Deià to Soller road was intended to give access to the proposed hotel, but money ran out and only the road was finished. Graves's and Riding's aborted effort to control development resulted in increased activity past his house each day as villagers and many more visitors, who had been unable to descend the steep paths in the past, began to frequent the cala via the new road. Naively, Graves prepared the way for the outside world to gain access to the cala of Deià and invade 'his privacy'. The road was to be the cause for conflicts between locals and foreigners at various times in the next fifty years (these conflicts will be discussed in detail in Chapter 6).[16]

We have discussed Graves's local friend and business associate, Gelat (Joan Marroig), who was involved in all of his business dealings and held control over a large percentage of the working men in Deià.[17] As Graves's and Riding's friend, one had access to any help one might need from Gelat as well, which meant that between them they had the village and the outside pretty much at their beck and call. In Graves's letters during the build-up to the Civil War in 1936 there are many references to the 'power' he and Gelat could wield. In one letter he wrote that Gelat 'any day now will be Mayor of Deya at the head of a council of his friends (and ours) appointed directly by the Governor who is also of course Left. Then Deya will begin to develop, we foresee, the first aim a telephone' (O'Prey 1982:269). The war prevented any such developments.

Graves had a marked effect on the social and economic life of both the local Deianencs and foreign residents during the forty-six years he lived in Deià. He employed village girls and women from the mainland in the house and as olive pickers during the season. He wrote to a friend in 1934 commenting that 'Maid Isabella is such a success that we are fetching her younger sister from the mainland to help her, and do the washing. They will have a room in the basement' (O'Prey 1982:237). Both girls married into the village in later years and, when their daughters were old enough to work, they took their mothers' places in Graves's house. He certainly increased the load of post that arrived each day in

Deià, and the postman was grateful that Graves developed his schedule around the *Correos* (the mail that arrived from Palma at 3:30 each afternoon on Gelat's daily bus). Graves could be seen unfailingly at 4:00 P.M. most days (except Sunday) striding up the steps to the post office. Visitors and friends learned his schedule, arranged to 'casually' bump into him en route and took advantage of the opportunity to get help from him or just have a chat. The importance of these encounters, to some people, can not be overstated. One Englishman who retired to Deià in 1969 kept a record of the number of times he had Graves over for tea after these regular post collections: it reached well over a thousand. Graves kept a punctilious schedule all the years in Deià. He always worked in the morning, walked to the beach at the same time each day, dived off the same rock after climbing to a preferred spot and returned home for his midday meal, a short nap, then to collect the post, etc.

Like the Archduke who held a yearly party for all his employees and their children, Graves's birthday was an annual celebration to which local and foreign friends, officials and acquaintances from around the island and the United Kingdom were invited. Graves and Riding and later Beryl (Mrs. Graves) accepted the roles of patrons with the associated reciprocities. Laura had a dress made for a local girl who was chosen to present flowers to a visiting Bishop; Graves contributed to Gelat's purchase of a larger generator to give the village improved electricity. There are some local couples who received wedding gifts and poems dedicated to the newlyweds by Graves. These gifts were almost all objects from the Mallorquin past which he had bought in an antique store in Palma. The carpenter and his wife have an oxen's yoke hung over their mantle with Graves's dedication framed beneath it. In some homes these are the only bits of the past that were held onto when interiors were 'modernised'. Clearly, because they were gifts from Graves and purchased in an antique shop, rather than found among discarded farming implements, they were given symbolic value despite their functional origins.[18] Today, whether from the attic, the cellar or a shop, anything to do with Deià's past is prized for decorative purposes.

The Archduke and Robert Graves and most of those later referred to as senyors maintained the differences that were associated with land- and house-ownership, employers, and patrons. Within the complex structure of landowners, tenants, employees, and day labourers, land remained an important instrument of social dominance. While villageness was still based on the ethos of large estates and the social and economic imbalance they maintained, locals had accepted outsiders as strangers and converted them into recognised gentlefolk, just as they had always accepted landowners. The 'new' foreign senyors included the Archduke, Graves, and those who followed. They combined work and leisure, had smooth hands, retained contact with the outside world and their home countries. They had innumerable foreign guests and lived up to the expectations associated with senyors by providing concern and employment for local people. They had very clear ideas about what they wanted from the place and the people and made their needs known. Those with whom they interacted met their requirements and often surprised them by unanticipated kindnesses.

When Graves and Riding had to leave hurriedly at the beginning of the Civil War in 1936, his friend Gelat vowed to watch over his house. After returning to Deià in 1946 he wrote in his diary: 'I can't think of anywhere in the world where one could leave at an hour's notice and come back after ten years to find everything waiting as if nothing had happened' (O'Prey 1984:343). The Archduke and later Graves were honoured for their contributions to village life by being made adopted sons of the village. Graves was presented with an official document stating that he was an *hijo adoptivo del pueblo de Deya* in a ceremony held in the summer of 1965.

During this period, a homeowner who sold or rented his or her house to a foreigner not only gained sorely needed cash but prestige among the other villagers. That person possessed inside knowledge about the stranger. The stranger in return gained entrée into the local world through his house and its owner. Bachelors and spinsters were among the first landlords for foreign tenants. Living with their siblings or elderly relations, they were the ones who had empty houses inherited from their parents or bought with savings. They cared for their tenants, the house, and garden as though the tenant were a family member. Single foreign men were pampered – they were an anomaly in this village where an unmarried or widowed man would not be left to live on his own but always taken into the home of his parents, siblings, or children. Single women who were widows or spinsters did not attract the same concern. Women were considered to be at ease in the domestic sphere. The effect of a few foreign residents in the village at this time filtered through to many levels. Spinsters and bachelors satisfied a need by being able to provide necessary services and accommodations. Their peripheral role within the family household became an important asset for welcoming and orientating foreign visitors into local life. The money they received was poured back into the family homes of their siblings; the information they gained was shared over dinner table; and their young nieces and nephews, siblings, and parents were introduced to the ways of the outside world through the stories their aunts and uncles carried home from the foreigner's house.

1940 to 1975

Some of the foreigners who came to live in Deià during the early part of this period had experienced the social upheavals that occurred in the United States and Europe during and after World War II. Inspired by French Existentialism each was seeking 'to realise himself through free choice between alternatives, through self-commitment. To exist, therefore, meant becoming more and more an individual and less and less a mere member of a group. It meant 'transcending universality in favour of individuality' (Kirkegaard 1968:335). One sought a precedence of existence over essence by accepting the Existential premise that, 'the individual is born in a void, from which point his life progresses as a series of free choices, decisions and actions, for which he alone is responsible. The individual is seen as a free agent in a deterministic and seemingly meaningless universe' (Sartre 1949:57).

Like the travellers of the past, these individuals felt 'truth' lay outside their home countries. They wanted to taste the joys of life that they and their generation had been denied. Deià became 'paradise', the place to find oneself, to recreate the ideal world each imagined. Those who followed in the 1960s added the 'peace and love' elements of the hippy movement to the previous decade's 'free agents'. Among the foreign community, sexual relations were a necessary expression of freedom of choice. Sexual activity was seen as 'natural', monogamy as unnatural and restricting. Sexual liberation meant personal liberation. Younger women brought laughter and lightheartedness back into the lives of the very intense men who felt they had lost their youth and dreams in far-off wars. One man's remembrances of that period show the pursuit of personal pleasure among the foreigners in contrast to the restrictive moral and economic aspects of local life:

> My God, that place was a paradise wasn't it? We were true hedonists, playing it up in one of the most beautiful scenes in the world. The greatest thing about it was that for a decade [1960–1970] it never changed – Spain never changed – and we played on, lolling on the beach all day and partying all night. Never did so many play so much

> on so little. I was living like a King on 3,000 pesetas [£15] a month. I had that big house over looking the Mediterranean and the tower for three hundred and fifty pesetas [less than £2] a month. In that milieu there was no such thing as a poor American. A three course meal with wine averaged about twenty pesetas. It was a place for love. I lived in places all around the world, but never did I see such beautiful and interesting women as there were right there in Deià ... I must have fallen in love at least thirty times.... Those were the days, my friend, as you well remember. Ah, wise were we to retire after our war, while in our physical prime. We were the lotus eaters in paradise. No one, not even the gods, can take that away from us. (A letter to W. Waldren from Brad Rising 1985)

The main feature of the groups that were formed and reformed during the 1940 to 1975 period was not merely the common interests that participants shared but the bohemian, eccentric, expatriate lifestyle they had all chosen. Outside the mainstream or accepted norms of their own and the local culture, each was endeavouring to create an identity based on the criteria of creativity, knowledge, and freedom of choice in all areas of their lives. Individuals were encountering others who shared their marginality. Together they reinforced one another's idiosyncrasies and helped to make these the expression of their independence. The ideal community of Graves and Riding demanded that its members, despite personal eccentricities, conform to certain literary standards that the two of them established. Those who came to Deià during the late fifties and throughout the 1960s were not willing to conform to fixed norms. Writing had no limits, art no set forms, and experimentation was essential. It was a time of anti-culture, any culture, and freedom from any sort of constraints.

A brief description of the foreigners who arrived before 1965 whose lives were intimately connected with Deià and Deianencs will reveal additional characteristics that can be associated with these early arrivals:

1929 to 1939: Graves (died 1985); a German artist, Lehman (who died in Deià at 102 years of age in October 1987), and his Mallorquin companion from another village, also an artist; a German antiquarian and his wife; a German artist, his wife, and their son born in Deià in 1935. Lehman and the antiquarian bought houses in the village, Graves built Canelluñ, and the last family rented a house.

1940s: A German philosopher and his wife; a Danish couple; Graves with Beryl Hodges (later to become his second wife) and their three children; a German merchant with his wife and son. Two bought houses and the other rented.

1950s: A French couple and a German woman as well as a large number of Americans came to Deià, some directly from the United States while others had been studying art in Paris (on the GI Bill). They came first for the summer holidays and later to settle. There were five single people (three men and two women), six married, and six small children. Two more children were born in Deià. Four couples bought houses, the others rented houses or stayed in the local inn. There were a number of affairs, a divorce and a marriage among this group that met in Deià during this period.

1960s: Twelve single people and twenty-two married couples settled in Deià or spent at least three months there each year. Five couples and two single mothers brought eleven small children with them, and thirty more children were born during this period. Six of them were born in Deià and the others were brought to Deià soon after their births. Five couples were separated and the husbands formed new relationships with the single women they had met in Deià. Three of the ex-wives remained in the village and two moved away. Four marriages occurred: one between two of the single people; another with a single American man and the Mallorquin village school teacher (from the adjoining island of Cabrera); two of the Graves children married Spaniards (from the mainland). Each couple had one child before 1970. Twenty of the couples and five of the singles bought houses; the others rented. Three of the divorced men bought second houses when they remarried.

This listing clearly indicates the self-contained quality of the foreign community and the complex internal relationships that developed among them. The number and variety of people increased dramatically from the 1930s to the 1960s. The only 'intimate' relationships formed with persons from outside the foreign community were with forasters or non-Deianencs: the doctor from Palma, the schoolteacher from another island, and Spaniards from the mainland. These were all forasters by birth and education who mixed as much with foreigners as they did with locals.

The Deianencs, who had been *curats d'espants* (shock proof) for over a century, were largely indifferent to the foreigners' eccentricities. Foreigners did not threaten the Deianencs' values or way of life. Their actions were too far removed from anything Deianencs valued. Foreigners lived their lives in public. Their everyday and nightly actions, expenditures, and lifestyles had become common knowledge. There was a mutual respect for one another expressed in greetings and actions, yet boundaries between them were carefully maintained: local girls did not frequent the cafés, and foreign men had little or no access to local women of any age. Local men mixed with foreign men and women in the café. Occasionally, a local man would dance with a foreign woman, using the excuse of being under the effects of alcohol, but the foreign women at this period had little in common with and showed no interest in local men.[19] The local repression of sexuality and the religious and political control of individual freedoms were in absolute contrast to the licence practiced by the foreigners who came to Deià at this time. The vast cultural differences that attracted foreigners to Deià also served to protect the local people from any intimate contact with them. As Simmel wrote:

> We confront the stranger, with whom we share neither characteristics nor broader interests, objectively; we hold our personalities in reserve; and thus a particular difference does not involve us in our totalities. On the other hand we meet the person who is very different from us only on certain points within a particular contact or with coincidence of particular interests, and hence the spread of conflict is limited to those points only. (1953:44)

Throughout the entire period from the arrival of the Archduke until the present there have been no marriages between a Deianenc and any resident member of the foreign colony. In many levels of Mallorquin society marriage to a foreigner was once considered tantamount to the loss of a child, although that attitude has changed over the past decades. The only marriage between a local girl and a foreigner during this period involved a fisherman's daughter and a German tourist whom she had met at cala Deià in 1960. He returned for a fortnight each year to court her the required six years before the family begrudgingly allowed her to be married. The couple moved to Germany after marriage, returning some years later when the husband found work on the island. The German husband has adapted to Mallorquin life. He speaks the language, works for a Spanish company, spends his free time with his wife's family, and has little contact with other Germans on the island. This marriage gained the approval of the girl's parents only after she went away. Her family was forced to choose between permanent loss of their daughter or compromise. The next marriage between a local and a foreigner did not occur until 1980.

Women have a key role to play in the transformation of themselves and society and each generation seems to make new advances. This marriage did not really alter the separation between the various groups in

Deià; it just pointed out the difficulties encountered when symbolic boundaries are transgressed. Daughters move away from their families, an 'outsider' has to learn to become an 'insider', and for all concerned the process is long and onerous.

Foreigners born, raised, and schooled in Deià say they perceived little difference between themselves and the local friends they made at school; however, the moment they went abroad to study, their relationship with village friends changed. They say there is a certain investment of time, when one learns to conform to local values, that seems to be an essential part of belonging. When people alter the status quo, they find they have to renegotiate their local role by subtle, constant involvement in local activities. One has to work at belonging.

Incorporation or Fictive Kinship

Foreigners have been incorporated into the village through the name of the House they occupy, through shared experiences with locals, and, for some, through a sort of fictive kinship that has developed through years of interaction with local families who cared for their children, built their houses, and continued to look after them. A mutual dependence and affection developed between these foreigners and locals.

The local cafés have always been the meeting place for foreigners and locals. Drinks were interchanged, there was joking and camaraderie among some, while others sat off to the side in smaller groups watching, talking, playing cards or chess. The foreign colony seemed to be formed and constantly reformed in the public arena. People met in cafés, on the streets, in the shops, or at the cala. No introductions or credentials were needed or requested. A new and attractive person was accepted at 'face value'.

The cafés were where local men got to know foreign men and women by observation and interaction. Cafés have always been places for cultural interchange and shared contact. Many a night foreign and local men would be seen leaving a café supporting one another down the winding roads to their houses after 'one drink too many'. Two foreign men were included in a dining club[20] organised by local workmen and honoured for their participation in 'real work' (each worked side by side with the builders on his own house). Men gained status among the village men through working with them. Before they met these foreigners, local experience had led most Deianencs to believe that class determined behaviour and that senyors left the physical and dirty work to the 'peasants'. If a foreigner combined the image of a senyor with real work (dirtied his hands and exerted physical strength), he was highly esteemed.

The early days in Deià for foreigners were bohemian, romantic, idealistic, poetic, and extremely cheap. There were twenty-five foreigners my first (1959) summer in Deià. They spent their days at the rocky cove and evenings in the cafés. Few Deianencs came down to the cove during the week, except the fishermen who sat by their huts mending their nets. The fishermen would pull their boats down the ramp each evening as the sun set to lay their nets in their allotted space a kilometre or so outside the cove, and they would set off before dawn the next day to pull in the day's catch. On Sundays the youngsters from the village and excursionists from Palma would add to the numbers at the cala. There was a café built into the cliff where one could have fresh fish and wine for 15 pesetas (about ten pence). Most of the foreign visitors stayed at *Sa Fonda* (the Pension Coll)[21] where Margarita and her daughters cooked local food which was ceremoniously served by her son-in-law Antonio (who had been trained in France and spoke French to most of the guests). Room and board was 60 pesetas (40 pence – $1) a day and included a bottle of wine.

The nightly gatherings at Sa Fonda were followed by a three-kilometre stroll to Ca'n Quet, a small hotel with a patio where a gramophone was wound up and we could dance under the grape-covered arbour until the early hours. At Sa Fonda, I met an American artist who had come down from Paris each summer for the previous five years and encouraged many expatriate artists and writers to follow. We were married the following winter. Although memory blends the harsher facts with the more pleasurable ones to create a smooth image of the past, I remember feeling that everything I saw and heard and experienced during that 1959 summer in Deià was unique and that my twenty-one years of life had little prepared me for the impact of the rugged landscape, the intense heat, and the beauty that surrounded me. The combination of cosmopolitan people and the simplicity of existence they chose for their summer holidays or for the rest of their lives contrasted markedly with my middle-class American background.

The following year, my husband and I rented the first floor flat over the local bakery and telephonist for 700 pesetas (£4.50–$10) a month. We had one of the few places in town with running water and a flush toilet. There was no gas (cooking had to be done on charcoal braziers), and electricity was supplied, for only a few hours each day, by the generator Robert Graves had helped his friend Gelat to buy. One learned to adapt to the local practices including running to buy fish at 7:00 A.M. at the sound of the conch shell blown by the local fisherman at different spots around the village, and going to the shops each morning to wait one's turn with the other village women in order to acquire fresh bread and vegetables. Meat could be had on Friday when a lamb was slaughtered. I often found just the ribs were left until someone informed me that you had to order in advance. One leg was always reserved for the Graves's Sunday lunch.

Living on the local economy, learning how to acquire goods, to cook and heat water for bathing on a charcoal fire in a tiny brazier, to wash clothes in cold water at the local *lavadero* (washstand), and to communicate with my new local friends and neighbours in what remained from my high school Spanish were exciting challenges in which I was aided at every turn by local women. When our first child was born, our landlady and the village midwife gave her her first bath as I stood by in horror (sure that they were going to drop her). Throughout the next months our landlady's unmarried sister Francisca cleaned and did our laundry and cuddled and cared for the baby at every opportunity. Our landlady brought me pots of lentils and beer (meant to improve mother's milk, to fatten the baby and me). The kindness and care that Francisca and the entire 'bakery family' shared with our growing family made me feel like a spoiled daughter, and our children still refer to the now deceased Francisca as *Tieta* (an endearing form for auntie) and to her sister as *Mama Mena* (a diminutive of Magdalena).

This brief autobiographical insight is meant to evoke some of the personal involvement one felt as a visitor and then a resident in the village during this period. Other foreign women who had children during the 1950s and early 1960s received similar support and care. Local families, usually landlords or neighbours, protected, adopted, and incorporated us into their lives, sharing what they had without expecting payment or conformity to their lifestyles. Children were adored and drawn into every aspect of daily life: 'We are going to feed the rabbits, can Tali come with us?' They would include the children when they made wine, picked olives, made sausages, and even when they went on excursions. We were invited to Saints' Day celebrations to share *ensaimadas* (the local pastry) and sweet wine. One felt welcome, non-intrusive, and 'at home'.

Since few foreigners went to church, it was always a special 'treat' for the small children to be taken there by their second families. Some foreign children convinced their parents of their wish to take first communion with their peers, and neither the priest nor the locals objected. In fact, they were delighted to see the children becoming part of their culture. Although we did not want our children to take communion, they were still included in all the other social and religious activities of the village. The children fit into local life as long as they participated in all of these activities; they were accepted despite their parents' lack of involvement. Few of the foreign children practised Catholicism or any other religion after they left local schools.

Foreigners participated in innumerable exchanges with local people and in this way learned about local reciprocity. For example, after living in Deià for a few months, I realised that I would have no need for some of the clothes I had brought with me from the U.S. My neighbours and friends were always pleased to receive any such clothes since ready-made garments (other than work clothes) were hard to find in Spain in 1960.

When I returned from a visit abroad and brought them purchased gifts, they were very uncomfortable. I did not realise at the time that they felt this put them in my debt because they had no access to anything commensurate with which to reciprocate at a later date. From my point of view, I could never repay their loyalty, care, and warmth. They put the gifts in a cupboard, embarrassed by their value but proud to use them to impress their neighbours and friends with the fruits of their 'outside connections'.[22] In his diaries from the 1930s, Graves describes how he and his friend Gelat 'are so mutually (or is it reciprocally?) grateful to one another for past services that it is almost uncomfortable', and he notes later that 'the trees are full of fruits and I can finally give something "from nature" back to those who befriended me' (O'Prey 1982:28). It took a while to gain this awareness that reciprocity had to be in kind and that something that was produced through the combination of human effort and nature expressed feelings of gratitude without seeming effusive.

Reciprocity was extremely difficult and one learned that it could only be accomplished through years of maintaining close relationships with these families. Friendship was based on mutual need and curiosity about one another. Sharing everyday contact, organised activities, simple shopping, and ample conversation, visits to the café or driving someone to Palma, all were more important than money exchanges. Unless one insisted on paying for things each day, accounts with the butcher, baker, or grocer were settled once a year, on St. Michael's Day, just like the locals. The rituals of daily life made one part of a community. Prestation and counter-prestation were ongoing, not just with gifts and food, but by adopting aspects of local culture which showed respect for our new friends and our identification with their way of life. Their recipes, local dress, names, and values associated with family and social life were often absorbed by us and combined with our own values and habits. The Graves's children were named Lucia, Joan, and Tomas after local friends; the only one of my children born outside the village is named Deia.[23] Locals, too, identified with and borrowed some of our customs and practises. Friends of my daughters tell me how they would convince the girls to trade sandwiches at lunchtime. The local girls said they loved all the mayonnaise and lettuce and tomato on my girls' sandwiches and the girls loved their *p'amb oli* (bread with tomato and olive oil rubbed into it). Some local children were named after their parents' foreign friends: Vanessa and Jimmy. (To be baptised, these children were given local names by the priest: MariaVanessa and Jaume – Mallorquin for Jimmy.)

At first, almost everyone except Graves lived in rented accommodations, but one by one foreigners found out about local village houses for sale and made private purchase arrangements with their owners. Relationships with Mallorquin neighbours, local shopkeepers, Antonio at Sa Fonda, Maria the dressmaker, or Graves led to information about houses for sale. Local friends would help one to negotiate a 'good price'. Although prices were extremely low by U.S. or British standards, if we did not rely on the help of a local, we were told 'you paid too much'. It was to our advantage to maintain these relationships which allowed the locals to participate and become brokers in our financial dealings. Some foreigners who had savings or inheritances were able to pay the £300–£500 price straight away, but others worked out payment plans with the owner and a notary public which sometimes extended for three of four years: e.g., £50 every six months for three years (for a house that cost £300) or £100 each year for four years for a £400 house. It is interesting that in 1933 Graves noted in his diary that he had arranged 'to pay just the interest on the money still owing on the cala road'. This suggests that his 'friend' Gelat was far more cunning than his less experienced neighbours. In the above long-term arrangements, when regular payments were met, most people paid no interest.

Some of the artists and writers who had settled in Deià on small incomes had to struggle to meet their payments but most managed to buy a small house. Land and labour were cheap (1,000 square metres of sea-view land was £250). Houses in Es Clot were smaller and cheaper than those on Es Puig and detached houses were more costly than semis or terraced houses. It wasn't long before open discussion of the price of the latest house to be sold allowed every seller to raise their price to that level, making almost all houses the same price. Almost everyone at that time had some notion of 'living among the locals' and bought houses inside the village. Living in the village made one part of a neighbourhood, and one learned about local customs and how to live amicably with local neighbours.

Today, despite the formality of bank loans, lawyers' contracts, and other forms of securing sales, defaults on payments occur, agreements are broken, and some building contractors have suffered great losses in advancing construction time and materials only to find that payments have stopped. There are few transactions anymore based on one's word or a handshake between buyer and seller. However, for those one knows, various payment arrangements can be made. Locals shared many aspects of their lives with their foreign friends in the past. Those foreign residents who have had long-term relationships with locals recognise the trust they were given. Increased numbers of foreigners seeking to buy property and its high value has caused locals to be more wary of foreigners and fewer enduring relationships between locals and foreign residents are formed today.

Among the fifty foreigners who arrived prior to 1975 and continue to reside or return annually to Deià, one notes that the majority have managed to buy at least one, if not more, house in Deià, and only five still live in rented accommodations for which they pay extremely low rents (based on 1960 prices). The relative value of property in Mallorca, as compared to England or America at that time, was very low. Many of those who bought houses during this period in Deià would probably not have been able to buy property in their home countries. Certainly, in the 1960s few home countries considered those who earned their living from selling paintings or sculptures or by writing books as safe risks for mortgages and loans.

During the 1960s, Spain was rapidly industrialising, there was migration from rural areas to cities and into other parts of Europe, foreign travel was becoming easier, and tourism was beginning to bring some prosperity to the islands. Madrid and Barcelona were once again becoming cultural centres with active modern art movements and galleries. Outside cultural influences were welcomed in the Spanish art world. A few foreign artists in Deià tried to create a local market for their work. Ten artists (seven American, one Spanish, and two British), whose abstract paintings had been inspired and created in Deià, organised a group which they named *Es Deu d'es Teix* (the Ten of the Teix – the mountain range behind Deià). As in much abstract work of the period, the aim of these artists was to express their personal dissatisfaction with the elite world of art and create form and content that could be understood by a wider audience. After an exhibit in a Palma gallery, they were invited to show in Barcelona and Madrid. These years were characterised by a number of Spanish artists working in collectives, and Es Deu d'es Teix was included among these groups in media coverage and in local and international newspapers and magazines. Their choice of a local name drew on the existing reputation of the village as an artists' colony (Rusiñol 1958) and reanimated the image both inside and outside the village. The prestige engendered by this group of international artists and by the well-known poet and writer Robert Graves drew many other artists, admirers, and collectors to the village. A limited internal market began to develop. As Coad writes in her work on Spanish art and artists during this period, 'Avant-guard work was highly valued, fetching high prices in Spain and abroad, and inevitably joined the body of work – and the capitalist dealer system – against which it was protesting' (1995:299). Resident foreigners had begun to purchase and renovate houses, and they needed the expanding audience and increased incomes the gallery system provided.

Es Deu d'es Teix lasted for about two years. The members had difficulty adapting to the idea of being a collective with rules and obligations and to the hierarchical and competitive relations that developed between them. Dealing with the commercial side of the art world required compromises few were willing to make. The independent spirit that had led them to leave their native countries in search of a paradise where they could find a 'utopian' existence did not fit with the demands of competition and made group identity and cooperation problematic. It seemed that group participation on any prolonged basis compromised one's sense of individualism.

In 1963 my husband and I bought a ruined flour mill midway down the Clot road. With the aid of a small grant from the United States and volunteer labour, we converted it into an art gallery and a small Archaeological Museum.[24] Whether for the exercise, the camaraderie, or a sense of common purpose, many of the resident artists and writers spent a few hours each week plastering walls or mixing cement in exchange for a simple lunch of macaroni or spaghetti. Graves donated a sixteenth century door and a local carpenter gave us a wooden screw beam from an old olive press. Although privately owned, the Museum was to be a showplace for Deià art and artists. Bi-monthly exhibitions were held for resident or visiting artists, with printed catalogues and a *vernissage* (opening night). There were poetry readings once a month and silent movies were shown every Monday evening. Various musicians including

Julian Bream (the British classical guitarist), the Valldemossins (a group of singers and musicians from the neighbouring village who popularised Mallorquin folk music), a Mallorquin sitar player, an Irish piper, an Argentine guitarist, and many others gave concerts. There were few diversions for the villagers during this period, and these activities brought visitors from all parts of the island, giving locals an opportunity to participate as well. Religious observance and festivals were the only break in what seemed like an endless cycle of work. The children loved the silent films and their parents, who came along to chaperone, fully enjoyed themselves as well.

Not everyone who came to Deià in the 1960s was an artist or pursuing purely creative endeavours. Axel Ball and his brother Klaus arrived in 1960 with the intent to reconstruct and develop a hotel at the site of the finca Es Moli. It had been purchased by a German company in which their father held shares. When the conversion of the old building and construction of new ones was completed, they hoped the hotel would provide jobs for many local people. As it turned out, few were able to take advantage of this opportunity. Most of the young had gone to the city to find work while those who remained in the village were committed to maintaining their own land or the land of others, or were employed in construction.

When the hotel was finished three years later, only six of the forty employees were from Deià. Axel had become a familiar figure in the property negotiations going on in the village. He began buying up old houses in and around Deià, renovating and improving the interiors and reselling them to foreigners. He made loans to heirs against later purchases of houses occupied by elderly parents and managed to acquire quite a few houses from 1962 to 1970 in this manner. Axel had come to Deià for a particular commercial project and proceeded to develop business and social ties with local people, foreign residents, and prospective house buyers which would lead him to become the major force behind village development during the next thirty years.

While the artists' group, Museum project, hotel and house construction, and increased house sales made the early foreign residents feel they were experiencing local life and contributing to it, in the eyes of the Deianencs these activities reinforced their image of the foreigners as senyors. The fact that a foreigner could purchase a house, renovate it, and pursue what seemed to the locals a leisurely way of life while most of them were working from sunup to sundown to maintain their families continued to be evidence of their differences, and they could easily fit foreigners into the senyor category. When an American who had barely been able to buy enough food to eat in 1964 returned in a motorcar with a wife and a child in 1965, his neighbours were astounded. How was it possible? He must be a Senyor.[25] Foreigners were welcomed as neighbours for these differences. They offered hope, experience with other people and cultures, access to income, information, goods, contacts, prestige or power not previously accessible to most insiders.

As Cela Conde notes in his study *Capitalism and the Peasantry in Mallorca,* 'The presence of tourism was an important factor in the sociological changes that occurred on the island during the 1960s. There are two hypothesis to explain the impact of tourism on Mallorca's peasantry. One suggests that mass tourism increased the demand for the islands' produce and that had a positive effect on increasing production and employment in the agricultural sector. The other sees the drain on human forces once involved in farming as disadvantaging the peasantry and producing a new social situation. Mallorca lost the character of a peasant society and became one dependent on the outside. The dynamics of conversion of a peasant society into a society dependent on mass tourism, and the role of the urban classes in the accumulation of capital produced by tourism are key issues in understanding the social environment of the islands' (1979:157). Most Mallorquin historians see the spread of small peasant land-holdings reaching its peak in the 1950s, followed by second residences for city dwellers and the 1960s influx of mass tourism. In this study of Deià, we see how early foreign investment provided capital on a small scale, benefiting only a few, and continued to filter through over the decades until it included almost everyone in the village. We are able to follow the transitions taking place and gain a fuller understanding of the process of change over time.

Graves was the main figurehead of the foreign 'colony' from its beginnings in 1929. His prolific writing from his house in Deià aroused the interest of young and mature poets and writers who came to meet their mentor. Many bought houses and returned yearly or made Deià their new home. Poetry readings and theatre productions were organised and presented in the small amphitheatre built into the hills below Graves's house in 1965. The plays were often written by groups of friends in the village and highlighted many recognisable village characters and events. In 1963 the entire play was based on the changes brought in with *Butano* (bottled gas), including light, heat, and cooking fires. The theme song, set to the music of 'Maria' from *West Side Story,* was sung by everyone for months after the performance, 'Butano, Butano, Butano, We live and we love by Butano, Life will never ever be, the same for you and me, you'll see. Butano', etc.

Graves bought the ruin across from the Museum known as *Ca'n Pintat Vell* and financed the building of a library and lecture hall there based on the concept and design of Bill Waldren. It was to be an extension of the Museum. Waldren brought in a few foreign artists, who needed to make some extra cash, to help with the reconstruction of the ruin. Graves inaugurated the finished library building on his seventieth birthday in 1965 with a poetry reading and dedication ceremony. This was envisioned as a centre for cultural activities, research, and social interaction between locals and foreigners. Family and money problems forced Graves to sell the building the following September, causing misunderstandings among all those involved. This was another in a long line of broken promises between Graves and his friends.

Graves gained a reputation for 'going against the grain' through his involvement in projects where he would overcommit his resources, always banking on the next publication to cover him. He entered into situations which provoked endless money problems and affected his relationships with Gelat and many of the foreign artists and writers he befriended in Deià: a visiting artist borrowed thousands of pounds from him and disappeared; Gelat's son reclaimed all the land Graves had purchased for the ill-fated hotel; Graves's son sold the house Graves had purchased for the Library project; one of Graves's protégés ran off with his current Muse[26] at the time he was giving his lectures as Professor of Poetry at Oxford University; and another protégé involved him in the *Rubaiyat* hoax which brought him great embarrassment.[27] All the difficulties friends and colleagues had with Graves seem to have been designed to question, contradict, or test the values and ideas he was endeavouring to project – a disregard for money, his belief in a Moon Goddess (ideal woman based on myth), and true poetry, 'the unimprovable original and not a synthetic substitute'. In each case, the person was able to assert independence, autonomy, and his idea of equality with his mentor only after confronting his 'idol', finding his vulnerable points (money, his muse, and poetry), and claiming them as his own. These confrontations and the resulting enmities brought about many realignments in Graves's social groupings over the years.

Another short-lived project designed to bring together the talents of Deià-based artists and writers with leading literary figures and university students and teachers was begun in 1969. Graves was invited to participate in a Mediterranean Institute organised by Dowling College (New

York). Leading British writers of the period – Anthony Burgess, Kingsley Amis, and Colin Wilson – were invited as visiting lecturers, and a few resident English and American writers taught courses. From the beginning there were difficulties and discomfort between resident foreigners and the visiting writers and academics. It was evident that local writers felt slighted when 90 percent of the staff for this program was brought from outside the village. Despite the fact that they might not have been amenable to the schedule and responsibilities imposed on the teachers, the foreign residents were offended for not having been consulted. By excluding most Deià-based residents, the organisers made it clear that they were coming for the beauty and tranquillity of the village, not for its resident writers. The resident foreign writers were experiencing the 'invisibility' that the local Deianencs had lived with for so many years. Unlike the locals, the offended writers spoke up. The tension created between the visitors and the resident writers was detrimental to the success of the programme. There were additional reasons for the failure of the programme; lodging, provided by Graves's son William and his wife in a small pension they ran, was unsatisfactory, and funding and organisation were poorly managed. A growing drug culture among some foreigners in Deià was also seen as a deterrent to success, and the program was not repeated the following year. The local writers regained their sense of personal importance by clearing out the competition, but they also closed themselves off even more from the wider world of literary exchange, production, and criticism.

In the late sixties a number of British 'hippy' bands rented houses and added a new dimension to the foreign scene. British musicians, such as Robert Wyatt and the Soft Machine, and Planet Gong with Australian David Allen, practiced their new sounds on the foreigners who chose to 'tune in' to this 'new wave' in music. Kevin Ayres, a successful British musician, bought a house in Deià in the seventies. A group formed by foreign resident musicians named themselves P'amb Oli (bread and oil). They brought 'live music' to the bars on Saturday nights and to some of the local fiestas, such as the Epiphany celebrations. The 1960s and 1970s also brought experimental drug culture to Deià. David Solomon, a disciple of the Harvard University 'guru' of psychedelic drugs Timothy Leary, introduced LSD to foreign residents and a few locals. Marijuana and hashish were also easily available. Smoking and 'tripping' became a way of life for some residents and for a few continues to be associated with artistic creation. This early experimentation caused some permanent damage to a few young people who became deeply involved in drugs during these years, but on the whole it was a passing phase for most people.

A good number of poets, writers and academics continue to reside in or are regular visitors to Deià: German philosopher and teacher Walter Bimel; Liverpudlian poets Brian Patten and Roger McGough; Austrian writer Jakov Lind; the actor Adrian Mitchell; journalists John de St. Jorre, Larry Malcolm, and the American writer Robert De Maria. A few of the painters have gained international reputations: Mati Klarwein, Annie Truxelle, Georges Sheridan, Norman Yanikun, Bill Waldren, and Mark Heine, Ross Abrams and Mary Tatum. Younger artists also are now residents and two galleries display and sell their work. Concert pianist Susan Bradbury and composer Carl Metzger are in residence between engagements. A number of well-known popular musicians have become regular visitors since Richard Branson of Virgin Records bought an interest in La Residencia Hotel. The Archaeological Museum and Research Centre continues to bring students from around the world to participate in their excavations and investigations of Balearic prehistoric peoples and fauna. The Deià Music Festival is an annual success with foreign musicians entertaining an international audience in Deià and other villages on the island. Narcis Serra, past Vice-President of the Spanish Parliament, spends his holidays in Deià surrounded by bodyguards. Michael and Diandre Douglas (who spent her formative years growing up in Deià) have renovated S'Estaca, one of the Archduke's houses, and spend a few summer months in residence. But among these people and their activities, no single name or activity has given Deià and its residents – local or foreign – a new figurehead to replace Graves. Values have changed, and although the village makes little of all the well-known visitors, the press and tourism offices still take advantage of their presence to promote the beauty and charm of Deià and its 'famous guests'.

Robert Graves withdrew into what many foreign friends believed to be his own self-conceived world of poetry, magic, and metaphor (a degenerating disease caused him to lose his memory, speech, and mobility during the last decade of his life). Nevertheless, he remained the central focus of the lives of his family and many foreign residents and visitors to Deià, some of whom helped his nurses to bath, dress, feed, and prop him up each day dressed in his favourite black jacket and Cordoba hat. His birthday celebration continued to be a highlight of the summer as it had been every year since 1950. There were poetry readings and plays performed by his grandchildren and other foreign residents. Only the guest of honour could not attend. A writer who visited in

1983 wrote that, 'At 88, the old warrior poet still sits atop his Olympus on Majorca, being crusty, godlike and protean' (The Guardian, 5 June 1983). It was apparent that Deià's foreign colony had developed around Graves and was doing everything possible to hold onto his 'image' as long as possible.

His funeral in December 1985 brought forth almost the entire population of the village of Deià. His casket (so light that some of the pallbearers could not believe that that was all that remained of the 'great man') was carried to the church from his house at Canelluñ on the shoulders of the sons or grandsons of the men he had befriended in his early days in Deià. Foreigners and locals stood side by side during the mass and marched one by one to give condolences to the wife, children, affines, and grandchildren standing in the front of the village church. Even in death Graves continues to draw admirers to Deià: his simple grave in the local cemetery often has fresh flowers put on it by visitors. Poems dedicated to him have also been found there. His widow Beryl and sons Tomas and Joan continue to be full-time Deià residents, while son William and daughter Lucia live between London and Deià.

The memorial service given for Graves's friends and family in London, who could not get to Deià within the few hours between his death and burial, was more a celebration of his life than a sadness of his death. At the wake after the church service, gathered together at the Royal Academy, were hundreds of close friends who had known Robert and, in most cases, had met one another through him. Almost everyone had been to Deià. People who had not seen each other for ten, twenty, even forty years met up again to bid their friend (and sometimes foe) a fond farewell. Robert Graves wrote *Good-bye to All That*, 'a story', he said, 'of what I was, not what I am' and set out with Laura Riding to find a place that was 'a concentration of the limited virtue and pleasantries to be found in the earth itself' (O'Prey 1982:94). Graves spent forty-six years in this mountain village, descending daily to the cove below to jump off his favourite rock, swim out a bit, and rapidly ascend the mountain path back to his desk. The impact of his presence on the social, economic, political, demographic, and ecological aspects of village life, both for the Deianencs and the foreign colony, cannot be overestimated. He brought visitors and residents to Deià, all of whom rented or bought houses, shopped in the village, drank, created, and often reproduced there. He defended local interests against impinging development and bureaucracy and sought to define what was natural and unspoiled, preserving some areas while developing and cutting roads through others.

Many say that while Graves was alive, no other leader was necessary. Although he did not hold any official position, Graves was the unspoken hero or 'charismatic figure' of the foreign colony. His autobiography *Good-bye to All That* became a model of bravery in war and disgust with war for the 'angry young men' of two wars. His withdrawal into expatriate paradise gave them an ideal to strive toward. Young poets came as pilgrims to Mallorca for his advice and encouragement. As one biographer wrote, 'Many younger poets have turned to Graves, a meticulous craftsman with words, who despised all schools and predetermined formulas' (Snipes 1979). Gaining his friendship or falling out of favour with him affected many of the social networks that developed throughout the past forty years. Some residents and locals chose to remain outside his social activities, not wanting to become involved in the erratic behaviour and attitudes of the poet. Experiences shared while living in the same village had shown them that some of those who became involved were admired for awhile and then passed from favour, carrying the scars of a deep friendship gone wrong.

For those who knew Graves and his Goddesses (the women who inspired his poetry and to whom it was dedicated), the mystic and spiritual associations he drew and the 'magnetic force like that at Delphi' he attributed to the mountains surrounding Deià were seldom convincing (there were few converts). However, these myths added an esoteric dimension to the new life some people were trying to create. The role of women in the foreign colony was very much influenced by his ideas about women and his concept of the White Goddess, 'more metaphor than mythology', who appeared variously as nurturing mother, seductive lover, and terrible death goddess. For Graves, she was the centre of wisdom and poetic inspiration – only she held the secrets of life, joy, and, finally, death.

The foreign men in Deià adored women, fell passionately in love, idealised the lady in question, and were deeply saddened if she had to leave the village. Like the poet, they relied on women for inspiration and soon another lovely visitor would fill the void left by the last. They shared the belief that Western society had lost ideas of intrinsic importance and that perhaps the myth, magic, and dreams of other people and places held some of the answers they were seeking. Deià was imbued with a magic quality that, like the Goddess, brought out the best or the worst in one. Paradise and reality were at times indistinguishable as each person experienced the wonders and inconsistencies of each day. 'Secret' knowledge, whether about mythological goddesses, 'real' characters who had been part of Deià's past, or gossip about last night's conquests, gave foreigners a sense of belonging to their own special community that had its own past, present, and future.

Most of the people who knew Graves well are still identified as senyors by the local people and see themselves as the early foreign settlers of Deià. These long-term residents feel they have made major contributions to the creation and maintenance of the village image through their writings, paintings, or poetry, by their involvement in social life, and in controlling building and development. They have experienced the opportunity given foreigners in the past to voice their opinions and to speak for those who felt they had no voice. On many occasions, their opinions were shared, repeated, or adopted by the locals; i.e., foreigners sought controls on building styles and development areas long before locals had time to consider the long-range effects of tourism. The image of the 'traditional' village, which is of primary concern to the locals today, has been nurtured and protected by foreigners for over a century.

During the 1960s and early 1970s, when Deianencs were beginning to modernise their houses, they threw out 'old' olivewood furniture, family pictures, farm implements, and granite floors and replaced them with formica surfaces, veneered furniture, mass-produced paintings or tapestries, and easily washed ceramic tiles. Foreigners quickly bought these 'old' objects and installed them in their houses as symbols of the Mallorquin past. Long-term residents have seen how house prices after 1975 were established by the price paid by each new foreign buyer regardless of differences in size, location, or condition of the house. From that time forward, it became more difficult for local Deianencs to buy a house in their own village because the prices were out of their reach and much higher than in the neighbouring villages of Soller, Biñaraitx, or Fornalutx. Increased house prices have altered residence and inheritance patterns, community structure, and the social relationships between locals and foreigners (as described in Chapters 2 and 3).

By the mid-1970s, long-term residents had become concerned about the increasing numbers of outsiders who were moving into Deià. After all the years of learning to at least understand the conventions which relate to hospitality and neighbourliness and feeling that one was incorporated, it was disturbing to see new projects and new arrivals upset their paradise, their hard-earned place in local life. A small group of residents tried to impose rules on the other members. They began to create their own insider-outsider valuations. Some set themselves up as the preservers and connoisseurs of local beauty. They felt they were protecting it from desecration by both uninformed foreigners and unconcerned locals.

One American denounced another for cutting down 'a very old and beautiful fig tree' (the man who cut it down said that it was dead). No action ensued. Then, two Englishmen and an Englishwoman, two American women, a German woman and her Catalan husband formed a committee which sent denunciations to *Belles Arts* (the Arts Council) whenever they objected to a project. They called themselves *Amigos y Residentes de Deià* (Friends and Residents of Deià). When it appeared that a building was not adhering to local requirements (unspecified by local building codes but established by this group), one or more of them would send a note or go personally to the Arts Council or try directly to make a person alter the offending details. The Arts Council would send a notice to the local council which might take action that could stop work on a house or enforce alterations.

Among the foreigners there had always been a lot of gossip about village developments. People liked to gossip but seldom bothered to find out the details before commenting on any matter of general interest. Most were surprised when fellow foreigners tried to control things and thought they wouldn't get very far before they gave up and quit. But some kept interfering. One small group voiced their objections to the way a foreign neighbour was enlarging a terrace wall. As he was accustomed to their critical comments, he took no notice. Three days later he awoke to find the wall knocked down. He could not prove who had done this until the next day when a group of small children came to play in front of his house and one was heard to say: 'Look what my mommy and yours did last night!' News travels quickly within this small village. These actions were discussed among the foreigners, each of whom had his or her own comment on the subject, but no sides were taken. The wall was rebuilt a few days later and seems to have survived despite the objectors. The criticism seemed to be as much a testing of one another's values and strength of purpose as of their aesthetic sense.

Most of the conversions during this period were done by foreigners except for two new houses built on family land by two local men. They, too, were subject to foreign criticism. Foreigners were relying on their status as outsiders to impose their value judgements on the locals. At the same time, the locals very generously turned a blind eye to the building being done by the Englishmen known as 'Yo quiero', who had set out to build his own house on a small piece of land in the village.

Most foreigners, whether they acted upon it or not, did feel that there were dangers in allowing building styles to be altered and were relieved when the state intervened and the entire area of Deià was included as part of the Mallorquin Historic and Artistic Patrimony, which meant that all building permits had to be approved by the Belles Arts. The only problem was that it left those who enjoyed assuming power over others, even occasionally, without an outlet.

The *Amigos* were the only ones who ever got so far as to take a name. This small group of long-term residents tried to impose their rules over others who felt equally capable of making such evaluations and, as in previous attempts at organisation or the imposition of hierarchy, their group was short-lived. Although foreign residents formed various coalitions to deal with specific problems in the past, they never formalised a Foreign Residents' Association. That would have given power to the few, institutionalised their outsider's role, and defeated the element of individual 'free choice' foreigners tried to maintain in their lives. It was more in keeping with this philosophy to have new groups forming as different issues arose. Also, the political system from Franco up until the new constitution of 1981 gave foreigners more autonomy to act than any locals. As Bailey so aptly wrote, 'Absence of normative rules allocating authority or even the presence of rules explicitly rejecting it, leave room for pragmatic rules which enable some men to coerce or influence others' (1973). Even the local mayor had so little power within the village that one could go directly to Palma or to the Guardia Civil to denounce another and get much quicker action.

1975 to 1988

With the death of Franco and the efforts to establish a new social democracy in Spain, local politicians gained more control over the affairs of the village. The foreign colony continued to alternate between a small number of artists and writers committed to their individual pursuits, who occasionally coalesced to deal with a local development that infringed on their 'privacy', and a large number of mixed groupings.

As the numbers of foreigners increased, the ritual sharing between locals and foreigners decreased. Locals began to put a price on the services once viewed as part of reciprocal exchanges, and their contact with new foreigners was mainly through commercial and financial transactions. The kind neighbour who once offered a homegrown cauliflower or freshly picked oranges now had foreign neighbours all around and found that he could put a price on these goods or just leave them to fall off the trees for compost. New arrivals who did not speak Spanish or Catalan became reliant on long-term foreign residents for information about life in Deià. The public arena in which so many casual interchanges took place was becoming too crowded.

A New Zealander opened 'Richard's Bar-Restaurant' which was welcomed by some locals and most foreigners while other long-time residents felt it had no local atmosphere. Richard's, which was the first foreign-owned bar, attracted locals who were interested and desirous of participating in foreign social life. Young single men, who fancied getting closer to the foreign girls who seemed so much 'freer' than the local girls, and the older men who knew some of the long-term foreign residents and had formed friendships with them through work and social contacts became 'regulars'. There was popular music, draft beer, chess games going on in the corner, people milling about drinking, laughing, and sometimes dancing or flirting.

By this time, some long-term resident foreigners had begun to spend less time in the cafés. Those who had arrived in the 1950s and 1960s as young men and women and found a few others with whom they could share youthful hopes, dreams, and aspirations had grown older together in Deià. They had left the regular 'café scene', with its heavy drinking and wild parties, to concentrate on their work and the maintenance of the lifestyle they had created. They had acquired property when prices were very low and had established a base from which to create a career and a family.

To the locals, the withdrawal from public spaces by those foreigners most familiar to them seemed like a rejection. Social boundaries were fluid within the café, where everyone mixed freely. People did not casually visit one another's homes, however, and boundaries became more marked as people were less accessible. Since invitations to one another's houses occurred only on special occasions, contacts were limited. If one did not live nearby one was seldom seen. Long-established modes of communication and adaptation between foreigners and locals had begun to break down, and an increased awareness of symbolic boundaries was beginning to separate them. Without knowing it, the long-term residents who were no longer easily accessible in the café became part of the large group of foreigners with whom locals had little or no contact. The foreign senyors had abandoned their regular haunts, withdrawing into separate worlds no longer bridged by meetings in public social space. The home of each was private and cultural differences were more noticeable, while the café had always been neutral territory. As the café became less of a meeting place, fewer casual encounters and interchanges between locals and foreigners took place. The foreigners that the locals found in the cafés were often newcomers, and the locals would retreat to their own corner of the café, mixing less and less with the unknown foreigners.

The foreign residents who had not succeeded in controlling the changes they saw occurring around the village withdrew even further from village life. Some sold their houses inside the village nucleus (at enormous profit) and moved to outlying fincas or neighbouring towns. They physically removed themselves from everyday contact except on their own terms and set up spatial boundaries that could be crossed only by invitation or infraction. One man, who had been a member of the Amigos group, bought an old finca on a hilltop between Deià and Valldemossa and converted it into a palatial manor with two smaller houses that he rents to the sort of people he wants for his neighbours. Another man bought all the adjoining houses on a terrace and has the equivalent of a private estate where once four neighbours lived. Others moved to Soller or mainland Spain.

Out of sight except on occasional visits to the post office, the long-term residents have become the subject of café gossip that mixes past with present and serves to entertain any willing listener. Their personal sense of leadership having been thwarted, some were able to rely on their economic privilege to move outside the village nucleus. Other foreign residents who had for so long lived with the villagers kept their special Deianenc friends and a few relatively closed circles of foreign friends but seldom met new residents or visitors. Long-term residents who have remained inside the village are content organising their work and social life around the people they already know. They meet newcomers through local and other long-term residents like themselves or not at all.

This separation of long-term residents from public places serves both to control access to them and to develop a greater interest in their lives by locals and fellow foreigners. Stories about them become part of Deià folklore to be recited to newcomers in the café. Separation adds mystique but it also calls attention to inequalities between locals and foreigners, as well as between long- and short-term foreigners. Foreigners have always been aware of the differences in backgrounds and incomes among themselves, but economic considerations were sublimated in the shared pursuit of a creative life, or at least such was the impression that many tried to maintain. Those who had 'remittances' from home each month or generous private incomes did not make this evident and seemed to fade into the crowd. Almost everyone presented a similar public image, wearing old sweaters and tattered jeans and voicing the same concern when cognac went up from six to ten pesetas a shot. They did not want to be seen as dilettantes or easy with their money and had tried to give no outward evidence of their superior incomes.[28]

The Deianencs knew long-term foreign residents by House names or nicknames and they, in turn, were familiar with most Deianencs. Their children had grown up inside the village and some of those born in the 1950s and 1960s formed relationships with or married Mallorquins from the city or neighbouring villages in the 1980s. Most of these foreign residents had participated in the preservation of Deià's past, contributed to its present, and hoped to be part of its future. Some had tried to control the negative effects of time and modernity on the village, or at least on their own lives. Despite their efforts, the materialism of Western society had begun to creep into Deià life and the 'idyllic peasant' was a figure of the past. The outside world was now accessible, attractive, and desirous to local Deianencs and to many of the long-term foreigners' children.

Long-term foreign residents' withdrawal from the public arena of café life provoked a reassessment of foreigners by other foreigners and by locals that required the development of a different set of relationships and social values. Long-term friendships with locals continued to be an important part of some residents' lives, but many saw less and less of the local men they used to drink with in the bar. The egalitarian, individualistic ideals that had led these early foreigners to Deià had been maintained while they shared similar values, attitudes, behaviour, and activities with other foreign residents and a symbiotic relationship with their local neighbours. However, changing local values and the arrival of different sorts of foreigners had begun to alter their paradise.

In retrospect, one can see that the Amigos group had focused on obvious ecological and aesthetic problems, like cutting down trees and building in stone, while a completely different value system was in the process of taking hold. In place of criticising those who did not conform, they should have queried why some people were not abiding by the usual building styles. Those who did not finish buildings in the correct manner were not rejecting the values but merely cutting corners to reduce the costs of their buildings. They were local men and women and long-term residents who had begun to build during a period of rising costs and had been caught short. Those who were carrying out every detail in the 'traditional' style were those who did not have to count pennies.

They were either persons of ample private means or developers who knew their market and could afford to do things correctly because they were building for profit. Their potential buyers knew little about the value of local properties and based their judgement on their home markets and their personal assets. While resident foreign critics were denouncing their own neighbours and community members, a German developer and local contractors were negotiating sales of land and houses to outside buyers with very different lifestyles, interests, and desires.

After 1975 there seems to have been a marked change in the values and attitudes of many of the foreigners who came to settle or visited seasonally. Those who settled in Deià after 1975 can be recognised by a number of shared characteristics: the majority speak very little Spanish and socialise almost exclusively with other foreigners like themselves, from whom they derive all their information about Deià life and people. Some are artists or musicians from English working-class backgrounds who set out to find an established art colony where there was no class consciousness and they could pursue their individual interests on a limited budget, drawing inspiration from those who had created the community before them. Some have been able to rent or buy houses while others have found accommodation with two or three homeowners who let them stay in exchange for doing odd jobs. A few artists among those who arrived after 1975 have formed various cooperative exhibitions with long-term resident artists. This maintains the ethos of the art colony with some familiar and some new members. One foreign artist has managed to create a demand for his work among the local Deianencs. He produces coloured sketches or oil paintings from old photographs of deceased relatives and of more recent communions and weddings. Drinking and the use of soft drugs is still common among some residents and visiting foreigners. For some, the youthful lifestyle developed in the 1960s is still part of the ethos of Deià.

Locals and foreigners are still side by side in the cafés, but they establish their own spaces and keep to their own company. Although foreign visitors and seasonal residents may be in the same cafés, few interact directly with villagers. Increased numbers of foreigners have bought houses for holiday use only. With café life only one of the focuses of social interaction, new homeowners and especially summer-only residents might reside in the village without ever getting to know either locals or long-term resident foreigners and vice versa.

There are a few exceptions. One example is Susie, an American nurse who came to the village in the late 1970s for an extended holiday. A physical therapist, she began to treat some of the women with arthritic joints and her holiday became longer and longer. She was asked to help a few hours each day with Robert Graves and was the main source of comfort for three foreigners who had terminal illnesses during the past few years. She lived with a local man for a brief period but said she found it too confining trying to be part of a Deianenc family while maintaining her foreign friends and activities. She stays in various houses while the owners are away and returns to the United States every year to visit her parents and 'to earn more money to live in Deià'.

The village learned to depend on her services and allowed her to continue practising informally (without a work permit). Her skills were needed more each day. Since the nuns left in 1986, she was the only person in the village who could go to visit homebound people and give them injections and a bit of cheer. She assisted the doctor with these pastoral duties and made her services quite indispensable to the village. She provides the gentle kindnesses that locals once offered strangers, but the increased demands on her time by both locals and foreigners puts a strain on her special talents. In 1993 a social worker was assigned to the village one day a week. She arranged for a health visitor to see the few elderly or infirm people in the village. A budget was also made available for the doctor to have a full-time nurse. Susie was pleased but did not want to apply for either of these positions. She knew that work permits for non-European Community members are very complicated and preferred to see a local person employed. She continues to assist many people on a casual basis.

A few foreigners have started businesses: a bar, an art gallery, an antique shop, and two boutiques. The new boutiques that conspicuously hang goods outside their entrances on the main street of the village and the two gallery signs make some people say that 'Deià has become an Artsy Fartsy Art Colony' rather than a place for quality work. All of these shops are seen as commercial ventures in contrast to the more 'cultural tone' of the early foreigners' projects: the Archaeological Museum, classical music concerts, a boutique with island-made *artesania* (clothing, jewelry, pottery, glass, and drawings), and a small art gallery on a back street jointly run by resident foreign artists since 1967. Nevertheless, these businesses are welcome additions to the village. It is quite a surprise for visitors to find Indonesian and Mexican clothing and gifts for sale in this Spanish-Mallorquin mountain village. The variety of ethnic fashion and art objects reflects the international composition of the village and creates a striking contrast to the natural landscape and pastoral image of Deià.

However, there are mixed blessings associated with some of the businesses opened since 1975. The loud rock music so loved by the young has become a source of increased income for three bar owners who compete to have live performances on the weekends, but is a nightmare for locals and foreigners who live near the cafés or visitors who come for a peaceful holiday. A local ruling was passed that all live music had to cease at midnight but that did not stop the blasting of recorded sound at the weekends until four in the morning. Young villagers identify directly with the newer residents and their activities. They share the same interests in fashion, music, having fun, and socialising. They have grown up alongside the children of long-term foreign residents and their lives outside the home are not really very different. They wear the same sort of clothes, work together in the hotels, plan activities together, and support one another's projects. In 1986 the young sons of a local grocer organised a live concert in the Deià park for Kevin Ayres and P'Amb Oli, two groups composed of English musicians. They borrowed money to set up a bar from their father. The entrance fee of 500 pesetas was split three ways with 50 percent for musicians, 20 percent for the City Hall (for the use of the park), and 30 percent for the organisers (from which they paid for two doormen and five barmen). Drinks were sold at a makeshift bar. Over five hundred people attended. The success of the concert meant the village could not ignore the presence and value of these resident musicians. It also revealed the common interests shared by local and foreign youth. Such annual concerts provide special late-night events that satisfy the young while keeping them in the village, which pleases their parents and all those who were previously disturbed by the nightly café sounds. Two or three times a year, concerts can go on until dawn. In 1995 a soundproofed jazz club was built in the village which means there is music almost every night and few complaints.

Many young foreigners who were born and brought up in Deià study abroad and long to return to Deià during the holidays, but after a month 'back home' new faces are a welcome change to the all-too-familiar ones they've known all their lives. The more time they spend away from Deià, the more they need new and different people when they return. Single people continue to use the café as a meeting place. There one can find the sixteen- to thirty-year-old children of long-term residents, newcomers, new homeowners, and tourists seated at the same tables, listening to the same music and interested in the same things. To the young and newcomers, the café still appears to be the centre of village life and the place where new arrivals meet others who can inform them about the ways and means of the village. Parties in private homes, once a regular form of foreign entertainment, occur less often since there are so many seasonal visitors in the village. Word of such gatherings would be passed from friend to friend until the host could no longer recognise half the people at his or her party. In contrast to these large open gatherings, young Deianencs organise group dinners and dances for themselves on various occasions.

The children of long-term foreigners become friends and informants for new arrivals. These young people become the interpreters of their own and their parents' society. For those who have lived all their lives in Deià, the separation between Deianenc and estranger is even more complex than for their parents. Those over twenty had more difficulty with their peers than the young foreign children who are now in school. But as adults they have begun to discuss these differences, and many have succeeded in forming and maintaining friendships with local people of their own age. They are all interested in understanding the family pressures and differing value systems that caused them to be so hostile to one another when they were younger and more vulnerable. Their differences do not disappear but they find common ground for working together to enhance village life, at least during the yearly fiestas.

One of my daughters has organised and directed a village theatre company which performs annually at the village fiestas, and the local cast is made up of many of her previous schoolmates (she is the only non-Mallorquin). The works they perform reflect their changing views of their own society and their relationships with outsiders. They began with plays by Mallorquin authors and have moved on to Spanish, French, and English playwrights. If the plays are not translated into Mallorquin-Catalan, they do the translations. Most of the major activities in the village during fiestas are organised by this group of twenty-two to forty-year-old Deianencs (fifteen women and three men). Their friendship is based on mutual interest and exchange, each gaining insights from the other. The theatre group has dinner together in one of the local restaurants a few times each year and spends at least two nights a week during three or four months rehearsing the year's production.

Some children of foreign parents want to return to their parents' home countries, somehow feeling that they lost out on their heritage and only by returning will they fully understand themselves and their parents. 'Returning' to a place they do not remember often increases the sense of marginality they experienced growing up in Deià. Others have identified so much with local life that they have formed relationships with Mallorquin or Spanish men or women and found jobs within the village. They, as the local Deianencs, are faced with the problems of living in Deià in the 1990s. Inflated house prices has made buying a house more difficult for them than it was for their parents. Some live outside the village in Soller or surrounding villages while others have taken on large mortgages to buy a Deià house.

The experience of being a visitor to Deià is quite different for someone under thirty than for those of other ages. While the young people tend to mix with new arrivals, their parents and other long-term residents do not easily include many newcomers in their social circles. They already have more friends and visitors than they can deal with. Time, once seemingly unlimited, is now seen to be fleeting. Most have established routines that give priority to their creative work and have come to place greater value on their privacy. Others do like to return occasionally to the cafés and try to attend gallery openings or other large social gatherings, cocktail parties, or concerts to see old friends. It is at such gatherings that long-term residents rekindle the spirit of their early days in Deià, reminisce about the past, and marvel at the experiences they have shared.

Changing Values and Expectations

Until 1976 foreigners had moved freely between the three cafés on the main road. Following the rising sun from east to west one would have morning coffee at Ca'n Pep Mosso's; midday beers, *cathalia* (local anise), or cognac on the terrace (weather permitting) or indoors at Las Palmeras; and early evening aperitifs at Richard's Bar. If one went out again after supper one made the rounds of all three. But at the end of 1976, Ca'n Pep Mosso's closed its bar and became a restaurant. As a result, the local cronies who used to play cards there all moved over to Bar Las Palmeras.

As more tourists and new homeowners began to frequent Las Palmeras, prices began to rise. Locals and long-term foreigners who still popped in for drinks complained to no avail and were forced to drink less or stay at home. Old men who played cards in the café only ordered a single coffee, cognac, or beer during a three- or four-hour visit. The café owner (a local) began to put pressure on them to spend more money or vacate their seats. During the winter of 1977, the old men were 'evicted' from their regular spaces and activities, not directly by foreigners but by the bar owner's stated preference for foreign clients who spent more money than the local cronies. The card players were invited to use the tables in Richard's Bar. Some played there but many of the regulars said they 'did not feel comfortable' and stayed away.

In 1980 Richard's Bar-Restaurant was sold to Christian, a German, and in 1981 Las Palmeras was bought by a man from Palma who had lived in the village as a boy. In 1982 the new City Hall was inaugurated, which included a *salon de juego* (a games room) for the displaced card players. They never used it. In 1983 Paco[29] opened a café-bar-restaurant in a converted barn just next to the carpenter's shop off the main street. The cronies were welcomed to the use of the tables he had in the bar and his prices undercut the other bars by 25 percent. Paco's café had no outdoor terrace so it did not attract many outside visitors or tourists. Paco's was referred to as 'the local's bar' and resident foreigners who usually preferred to have their morning coffee or beer on the Las Palmeras outdoor terrace only went to Paco's on Mondays when Las Palmeras was closed.

For awhile, Christian's was the only bar open late at night. Then Sa Fonda, the old inn, was reopened as a bar and La Fabrica (the old icehouse) was converted to a bar. Local workmen, young locals, and visitors from Palma like to join with foreigners in all of these places on the weekends when the crowded atmosphere gives the impression of a lively cosmopolitan village. Under new ownership, Las Palmeras became a halfway point where both local and foreigners stopped for a drink but did not really settle in for the day. During the warm months, Las Palmeras is the preferred setting for outdoor drinks and a good place from which to view passers-by. The large open terrace of Sa Fonda is ten steps above street level and offers more privacy from gazing tourists than Las Palmeras. Each bar closes on a different day, which allows regulars to use all four and spreads the profit.

The displacement of the card playing men in 1977 from their preferred locale by one of their own members brought everyone's attention to the changing values that had developed over the previous years. Profit and personal interests had begun to replace social reciprocity and exchange, not just between foreigners and locals but between Deianencs. During the brief period from 1975 to 1982 a schism had developed between Deianencs and foreigners, which had begun with the eviction of the old men from Las Palmeras and expanded as each new problem seemed to focus more and more on foreigners: the noise from the bars at night was getting out of hand, cars were parked on sidewalks and blocking access roads, the price of property was rising, newly married Deianencs were having to live in Soller for lack of accommodations in Deià, etc.

The first democratically elected mayor took office in 1977. He began a program of village development which included the introduction of a rubbish collection service and two municipal policemen to deal with increasing parking problems; the construction of a water-bottling factory, a bank, a bakery, a pharmacy; and plans for enlarging the City Hall, increasing the size of the cemetery, and asphalting the road down to the cala. Long-term foreigners were once again agitated by village developments. Social gatherings during the next few years were dominated by gossip about the way the new mayor was 'ruining the village'.

An old man sold a house to a foreigner that the new mayor had been trying to buy.[30] The mayor's fury led to the closure of an access road to the foreigner's newly acquired property and accusations and denuncios went back and forth for months. It was not long before the mayor began to imply that long-term foreigners were preventing Deianencs from progressing. He made it clear that foreigners' efforts to influence village development were no longer welcomed. He presented foreigners as outsiders intruding in the affairs of the villagers, clearly the insiders. After many years of symbiosis, the greed of a Deianenc bar owner combined with the new mayor's fury sparked off a series of conflicts that would develop into open confrontation between groups now identified as Deianencs-Insiders and Estrangers-Outsiders (see Chapter 6).

Eternal Youth

A good many of the men and women one finds in Deià today are the foreigners who arrived in Deià during the period just described. While most have mellowed with the years, some of the men who were referred to as 'lotus eaters in paradise' continue to portray the role of carefree playboys, making suggestive remarks and eyeing any young woman who crosses their path. Now that they are older, their partners must be younger to provide the beauty, zest, and youth they feel slipping away. Some of them have married between one to four times, fathered many children, and continue to enter into the social scene of café life. Others are loud and conspicuously rude to one another and anyone else who happens to be around. Public social life appears to be composed of staged presentations where some performers act the part the audience anticipates and others create their character as the scene progresses.

Those who frequent the café enjoy sharing the latest gossip about last night's conquests and little of people's private lives remains 'private'.

Foucault's comments on this practice suggest that it is a common feature of 'modern societies': 'What is peculiar to modern societies, in fact, is not that they consigned sex to a shadow existence, but that they dedicated themselves to speaking of it ad infinitum, while exploiting it as *the* secret' (1981:35). 'The secret' discussed among the foreigners who frequent the café in the morning is what everyone is talking about by noon each day. In their youth, these men and women sought self-knowledge through intense or frequent and exciting sexual liaisons; they were encouraged to see themselves in terms of their sexuality which was interpreted as the core of the self (Caplan 1987). With added years (and less stamina), most have sought additional understandings of selfhood. However, a few still thrive on new conquests and share their latest adventures with anyone willing to listen.

Some of these men maintain an image of the rugged outdoors type – bearded, wearing blue jeans and boots – while others present the picture of the 'colonial gentleman' in white shirt, pants, and shoes or retain the hippy look of the sixties with flowered shirts, scarves, necklaces, and an earring. The contrast between the modes of dress is evidenced in the lifestyles each has chosen. Those in jeans are actively painting, writing, sculpting, or excavating; they are physically involved in the arts. The updated hippy look is maintained by those who spend the winter months travelling to Bali, India, or Bangkok and return with art objects, clothes, and jewelry from these areas which they sell to local boutiques, display in the hotel, or sell at village jumbles held occasionally in the park or at one of the cafés. Those who dress mainly in white (which soils easily and requires regular care) are seen to be simulating the look of a senyor. They have become the purchasers, planners, organisers, developers, and promoters of Deià, its architecture, artists, businesses, and the local people.

Foreign women are fancifully dressed and frivolously feminine, tediously tattered, or in the background. Somewhat confused by their role in this foreign, male-dominated society that places youth and motherhood on a pedestal and makes wives anathema, they sometimes seem like the pawns in the men's ongoing chess game. Young women are valued and protected by one player, then won by his opponent, only to be lost in the next game to another. Single women residents either have financial means of their own and attract men of lesser means, or are in difficult economic situations themselves and therefore gravitate toward those men who have reliable incomes. Marital difficulties and separation leave women without adequate means of support.

Perhaps the colourful appearance and 'performance' of the men make the women seem less important than is the case. The women who have been residents for a long while don't seem to need the theatre of public life as much as the men do. They are involved in educating children, expanding their own creative or artistic horizons, and maintaining a home. They are seen in the same social spaces that local women use and like local women have little time for café life. Women, both foreign and local, provide the support system that allows their men to enter into public activities.

Women often identify themselves as wives or mothers rather than as individuals. A young woman artist (who has grown up in the village and whose parents own a house there) was heard introducing herself as 'Mati's wife' to someone who knows neither Mati nor herself. She is establishing her personal sense of identity in the foreign community (of which she has been a member for over thirty years) through her relationship to a veteran member of the artistic element of that society rather than through her own accomplishments or those of her parents. Women brought into the resident social circles will often comment on how hard it is to find a place in a society where everyone knows everything about one another and doesn't seem to be interested in someone new except as so-and-so's woman, wife, or the mother of his child.

Today, most of the long-term residents list different priorities than those which were expressed when they first came to Deià twenty to fifty years ago. For most, free love and sexual freedom have been superseded by the search for, or discovery of, a caring relationship, parenthood, professionalism in their pursuits, and at least some form of continuity in their life. Some have formed kin groups: extended families, nuclear families, or single parent families. Children were born and relationships maintained with or without marriage. In these relationships both men and women contribute to the welfare of their families. The realities of responsibilities and the increased cost of living in Deià require more effort and planning than it did in the past. Social groupings – close friends (local and foreign), neighbours, activity groups, age and gender groups – have been formed and reformed over the years as some people leave the village and others return.

Social group composition can alter as people's priorities change. Groups are created and maintained by a number of people following someone who exhibits characteristics they value. Newly arrived artists find their way to other artists through a long-term resident painter who holds drawing classes in his house, befriends young artists, gives them odd jobs if they need money, or buys a painting from them. His patronage makes their stay in Deià possible.

The desire to purchase and partake in drugs (marijuana, hashish, or cocaine) draws other people together. Heavy drinking makes and loses friends as one challenges the patience of anyone near by. Although some long-term residents would like to make their groups exclusive, it is difficult to maintain such exclusivity during the winter when numbers are so small. Indeed, it reaches a point of accepting anyone who is on hand when one visits the café hoping for a game of chess or a chat.

Professional groupings of artists, writers, musicians, or business associates vary in composition over time. One group of three painters has managed to maintain a permanent exhibit in a small house they rented many years ago. Other artists join up for group shows or have one-person exhibits at Gallery Max, owned by an English woman, or in the small gallery at the Hotel La Residencia. The pop musicians have formed two small groups and will join up with others when there is a visiting professional who will not only stimulate the band but may agree to perform and help them bring in ever needed funds. The classical musicians are dependent on visiting professionals to carry out the concert series they organise each week. Exhibitions, concerts, and café gigs are all improved by the addition of new talents. By including outside talent, local artists and musicians give the impression of keeping up with current trends in their field without actually having to reenter the competitive world. Deià has always attracted a variety of people, and there are few places in the world where one can be surrounded by such an assortment of politicians, royalty, theatre and motion picture actors, artists, writers, designers, photographers, shop assistants, farmers, office workers, and others, all gathered on a terrace, under the stars, listening to music, idly chatting or intensely conversing, and taking no notice of one another except as social beings in a special space.

Activity classes of various sorts have been organised over the years and those still meeting are: a sketching class with a model held on Friday mornings at an American artist's house where the participants and model are all foreigners; a yoga class attended by three local women and five foreign women and taught by a Mallorquin from the centre of the island; a Mallorquin folk dance class taught by the leader of a Soller dance group. When the dance classes were begun in 1986, twenty children (about twelve local and eight foreign) and fifteen adults of which three were foreign women attended each week. All of these activities are paid for at each meeting. The dance group performs with other groups from around the island once a year in Deià for the St. John's Day fiesta. Folk dance performances like these are enjoyed by older local people who remember the dances from their youth and offer the young and foreign a taste of 'traditional' Mallorquin culture.

By summer 1995 the numbers attending the dancing classes had dwindled to ten women over thirty and the occasional visitor. Most of the others were too tired after their workday while the children preferred to ride bicycles and play with their friends. Those who have continued to attend form a cohesive group with some participating regularly in performances with a Soller group and the others enthusiastically supporting these activities. The dancers have an annual get-together when each woman brings food and it is shared among them. Dancing follows. The food is sometimes cosmopolitan, but of late, local specialties have been preferred.[31] The theatre group, the dancers, and the yoga class bring local and foreign women together and keep alive essential interaction between foreigners and locals. At these times, Mallorquí is the dominant language. The English, Australian, and Spanish women in the group reply in Spanish to the Mallorquin speakers.

The membership in most of these groups overlaps. For example, I am an American, who speaks English as well as Spanish, French, and Mallorquin, an anthropologist, a daughter, mother, wife, property owner, and long-term resident who sometimes dines with Mallorquin, Spanish, or foreign friends and attends Mallorquin folk dance classes with Deianencs and one or two other foreigners. I will be identified by only one or two of my multiple roles, those which are most relevant to the associations in each context. Each group has more or less personal subjects of gossip and inner group tensions, hostilities and conflicts particular to themselves, but they would also have many common subjects to discuss owing to the close living conditions in Deià where almost everyone knows everyone else and enjoys talking about them.

Seasonality affects the size and quality of groups. The regularity of meetings and duration of these relationships vary from formal contractual relationships, as in a marriage or a business, to informal one-night gatherings, to temporary coalitions, organised to deal with a particular situation, that are then dissolved. The strength of group ties can be seen by who comes forward when a member has a conflict with another person. In most conflict situations, friends and acquaintances will prefer to remain neutral rather than commit themselves to either side, keeping their relationship with both parties on an even keel.

English is the lingua franca of the foreign colony and it is the commonest means of communication within foreign groups and between groups. Among the English speakers there are some who have been friends for twenty or more years. There are three neighbourhood groups (who live within the named areas of Es Clot, Es Reco, etc.) composed of people of similar ages and status who have formed social groups that combine professional interests and day-to-day matters. One group is composed mostly of writers, with a few painters, an architect, a weaver, and their children. They share meals when they get together at least once a week when in residence. The separation between writers and artists is not so marked today as it was when Robert Graves formed his 'ideal community' in which he made it clear that writers were the only people who knew how to use words. Artists were told to 'stick to painting and leave it to the writers to explain it'.

Expatriates, people away from home, are notable for their tendency to clump together with their fellows, and English-speaking foreigners who have met in Deià have developed social networks that span three continents. There are a few Germans, one Dutchman, an Austrian, six or seven Spaniards, one Chinese, two Italians, four Frenchmen and women, two Israelis, three Argentines, and two Icelanders, as well as many American and English nationals who are part of these English-speaking groups. Within these groups one finds long-term residents, property owners or renters, young, middle-aged, and retired persons, and their children. Besides regular encounters in Deià, one group has managed to meet up in various parts of the world over the years since they first met in Deià in the 1960s.[32]

These groupings are not absolutely fixed, and there are people who interact with various groups. There are encounters between members of different social groupings at gallery openings, in the cafés, at concerts, at theatre performances, in the shops or restaurants around the village. If a conflict occurs within a group, some of its members will temporarily drop out and revive their relations with other groups. This 'toing and froing' keeps the separate groups in touch with one another. Those who have been in the village a long while know all the members of other groups either by direct contact or as acquaintances about whom they have been 'filled in' by mutual friends over the years. This makes access to almost any group possible for long-term residents.

Nationality is seldom a criteria for grouping, although locals and English speakers have been heard to refer to 'the Germans' or 'the French'. These are the groups whom they know least, who do not speak either

Spanish or English, and who keep to themselves. The locals will sometimes distinguish various groups of outsiders by nationality which they base on language and association. 'The English' actually derives from when Robert Graves and Laura Riding arrived and a small contingent of British and one American formed a rather select group of 'literati'. Today, 'the English' no longer refers to one nationality but to all those who speak English.

Only an informed observer would discover that perhaps the most salient feature of the long-term English-speaking groupings is the professional background of many of the members. The majority are writers who have university degrees and have published works; painters who attended art schools and have exhibited in major cities; professional musicians; Doctors of Philosophy, Literature, Psychology, Anthropology, and Prehistory. The village medical doctor is an educated Spaniard who spends all of his social time with foreigners. His wife and children are bilingual. A number of women who have been busy wives and mothers until recently have now begun to contribute to poetry and prose readings. Reading is a way of life for most people, and newspapers, journals, and books are circulated among friends. A few are self-taught, widely travelled, and well read. If one were to overhear the usual conversations in the café, it would seem that all of the above were a fiction or wishful thinking! Credentials are not important within the groups and are seldom discussed. Indeed, there is an unspoken rule that the café is a place for casual conversation and repartee rather than meaningful discourse.

The foreigners have developed a sort of 'barter economy' over the years that brings different people into contact as the circumstances of their lives change. When the Deià Music Festival was begun by an American couple, an English writer was given lodging in their house in exchange for writing publicity. Artists and writers plastered the museum walls in exchange for lunch, and two young women have managed to stay in Deià by living as caretakers in ten different houses during the time the owners were away. One artist traded a painting with his dentist for his new teeth, another for meals in the local restaurant. This casual but ongoing 'self-help through prestations' is an essential aspect of the foreign colony and one of its defining elements. In the 1980s three foreign women and a man had terminal illnesses, and many of the foreigners in residence rallied round and provided round-the-clock nursing and meals-on-wheels for them. All but one were given a 'Deianenc' funeral, their caskets carried on the shoulders of their friends[33] from their homes to the church where all the village, both locals and foreigners, came together to bid them farewell. The third woman was offered similar treatment but had requested cremation.[34] The two women – Oma, a Dutch Indonesian woman, and Maggie, an American woman known as 'the Cat Lady' because she cared for all the stray cats in the village – and the man – Norman, an American artist – were buried in a communal grave in the village cemetery that also contained the remains of an American priest who had died the previous year and Sebastian Boi, the man from whom the pensioners bought their new centre. The long-term coexistence of Deianencs, forasters, and estrangers is easier in death than it was in life.[35]

The rituals associated with Norman's burial were different than the others with whom he would share the tomb. Norman's friend, a Rabbi (and seasonal visitor), performed a Jewish burial for him over the grave in the Catholic cemetery. It was the first time that many of the local mourners had ever seen a Jewish burial, and they seemed to take it for granted that as long as there was a ceremony it was a fitting burial for their neighbour and friend. No one seemed to mind that the Rabbi spoke in Hebrew and in English, and they all turned toward the east (as requested) when he recited the final prayer.[36] The village priest was pleased that there was someone of Norman's own faith to guide these final moments.

Unlike local associations, there is little social pressure for individual foreign interests to conform to local social values. However, by participating in the theatre or dance groups and in rituals of death, foreigners are momentarily adapting to local values and cultural patterns. Although the adaptations mask differences in belief or interpretation, these differences are seen as unobtrusive when the overall patterns followed are similar.

The Past in the Present

For those who reside year-round, the seasonality of the community means that from dozens of close friends and family as well as other social groupings in the summertime one is left in the winter with twenty or thirty foreigners. New faces are sometimes refreshing after a quiet winter or after months of seeing the same people all the time. With newcomers one can at least answer questions about the history of the foreign colony and tell stories from the past. The sense of a community of foreigners over time is kept alive by this seasonality, the constant coming together and moving apart, with redescription by a few foreigners to others who perpetuate the myth of the creative past of Deià by recounting these tales. The reality of dispersed groups, conflicts, and tensions is balanced within this ongoing story of the scandals, struggles, and successes of the changing characters in this artists' colony whose myths, magic, dreams, and realities have been lived or lost over time.

Most people who have lived in Deià for any extended amount of time (six months or more) and then gone away, return at some later date. Even those who have had traumatic experiences there – marriage break-ups, alcohol or drug abuse, or merely running out of money – are drawn back to see if it remains as they remembered it: a beautiful setting where knowing everything about one another (or at least thinking one did) gave everyone a sense of belonging to a 'pseudo-family' of foreigners who formed a community, although without the responsibilities, ceremony, and obligations usually expected of one in such places. They find that they just seem to pick up where they left off with familiar faces nodding in recognition, no questions asked, as though time had stood still. People they hadn't seen for years acted as though they had seen them just a few days or weeks before.

In this manner, long-term residents have so succeeded in separating themselves from all the conventional ties and values of their 'other worlds' that they no longer acknowledge another's absence as 'time away' but rather as some 'other time in some other place' which really has not affected the timeless image that they hold of Deià. The repetition of ideals formed in one's youth and realised in Deià and the 'indoctrination' of younger people with these past thoughts and times brought into the present add to the ethos of eternal youth and timelessness that so many foreigners associate with Deià. Paradise and reality flow into one another and the ills of the outside world are temporarily closed out by recalling exciting moments and beautiful memories through 'myths' of Deià's past.

Daily encounters in the café or along the roads present people as they really are: unadorned, preoccupied with mundane matters like excessive telephone or electric bills, children's studies, worries, etc. Everything becomes slightly exaggerated, dramatised to derive sympathy or at least empathy from one's friends. On evenings and weekends some people 'tart up' (dress more colourfully). The bars and cafés become a party scene with music, dancing, and drinking (and perhaps some marijuana or cocaine), all lively expressions or dramatisation of cohesiveness (Turner's 'communitas'). There is a celebration of a free choice of lifestyle in these evening rituals that create a momentary avoidance or closing out of everyday problems: boredom, frustration, or loneliness.

The outside world becomes more and more distant as the inside becomes larger and more complete. For some people it has become more and more difficult to leave this timeless world which they helped to create and to which they are now so attached. A trip to Palma becomes a major excursion and anywhere beyond 'unthinkable'. Telling visitors about the people one knew, the events that occurred, the funny things that have happened to oneself and others over the years recalls the circumstances, the ideals, the hopes and visions that led one to Deià. Each person, from a different angle, retells these stories: the insecurities, the ambivalence, the difficulties as well as the rewards of living an 'expatriate' life. These individual retellings come out as 'one story and one time' and express the importance of Deià in all of their lives. One is expressing belonging by one's ability to describe past events and personalities and to be described by them.

Stories about the Archduke, Robert Graves, and other well-known persons have become the basis for the myths of the past around which the foreign colony has formed. Anyone with inside information about the well-known characters is in a position to pass that information on to others. What began as whispers is soon part of popular transmission channels. After the famous are gone, little events become big ones, gossip creates importance. New arrivals grasp onto every bit of information they can glean about long-term foreigners so that they can become the informant of the next group of newcomers. Embellished, distorted, edited, these stories of foreign exploits in Deià become enhanced with each retelling. The myth celebrates the separateness of Deià from anywhere else, a self-conceived world of poetics, myth, and metaphor created by those who are able to describe it. They perpetuate the myth of one particular 'paradise' where youth and creativity, fun and wild living become the image that is presented to newcomers and sets the standards for their visit. Like any image, it hides as much as it reveals.[37]

Today

Brian Patten has well captured the contrasts one finds in Deià today:

> I thought, as I left the village, that if God had wanted to spoil a Garden of Eden without involving Adam and Eve in the plot, He could have a) opened a five-star hotel, b) used the location for a German soap opera, c) sent the travel writers. The village has somehow managed to accompany all of these as well as the million and one follies of

> its resident cast. It sits on a hill in a place I was asked not to name, part lunatic asylum, part paradise. (The Independent, 7 October 1988)

Edna O'Brien's novel *The High Road* (1988) was inspired and developed during her six-week stay in Deià. Although she does not use the village name, her descriptions certainly reflect some of the aspects of the foreign community I have described. One reviewer, Lorna Sage, wrote the following critique of O'Brien's book:

> The characters here have nearly nothing to lose. They're a collection of ageing wanderers, mostly women, who've been cast up like brittle cosmopolitan dreck on a Spanish coast. The nameless flower-scented place does prove to be full of dubious magic. This is the kind of paradise where lost souls can savour their exile from innocence even more keenly than usual, and where, even worse, they see themselves in each other's cruel reflections. One of the reasons why the Spanish setting here is so strange is that it's not Spain, but an island of the mind. (Observer, 9 October 1988)

For the locals and those of us who recognise some of the real and fictionalised characters in these writings, it is fascinating to see the impact Deià makes on its visitors. We have lived through the episodes and the processes of change that are not reflected in these articles. This spate of writing about the village is seen as another stage in the ongoing story of Deià. I hope the fuller picture has been revealed in these pages.

The idyllic village in the mountains is not what it used to be, but for many people this is not a problem. Since 1980 Deià has become a 'chic' area of Europe where young, upwardly mobile, and retired people are buying second homes in which they can combine elements of the past with artistic design and bohemian lifestyles. Swimming pools dot the landscape and use up much of the water that is meant to supply the orchards and gardens of their neighbours. The demand for houses has increased to the extent that prices double and triple each year. Foreigners compete to buy houses with sea views and no modern conveniences for £300,000. Two or three resident foreigners have been renting their homes in July and August (for £1,000 to £5,000 per month). They use only a portion of the money to go to quaint villages on mainland Spain, returning when the 'fancy' visitors have gone. The fancy visitors enjoy the peaceful walk to the pebbly beach, the relative quiet of the hills and valleys, and the access to a cosmopolitan group of people when they feel like socialising.

Axel Ball has brought in German buyers for house conversions and new chalets. During the holiday periods, other foreign residents joke about these "Dusseldorquins" (Dusseldorf-Mallorquins) that fill the cafés in their trendy fashions, drinking champagne for breakfast. When a long-term resident does decide to visit old haunts, there is hardly a familiar face and one finds the price of a shot of cognac is now as much as one once paid for a bottle.

In 1984 Axel organised a purchasing company and directed the conversion of two large farming estates into La Residencia, a five-star hotel which combines the finest of Mallorquin decor and fittings with modern paintings and comforts. In the process of constructing this hotel he acquired two-thirds of the local water rights (from a dozen different owners) and created jobs for thirty young Deianenc men and women.

There is hardly a family in Deià today who does not have some relationship with Axel. Among the Deianencs, he has employees, contractors, builders, gardeners, hotel personnel, property sellers, caretakers, baby sitters, borrowers, parents of employees, and others. He has kin among the foreign residents: his mother, for whom he built a house, his brother and sister-in-law, two ex-wives, two daughters, a stepson, his present wife, her daughter, and their two sons. There are twenty-five Germans and their respective families who have bought houses from him. There are also artists who have sold him paintings and exhibited in the hotel, musicians who perform at the hotel, and foreign residents who have invested in the hotel. The hotel has brought many changes to the village. More young Deianencs are able to find work and thus remain in the village, and the hotel's occupancy of over one hundred clients each day has added a prosperous potential clientele for shops, restaurants, galleries, and property. Axel's impact on the village cannot be underestimated and could easily be compared to that of Graves and Gelat forty years before him, but on a much grander scale.

The continuing success of La Residencia, Deià's now world-famous, German-built luxury hotel, served as the theme of the Graves grandchildren's annual play in 1990. Maureen Freely, a regular visitor to Deià over the past sixteen years, described this play in an article she wrote for the Independent:

> *Hotel Parasite* was a vicious and clever satire about a village overrun and ruined by fascist German developers, rich American bitches, dark Argentine sorcerers, grasping Spaniards, air-head hippys, pretentious French chefs. What impressed me most was that the audience, made up of all the targeted nationalities, was so delighted to be lampooned. I saw Germans howling with laughter at the sight of the Dusseldorf developer trying to stop his arm from doing a Heil Hitler.

> I saw Mallorcans wiping tears from their eyes when the Deià shopkeeper grovelled for profits. Wealthy divorcées from all over the northern hemisphere were rolling in the aisles when their rich bitch counterparts gossiped crassly on the phone to their friends in L.A.

The play revealed the conflicts of everyday life in Deià in the late 1980s. Despite the notoriety and improved local market for jobs, art, and other consumer goods, long-term residents, especially the artists and writers, feel compromised. They know the village needs the revenue provided by the new amenities and increased numbers, and that visiting collectors and the new moneyed can also benefit them, but they resent the intrusion of these less than desirable types into 'their' village. They fear that a price tag has been put on all aspects of life in Deià and no one can ignore the changes.

Long-term foreign residents do not want to see the village opened to any more outsiders. They see progress only as destructive to the idyllic setting they so admire. However, they no longer hold the power to influence those in charge. Locals want to open the village to more investment because it will produce jobs, housing, and livelihoods for their children and grandchildren in Deià. When foreigners try to tell them they are not going about it in the right way, the separate perspectives of the two communities once again become evident. The Deianencs have reached a point in their social and economic development where they feel fully capable of dealing with their future, based on their experience of living side by side with foreigners throughout this century and on their own appreciation of the qualities that have attracted outsiders to their village. Old-timers say their grandchildren don't need the past except to remind them of how fortunate they are today: 'The past was just endless hard work and struggle and it's best left to lie.' Foreigners reminisce and romanticise the past that is disappearing before their eyes. What they do not realise is that this view relies on one group remaining unchanged so that the other can benefit.

Today, the experiences shared over more than sixty years are enriched by three generations of interaction. The difference is that instead of an unquestioning acceptance of dominance, the local Deianencs have gained a long overdue opportunity to find their own voices and are expressing themselves on every subject. Foreigners are told that if they don't like what is happening to the village they can leave, while they, the Deianencs, must stay no matter what happens.

The foreigner no longer represents the unknown, outside connections, superior knowledge, or means. The local Deianencs (and many other Mallorquins) have reached what they believe is equal ground – they too have access to the outside, superior knowledge, and funds. There are no social or economic boundaries around Deianencs which prevent them from feeling equal to anyone who visits their village. There is a psychological awareness of belonging that makes them feel in control of their village and its future. Like foreigners, they travel, their children have time and means to attend university, and they have more than enough money for all their needs.

The difficulties lie in the necessity to compete on different terms than in the past by placing all foreigners 'outside' the social relations of the village. This separation of insiders from outsiders would mean that the rules of action pertaining to outsiders do not have anything to do with internal social organisation. After almost a century of dealing with strangers by incorporating them on one level or another, Deianencs are seeking a means to continue to interact on social and economic levels while controlling the involvement of outsiders in local politics. Deianenc solidarity has been formed in contrast to foreigners and outsiders. Indeed, the events of the last few years have expressed this renewed awareness of Deianenc identity.

This reestablished sense of solidarity is, of course, partly a result of the 1981 democratic constitution that divided Spain into seventeen autonomous regions, forcing each area to rediscover symbols of their separate identities buried for forty years under Franco's 'unified' Spain. Rather than choice not being a relevant factor in their lives (as under Franco), the locals complain of being confronted with too many choices. Long-term foreigners value the locals' hard-earned freedoms as they were well aware that for years they had 'free choices' that their neighbours were denied.

As a result of their previous interaction or 'incorporation', some foreigners today feel less foreign than the term estranger (stranger, outsider) implies. There is a perceived social distance between themselves and those foreigners who arrived after 1975 that they feel is even more significant than the differences they acknowledge between themselves and the Deianencs. The Deianencs have become accustomed to outsiders and have devised ways to hold onto their culture despite the intrusion. Long-term foreigners, however, relied on an image of timelessness that is fading and may not be replaceable. The changing composition of those who are considered insiders and others who are seen as outsiders reveals the complexities of Deià society and the ambiguity of these terms.

Despite long-term residents' fears that Deià is being ruined or spoiled, the foreigners who discover Deià tomorrow will see the village as it stands, a place of beauty and calm still sufficiently different from the places and people of their home countries to be attractive. Future visitors may easily confuse some of the long-term foreigners as natives because they are the only ones who will still be wearing skirts or shirts made of local 'vichy' materials, espadrilles (rope-soled shoes), and straw hats while the locals wear the latest fashions or Levis, Lácoste, and Gucci.

There are few senyors or peasants left in Deià, and Deianencs are equally capable of being hosts at home and guests in another land. Deianencs are travelling much farther afield than the European travellers who ventured south to Mallorca just a hundred years ago. They go to England and Germany to learn languages, holiday in other parts of Spain and Europe, and venture to the Caribbean, India, and Africa to see how other people live. They, too, have become tourists in another's land. Mallorca has become the summer 'capital of Spain' with King Juan Carlos spending three months with his family at Marivent Palace in Palma and entertaining the royalty of Europe[38] as well as holding meetings with the Spanish Prime Minister Felipe Gonzales and many of the cabinet ministers. The new Prime Minister, José Aznar, will be his guest in 1996 if he manages to form a coalition with members of other parties to gain a majority in parliament.

Instead of automatically giving strangers a higher status by including them in the group composed of senyors and senyoras, Deianencs have now reached the point of questioning just which, if any, of the familiar social categories an outsider may fit into. If, like Axel Ball, one has earned respect through providing increased opportunities for village members, there is no problem in continuing to consider him a senyor. On the other hand, the men and women who once employed builders and housekeepers and baby sitters no longer rely on those services, and those who provided the services have retired. If a minor repair is needed on one's house, the retired builder will send one of the younger men who have replaced him. The young man will do the job and leave, having no common experiences to recall with the foreigner. The women who cared for the house and children are also older, and most of the children they cared for are married. Affection still survives, but time to share it is limited.

Young Deianencs do not need or want to work cleaning someone else's house a few hours a day when they can be employed in the hotels full-time, work among friends, and receive a decent salary, social security benefits, unemployment compensation, and double pay two months each year. Many Deianencs have decided that it is easier to separate work and social relationships. They no longer feel obligated to extend hospitality to a stranger. They have learned to get on with business, collectivise their customers as tourists or outsiders, and keep personal associations separate. Many of the caregiving and cleaning jobs in the village are done by women who come over from Soller. There are also a few foreign women who help other foreigners to clean houses, paint, baby sit, etc.

Except for a few cases, the relationships that developed between foreigners and locals prior to 1975 are no longer possible or desirable for most Deianencs. Those relationships that have survived are based on the memories kept alive by those who shared them and their sensitive awareness and adaptations to the changing conditions of their respective lives. When a long-term resident hears the word estranger used by a local, he or she just has to remember how many people they spoke to on the way up or down the hills, how shopkeepers still extend them credit, and when they were last asked to pay a bill in order to feel that they are not included in the term.

In the midst of the village's renewed sense of solidarity in a period of accelerated socio-economic change and increased visitors and tourists, resident foreigners feel they have been displaced. Deianenc identity has been used over the centuries to mark off locals from others within the village but never before has there been the power to counteract these intruders. With increased prosperity, democracy, and more local autonomy, Deianencs can at last express their ambivalence toward a history of intrusions. Resident outsiders are no longer necessary as an income source, as buffers during social upheaval, or as mediators between the outside world and the inside.

The new-found powers of Deianencs have forced foreigners to re-evaluate their idyllic view of paradise. Now it is they who must find a way to 'carry on and be counted' without offending their neighbours and friends or losing the values that brought them to Deià in the first place. The European Community offers legitimate status to citizens of member countries who gained voting rights in local elections in 1995. This right may encourage some foreigners to take a more active interest in local politics, but no signs of such have yet emerged.

We have seen how experience with different groups of outsiders has formed the history of Deià and continues to be an issue of great importance. The present is understood through this past experience. It is not the actions of any one particular group of outsiders that has brought about the present antipathy but a cumulative experience which has only now been allowed to surface. Just as this is occurring in the 1990s, social memory will reconstruct local history to meet the needs of the future and, no doubt, the conflicts I have presented here will be reinterpreted. Insiders will continue to change in composition in terms of those they choose to identify as outsiders.

Notes

1. Hospitality not only reflects the welcome of the host but also of the village. Pitt-Rivers writes: 'The pueblo as a village is congruent with the larger pueblo of the district' and 'the family home is metaphorically the nation'. This might have been the case when Pitt-Rivers did his fieldwork. It is what Francoist dogma tried to preach. Franco himself said: 'only those capable of loving the Fatherland, of working and struggling for it, of adding their grain of sand to the common effort would be tolerated.' Many felt the home was not a metaphor for nation by choice but due to political coercion. The supply of food was influenced by political considerations and controlled by a local board in each town or village made up of the mayor (usually a local industrialist or landowner), the parish priest, and the local head of the Falange party (see Richards 1995).
2. Mallorca was 'exotic' at the turn of the century and well into the 1950s before modern transport and roads were developed. In fact, Francoism stressed the exotic aspects of Spain's 'traditional' social structure and Catholic ideology in contrast to European liberalism. Graham and Sánchez note that, 'the 1960s tourist slogan "Spain is different", while intended to appeal to the desire for the exotic "other", also referred back ambivalently to the idea of a national identity threatened by outside forces' (1995). In Francoist Spain of the 1960s, the 'other' was both feared and desired. Deià is still presented as 'exotic' in contrast to those areas of the island that have been modernised and overdeveloped for mass tourism.
3. The Archduke purchased agricultural estates during the period of poor harvests and perpetuated the existing senyorial system by replacing the monks, nobles, and city owners with a foreign owner.
4. This reference is still commonly used. When we recently visited the man who built our house, he was telling us about his long stay in hospital. He held up the palms of his hands and said, 'You see, I've become a senyor' (he'd been there so long his hands had become soft).
5. That is, they had no voice in public policy. Those who owned or controlled land controlled workers. There have been only two peasant uprisings in the six-hundred-year history of this area. Land-ownership or control remained the dominant criterion for political office, local power, and authority.
6. In the census of 1930 there were many foreign men and women in Palma but only three foreign women and fifty-eight men in villages around the island. Laura Riding set a precedent in Deià.
7. Pitt-Rivers and Lison Tolosana (and others) have written at length on the concept of the term 'Señorito' on mainland Spain.

8. Mallorquí (a dialectal variant of Catalan), although spoken in all local homes, was not spoken to foreigners or officials until 1974 when Franco allowed regional languages to be used publicly, taught in schools, and used in print.
9. Canelluñ was a misspelling of *Ca Na Lluny* (the House in the Distance). When Riding, Graves, and their friend Gelat named the house, few people knew how to write Mallorquí so they spelled it phonetically.
10. Nicknames during this period were in Spanish (Castilian), the language spoken to foreigners.
11. Edwin Ardener describes this invisibility in his article 'Remote Places': 'Natives to such an area sometimes feel strangely "invisible" – the visitors seem to blunder past, even through, them.'
12. MacFarland suggests that 'the gross category incomers (used by Shetland Islanders) helps cope intellectually with the increased anonymity' (1984:15).
13. Among the biographies of the Archduke are those written by Mallorquin writers: Quadrado 1932, Ferra 1959, and J. March 1986. March cites letters between the Archduke and various lovers and has named several direct descendants in his book. The listed 'heirs' are contesting March's sources. March claims to have been given a major portion of the Archduke's correspondence from one of the heirs and to have found letters in the attic of his own house, Son Galcerin (formerly one of the Archduke's houses), which he bought in 1962. It is not uncommon for the owners of large estates to leave behind furnishings and boxes of what they think is debris. A local historian has remarked that the 'real' history of the island is buried in the attics of these old houses, especially those that have remained within the same families for generations.
14. Sureda Blanes, in his introduction to his translation of the Archduke's *Die Balearen*, writes that 'the inventory of items in the Archduke's collection allows one to contemplate the aesthetic value in small items, and the emotion of humble things'. Joan Bestard describes the Archduke's methods as 'an obsessive precision of demonic ethnology – looking for nostalgia in objects – he collected artefacts in order to reconstruct a group's lost origins'. Although I think his detailed inventories in *Die Balearen* of objects concerned with the Mallorquin past are invaluable, I must agree with Bestard's criticism when it comes to his collection of erroneously labelled artefacts on display in the small Museum at Son Marroig: Greek vases labelled Etruscan, Punic glass beads labelled indigenous, etc.
15. Graves's judgements of people can be understood if one considers his interpretation of poetry and rational thought: 'The difference between poetry and rational thought is that rational thought goes in straight lines and poetry like nature has no straight lines.' His relationships were poetic.
16. Joao de Pina-Cabral (1987) has written about the symbolic nature of paved roads as opposed to *caminhos* (paths or old roads) in his article in *Man*, December 1987. This will be discussed more fully in Chapter 6.
17. Graves describes Gelat's conversion: 'Gelat in order to defend himself against the machinations of that awful doctor has had to turn Left and any day now will be Mayor …' Most of the reports I collected on this period paint the doctor as pro-Franco and Gelat as equivocal. This is another of Graves's misreadings of character. His faith in Gelat would have its backlash in the next generation (see Chapter 6).

18. Graves recorded the purchase of an antique oak table from an antiquarian in Palma for 30 pesetas (approximately £1 in 1934). Over the next forty years, Graves was one of the shop's regular customers. Labanyi describes an anachronistic survival in contemporary Spain of cultural relics from the past as 'freezing time to turn reality into a slick art object'. She cites McHale's suggestion that 'this anachronistic juxtaposition of different stages of historical development has led to a post-modernist fascination with the coincidence of different worlds, putting an "end to history" in the sense that linear time is experienced as synchronicity' (1995). It is useful to consider these approaches in relation to House names as discussed in Chapter 3 and in the section 'The Past in the Present' in this chapter.
19. I was told by a number of different sources that there was one very colourful exception to this rule. During the 1930s, a woman known as *La Inglesa* (the English lady) lived in a house called *Salarosa* (Red Room). The facts of the story may suggest that the house gained its name from the English woman's activities. When the butcher appeared to collect the yearly accounts on St. Michael's Day, he was informed by La Inglesa that she had no money but could perhaps pay in kind. According to the story, the young men who came of age each year were sent to Salarosa to collect the tradesmen's bills. When she left, boys had to be taken into Palma to the *Barrio Chino* (red light district) for these initiation rites!
20. This club was organised in 1969 and lasted about three years. Unlike mainland Spain (especially in the Basque regions, Galicia and Cantabria – see Douglas, Ott, Greenwood, et al.), dining clubs are not common in Mallorca. Since that period, few if any foreigners have worked side by side with local builders. During the past ten years, some foreigners who built or renovated their own houses have hired other foreigners who needed the extra money, worked for less than the local hourly rate, and did not require tax and VAT payments.
21. This is Sa Fonda where Rusiñol stayed in 1896 to 1897 and about which he wrote in 1905 (1958 English translation). Antonio has a fine collection of paintings by the various artists that stayed there during its existence from 1887 to 1967. The last owner's grandson opened a café there in June 1988.
22. Kenny (1961) noted that 'immigrants reinstate themselves with gifts to reduce envy and their association with the outside'.
23. This was meant to be an adaptation of the village name, which was spelled Deya (Castilian) at the time (1961). I thought my spelling was quite original until many years later I discovered I had unknowingly used the correct Catalan spelling of the name. The village name was officially changed to Deià in 1977.
24. Excavations of a cave site and a rock shelter with the Museum of Mallorca had begun to turn up unique evidence of prehistoric life on Mallorca.
25. The Archduke arrived dressed as a simple man and turned out to be an important and wealthy person. They assumed that the American must have been in disguise on his first visit because it would be impossible for anyone to acquire as much as he did in such a short time.
26. Graves believed that 'the language of poetic myth anciently current in the Mediterranean and Northwestern Europe was a magical language bound up with popular religious ceremonies in honour of the Moon Goddess or Muse, some of them dating from the Old Stone Age' (Graves 1948). The most popular idea of

the Muses comes from the Greek and Roman myths. They were the goddesses of myth and the inspirers of poetry, music, and drama. Graves would take an interest in a young woman and she would become the inspiration, the Muse, for his work.

27. An Afghan 'friend' brought Graves a manuscript of the *Rubaiyat* by Omar Khayam which he said came from the tomb of one of his chieftain ancestors. He said that he and his brother had done a rough translation from this original and would appreciate it if Graves would improve their English and join them as coauthors in this new translation. It turned out that the manuscript was a fake, the translations had been distortions of those made by an earlier translator, Robert Fitzgerald, and Graves was accused of everything from plagiarism to misrepresentation. The entire affair was highly embarrassing for Graves, his editors, and future publishers of his works.
28. An American artist who had lived for fifteen years in a rented house for which he paid £9 (1,800 pesetas) a month (no running water or indoor plumbing) died in May 1988 at the age of 72. It was discovered he had about $65,000 (£42,000) in the bank. He had denied himself any comforts during the last year of his life even though diagnosed as having inoperable lung cancer. He willingly accepted hand-me-down clothes from friends. His Deianenc landlady felt so sorry for him in his tattered and paint-splotched clothes that when her husband died in 1974 she gave Norman her husband's Sunday clothes. He had established a way of life back in the sixties in Paris and then in Deià and had not altered his habits since then, despite his receipt of a veteran's pension and social security during the previous twelve years.
29. Paco was the man who had run Ca'n Quet for many years. When that was sold to Es Moli, Paco opened a bar-restaurant in the centre of the village.
30. This was the derelict house of the mother of Sebastian Boi (he is discussed in Chapter 3).
31. Tastes in food also reflect the changes in insider-outsider relations. For awhile during the 1980s there was great interest in preparing 'foreign' dishes. In the 1990s there has been a resurgence of interest in Mallorquin regional cuisine.
32. Fifteen members of the group from Es Clot spent a week in Paris in November 1987, celebrating the fiftieth birthday of one of the members. Six of them also visited Greece for three months instead of returning to Deià one year. Three of the couples who own second homes in Deià are now working in London and two others (who have private allowances) have taken flats near to them. Parties called 'Deià in Maida Vale or Greenwich' were regular meeting grounds for anyone from Deià who was in London the past few years.
33. The death of Maggie 'the Cat Lady' occurred a few hours after that of a local man. His funeral was arranged in the usual manner and local neighbours of Maggie came to see what her friends would be organising for her. Her foreign friends and local neighbours decided that they would like to carry her to the cemetery like other Deià residents. As her Deianenc neighbours would have to be in the church for the other funeral at the same time, her foreign friends agreed to carry the casket up the hill from Es Clot. The local men offered to meet her pallbearers at the bottom of the steep climb to help them up to Es Puig. When the friends arrived with Maggie's casket on their shoulders, one of the village men pointed out (very discreetly) that it would have been easier to

carry had the casket been reversed with her head (the heaviest part) at the top as they went up hill. This was carried out in order to make the final part of the journey easier. It had not occurred to the foreigners to ask the locals for helpful hints; they just assumed they 'knew' how to do it. The locals were pleased to see the foreign men trying to emulate their customs but even more pleased to be able to teach them the correct way to do them. The catch-22 quality of coexistence is ever present. If an outsider does something as well as or better than an insider, he is resented, and if he can't do things as well, he's another class of person.

34. The closest cremation facilities were in Madrid, and her son returned the ashes to Deià. The ashes of a German woman who had been resident in Deià for ten years and died in the United States were brought to Deià by her daughter some years later and buried in a small plot in the cemetery.
35. Having just finished writing about Maggie's funeral, I came across the following in an article in The Independent, dated 7 October 1988, by Brian Patten who had spent the previous June in Deià:

    Poetry in Paradise

    Sunday. Sadly, Maggie the cat lady has died. A relay of friends carried the coffin up the valley road to the tiny cemetery that surmounts the village. She is buried in a communal grave, four layers of niches on either side of a deep shaft. Maggie's niche is across from that of Norman, an artist who died in the village last spring. He didn't like cats and she didn't much like his paintings, but there they both are, insulated from the sound of Vespas and motorbikes and all the other clatter that now disrupts the peace that brought them to Mallorca.
36. When discussing the details of the Jewish funeral with the Rabbi, he expressed his utter astonishment at the fact that the grave Norman was being lowered into was not actually in earth as required in orthodox burials but rather in a completely cement-lined niche.
37. Deià seems to be 'in the news' a great deal of late. A German soap opera, Hotel Paradise, has been filmed there off and on since June. Travel writers from Europe and America have recommended La Residencia and the village to readers. Television interviews with Richard Branson, major shareholder in La Residencia, were filmed in Deià. The centennial of Robert Graves's birth was celebrated during 1995. There was a surge of newspaper and journal articles in the UK and the United States. BBC ran a special film of Graves's life, and four biographies appeared.
38. Prince Charles, Lady Diana, and their children were guests of King Juan Carlos and Queen Sofia at their summer residence in Mallorca in 1986 and 1987. They returned in the summer of 1988. Queen Elizabeth and Prince Philip spent the last day of their first official visit to Spain in October 1988 in Mallorca with the King and Queen. The exiled King of Greece and his wife, a Danish princess, are regular visitors.

6. Roads

Wandering Without a Clear Direction

The mass immigration of Spaniards from the mainland and increased numbers of foreign tourists and residents from all parts of the world are major elements in the social transitions that have occurred on the Balearic Islands during the last forty years. We have seen that until the 1950s Mallorca had all the characteristics of an underdeveloped country: a fundamentally agrarian economy with strong autarchic roots, despite markets being opened to the outside in the nineteenth century. Industrialisation was slow and based on mechanisation of artisanal activities. Population increase in the early part of the twentieth century had forced emigration to distant lands in hopes of finding work and a means of securing a viable economic future. The social upheavals of Republican modernisation, a devastating civil war, Francoist repression, and exile for many were followed by economic development through tourism and industrial expansion. Through the 1960s and 1970s, the impact on values and lifestyles from regular interaction with increasing numbers of outsiders was becoming evident.

The number of foreigners in Deià has risen steadily since those early days, and it was not until the 1960s that additional and upgraded amenities were established for their comfort. New economic opportunities were created for local men and women in general, and for bachelors and spinsters in particular. Local people who had small houses inherited from their parents or bought over the years from savings were able to make more money from the sale of property than they had earned or could hope to earn from years of labour on the land. The traditional rewards of patronage and social prestige became less relevant as many Deianencs began to move away from agricultural employment and into the service sector. Working in hotels, cafés, restaurants, letting rooms or houses, they provided comforts, accommodation, properties, and caretaking services to a growing foreign population. The main attraction of Deià to outsiders was no longer the search just for an idyllic setting for their artistic pursuits but also for a place in the sun to pursue leisure and recreation. Among some local Deianenc families materialistic values and market exchange began to take precedence over ties of friendship and reciprocity. Foreigners once greeted as guests and incorporated into village activities through their host or the ownership of a House began to be indiscriminately grouped together as outsiders rather than individuals.

Social relations were altered as more foreigners moved into areas once known as neighbourhoods in which being a neighbour meant geographical proximity, reciprocity, and some form of kin link between the inhabitants of the various houses. The term neighbour was soon replaced by direct references to kin or family in different areas of the village, and the flow of conversation and reciprocity between people living near one another was replaced by awkward relations with unfamiliar people who had completely different habits of waking, working, and sleeping, who spoke unrecognisable languages behind closed doors, and who installed gates and walls between their houses and those of their neighbours.

Those who regularly dealt with outsiders were joined by others who had gained access to the benefits from foreign investment and daily expenditures. Rewards from increased spending by foreigners filtered through the village and beyond. Bar owners, landlords, and shopkeepers gained financial strength. Property sales began to create new 'bosses' with foreign investors bearing the major financial burden and local builders organising employees and materials. The ownership and control over land, houses, and property became more and more the terrain of foreigners.

Paving the Way to the Future

The conflicts and tensions provoked by the plan and construction of roads over the last century reflects the varying ways in which different individuals and groups have responded to change in village affairs. Road construction became a symbol that triggered social action. This inanimate object and the space it encompassed became a symbol of the thoughts, hopes, dreams, mobility, and technology of the local people at different periods. The construction and development of roads during a period of social, economic, and political restructuring embodied the process that led both to the opening up of the village to the outside and to the rearrangement of social relations inside. Roads became the focus of local, foreign, and national interest, and the varying opinions expressed reflected the changing concerns of the village.

It is interesting to note that many idiomatic expressions use the word *cami* (road): '*caminant sens cami*' (wandering without a clear direction), '*obrir cami*' (to lead the way), '*prendre cami*' (clear out), '*ésser en cami*' (to be on one's way), '*fora del cami*' (off the track), '*va per bon cami*' (have the right idea), '*cami tancat*'[1] (literally, closed road but it also means no alternative, no escape, no exit). Roads bring contact and expand the horizons of a village. Overgrowth is cut away, hidden or closed spaces are uncovered, and nature is altered, controlled, and adapted to human needs and desires. Roads bring the outside in and allow the inside to go out and to return. Roads encourage movement, inspire action, offer access to different places, people, and activities. Roads are usually constructed because a need to make one or more places accessible has arisen. Changes in activities and economic, social, or political life may make roads necessary. Their creation makes many other things possible.

Brunet notes: 'As routes to other parts of the island were created and improved, a system of complementary services appeared. Hostels, inns, and post stations, whose first functions were as rest stations where drivers could change horses, deposit goods and collect post to be transported to nearby areas, were adapted to meet changing modes of transport. In 1846 a program of construction and conservation of roads was begun all around the island. Work on the Soller to Palma road had begun in 1830 but no passenger services could be inaugurated until 1850. *Tartans* [*diligencias* – horse-drawn carriages] made the trip four times a week. In 1855 a new carriage pulled by just one horse was added to the service. This one went three times a week from Soller to Palma and three times a week from Palma to Valldemossa' (1984:103–132). A vivid description of the poor conditions of island roads in the early nineteenth century appears in a letter from the composer Frédéric Chopin to a friend in Paris in 1838: 'Every time I come from Palma I have been driven by the same coachman but we never used the same road twice' (Ferra 198:67). Mudslides and collapsed terrace walls would make the rugged roads impassable.

The highway built by the Spanish government from Palma through Valldemossa to Deià and Soller was finally completed in 1903, allowing many more visitors to the island to reach Deià as well as making the trip to the city a great deal easier for Deià merchants. Trade between Deià and Soller and Deià and Palma became easier and more direct for many small producers who had previously depended on shopowners to get their goods to market on their weekly trips over the rough tracks to the city.

With the new road, anyone with a mule and a cart could take his own produce to market. The internal tensions of local life could be reduced through this opening up of connections to other villages, markets, and commercial centres. Instead of walking for two or three hours over the mountain trail to Soller market on a Sunday, excursions by *caro* (mule cart) were arranged by the local grocer and five or six others who owned mules and carts. No longer dependent on a few powerful local entrepreneurs for transport and sale of their goods, patron-client relations diversified, as did the political alliances previously based on the dependency of workers on landlords. The road encouraged small-scale private enterprise.

Until the highway was built, one had to pass through the residential areas of the village in order to get to Soller. The road from Valldemossa descended into Es Clot and continued up through the Costa d'en Topa, Es Porxo, and on to Soller. The siete palmos widths (seven spread-hand widths) of these roads was determined by the average width of a mule carrying two packs. The needs of the users were the basis for the dimensions. All the roads within the village were dirt tracks of this width. One came up or down from the neighbourhoods that were formed around the village centre to the shops and cafés, on to Es Porxo, and up to the church on Es Puig. These roads were the scene of and routes for *rites de passage*, and village life revolved around them. All the village fiestas, dances, and gatherings were held in Es Porxo or Es Puig.[2] People from various parts of the village were drawn to these areas to celebrate the shared beliefs and values that identified them as a community. Anyone who came through the village was seen by most of the local people as she or he passed their doorway or fields. The young men and women of the village strolled together along these dirt roads during their Sunday outings in front of the curious and protective eyes of the rest of the village. Religious processions followed the road down from the church along the stages of the cross and back up again; funeral processions began at the house of the deceased and followed along the dirt tracks that led to the church and the body's final resting place in the cemetery. The road area was 'village space', a proper place to be seen on one's way home, to the shops, out courting, to the church, and being carried in a casket on one's final route to eternity. The process of life took place along these roads.

The new highway depended on some cooperation between property owners and the government. It had to be cut through privately owned lands, and owners had to decide which areas could be sacrificed to the cause of progress. Two houses that now open directly onto the main highway agreed to give up land in front of their houses rather than the land behind which was, by far, the more productive. One can say that the shape of the highway was determined both by agricultural priorities and the social status of some owners who had the power to influence decisions.[3] The highway not only facilitated more rapid and convenient access to other places but also improved the services available within Deià, where a mail coach, Correos, ran once daily between Palma and Deià carrying post, foodstuffs, residents, and visitors. Today, there are six trips daily between Palma, Valldemossa, Deià, and Soller. Children walk or ride their bikes to school and play along the main roads, and old men tap their canes as they stroll together along the roads that mark the periphery of the village. They stop to rest and catch up on local news at benches built at a number of spots along the way.[4] During this comfortable respite, the old men draw strength, share ideas, and gain a sense of movement and renewed experience. The traffic going north or south does not just pass by them but carries them through their memories to the places they knew so well. Without the effort of dressing up, travelling, or changing daily rhythms they are able to observe the movement of people, vehicles, and goods in and out of the village.

Roads: A Source of Conflict or Crossroads in Time?

Thirty-two years after the highway was finished, Robert Graves financed the building of a road to the cala, which was meant to be the first stage in a planned hotel project with Gelat. At that time, anyone with transport could come into Deià, descend to the cala, and become more familiar with the beauties and pleasures experienced by those who lived in Deià. Had Graves's plans materialised many tourists would have been able to stay in Deià for extended visits but, as his money ran out, the planned hotel was never built. The increased number of visitors seeking leisure, recreation, sun, and sea were kept away for another twenty-five years. The effect of increased numbers of visitors during this earlier period of social and political upheaval might well have resulted in a very different type of tourism developing in Deià.

The cala road served to give visitors and locals an easier approach to the sea and made possible the establishment of two cala cafés and the broader distribution of fresh fish. Larger quantities of fish could be collected and easily delivered to Palma and Soller markets, and goods and equipment could be transported by road rather than only by sea as in the past. This cala road reached the sea by joining the footpath from Es Clot. The connection of the highway to the cala road and the path from Es Clot brought together and encircled the various parts of the village, the highest point culminating in Es Puig and the lowest in Es Clot. The 'world of Deià' as people experienced it in the 1930s was formed by the combined forces of the villagers, the government, and foreigners. The roads that surrounded and enclosed the village symbolised this cooperation. First the village people, over generations, trod the paths that led over the mountains to Soller, back to Valldemossa, and down to the sea. Then the government built the road that connected Deià to its neighbouring villages, Soller and Valldemossa, and to the city of Palma. Finally, Robert Graves's cala road made possible the link between the two others. Just as the foreign-financed cala road connected the footpaths people had used to the government highway, foreigners mediated with government officials in Palma on the villagers' behalf, and locals helped foreigners to purchase property.

The cala road was washed away by a storm just six months after its opening. By the time Graves managed to raise sufficient funds to begin repairs on the road[5] political tensions were rising in Deià as in the rest of the country, and the progress of the road was dependent on developments in local and national politics. Gelat and Graves knew that the repairs on the road would be approved only if Gelat remained a powerful figure in the village.Through the excuse of making inquiries about the future of the road, Gelat was able to glean information about the rapidly changing political climate in Mallorca, was made aware of an enemy faction within the village, and was advised to transfer his party allegiance before his critics could act. His three months as Republican mayor of Deià was not long enough to get the road repaired before he was forced to resign and a nationalist government was claimed. The last note concerning the road appeared in Graves's diary on 28 June 1936; 'The question of the road has been put to one side' … and there it stayed for almost thirty years.

In 1965 Gelat's son claimed the land and what remained of the road as his own, based on the inheritance of his father's holdings in Deià. He had all the legal papers in his father's name and requested permission from the City Council to build ten houses on either side of the road. Graves's claim to the land was based on his friendship and trust with Gelat Sr., who was now dead. He had no papers to prove his part in the purchase. He took the case to court, claiming that foreigners were required to put properties they purchased into the names of Spanish citizens but that, in actuality, he had put up all the money. The court, having only Graves's word and Gelat's contracts, gave the majority of the land to Gelat Jr. but agreed to leave to Graves a small area of terraces just below his house on the grounds that any building there would obstruct his view and privacy. The village council supported Gelat's claim because he promised to give them access to the road in exchange for the building permits.

The cala road not only symbolised the period of symbiotic relations between the village, state, and foreigners, and the past relationships of trust between foreigners and important village persons, but also served to enforce the value of blood ties over friendship despite the inherent conflict in interests between the generations. The mere mention of the cala road today brings forth allusions to the misgivings people have about business partnerships formed with other than family members, and that parents have about giving children their inheritance before they die.

By the late 1960s, Axel Ball had begun to organise purchasing companies and to form business relationships with builders. Formal contracts and the establishment of corporations, S.A. (Sociedades Anonimos-limited companies), were possible. Axel's dealings brought outside interests, people, materials, and techniques into Deià. His project to convert Es Moli into a hotel expanded the horizons of the village. Axel offered the village an opportunity to be associated with a major business venture in European tourism. During this period, development aimed at attracting the increasing number of Europeans who were travelling to sunny areas for holidays of leisure and recreation was completely financed by outside (foreign) investment, with little concern for the local people. Some areas of the island were transformed from forests and wasteland to tourist centres with high-rise hotels and shops designed to cater to the tastes of tourists. Like these developers, Axel had come to do a job and knew very little about the local people or place. His interests were to provide comforts for German (and other European) clients in the Mediterranean sun. The personnel and time needed for this project put a strain on the Deià work force and many workers were brought in from outside the village. During the construction, the Ball brothers were drawn into local life through their contact with complex networks of workers, neighbours, families, friends, business acquaintances, and investors.

There were only four master builders in Deià. Each had three to six men working with him and were involved in maintaining local houses or renovating old houses for the foreigners who had begun to buy houses in Deià during the previous decade. Axel was not concerned that there were no builders in Deià experienced enough to carry out his plans; he could negotiate with companies anywhere on the island. Although there was no room for personal animosities or emotional ties in these strictly business ventures, employees were generally drawn from families he had associated with in his early ventures. When the village vetoed his request to bus the hotel visitors at Es Moli down to the cala, despite his offer to improve the road, Axel was forced to go further afield to find sea-front space for his hotel clients. The decision to deny permission in Deià was partly due to military controls on coastal development which lists Deià cala as useful for defense (although jagged rocks jut above the water in many places and only small, short-keeled crafts can come onto the shore). More likely, it was believed to be too valuable a link in the still active island contraband operations.

Unable to secure beach access in Deià, Axel merely expanded his horizons by drawing the Soller council and builders into his plans. A Deià contractor and a Soller carpenter had taken an option on land at Muleta, a promontory marking the beginning of Soller, but they had been unable to finance the necessary roads to promote their project. Axel offered to build them an access road to their building sites in exchange for permission to bus the Es Moli clients to the sea, using the road. Although military permission was required, this was not a port like Deià, and the military agreed to give permission to the builders. Axel's help facilitated the realisation of an urbanisation and gave his clients access to the sea. The new homeowners were given use of the stairways to the sea built for Es Moli clients, and weekend visitors found the descent over the cliffs made easier by platforms built for Es Moli along the way. Once more a foreigner had combined his financial resources with the political clout of local contractors to open up areas that had previously been quite inaccesible. Muleta could now be easily reached by Deianencs, and the new road to the beach there offered a convenient halfway point for Soller and Deià friends or relatives to meet for a Sunday outing.

Developers and builders in Palma, Inca, and Soller enlarged their firms through foreign investment in development. The builders with the most employees could handle more and bigger jobs. Family members helped businesses branch out. Builder's sons or sons-in-law might take on special aspects of the work (like stonemasonry) or form separate crews with their own employees. A builder chose his carpenters and plumbers from among his family or close friends. As the work in Deià increased, the contractors had to bring in workers from Soller and Fornalutx.

Neither Graves nor Es Moli S.A. (A. Ball and associates) could have succeeded in carrying out their projects had they not been able to form associations with influential local citizens. We have seen how the relationship between Graves and Gelat developed and was sustained over many years. Axel began his projects with outside firms only after he had gained the proper permits and village sanctions. Gelat needed Graves and vice versa. The City Hall needed Axel's investment (and taxes) to grow. The local associates gained standing through their involvement with these projects that opened the village to easier contact with the outside and provided facilities which brought increased numbers of visitors and income to the village. The steadily developing 'new' industry of tourism had taken many people on the island away from their natal villages, causing demographic redistribution that had resulted in some villages becoming 'dormitory towns' while new areas by the sea were becoming heavily populated.

In the 1940s and 1950s, when a man or woman was old enough to work, many went to France. After 1960 Deià's young working population went to Palma or other developing tourist centres to find work. When Es Moli opened there were very few Deianencs available to work and few of those were trained for other than manual labour. One local man, the fisherman's son, who had picked up languages working with his parents at the café they ran during the summers at the cala, began to work as a waiter in the new hotel's dining room a few years after it opened. Two local men did the gardening and a few women worked in the laundry. The rest of the staff was brought in from mainland Spain and Germany. After 1965, between the construction trade and the opening of Es Moli, jobs in Deià were on the increase but they would not be filled by many Deianencs until the generation born in this period was ready to go to work. In the interim, like their parents before them, most of the young men who remained in the village continued to work in construction or agriculture and the women in part-time domestic jobs.

The housing development that Gelat Jr. began brought ten new homeowners into the village, some as permanent residents and others for between one and three months each year. They relied on local shops for their provisions and local people to work for them in their houses and then to look after the house and garden in their absence. By the mid-1960s, Es Moli housed and fed 180 guests a day from April to September each year, but their contact with the village was barely noted except in the employment their visits required and minor increases in sales of post cards, souvenirs, and sundries at the local shops. Most people came for a two-week holiday and spent their time sleeping late, basking in the sun around the swimming pool, being bused to the Es Moli beach, reading fiction and detective stories, and drinking and dining in the hotel. One or two morning or early evening walks through the village sufficed to see the sights: the church, cemetery, City Hall, school, museum, gallery, and shops. For the villagers these were stimulating improvements and profitable ventures. They still recognised most of the people on the streets, shops had a bit more variety as resident and holidaying foreigners requested goods the locals seldom used: post cards, foreign *rubio* (blond) tobacco, mayonnaise, ketchup, peanut butter, sterilised milk (rather than the kind sent up from Palma each day that had to be boiled before use), and vegetables, such as mushrooms which were common seasonally in their wild form but not previously available in the shops.

The reference to tobacco as *rubio* reflects an interesting choice of comparisons. 'Blond' rather than white or bleached evokes a myriad of binary oppositions: *rubio*-blond/*moreno*-brown, *claro*-light/*oscuro*-dark, *norte*-north/*sud*-south, *frio*-cold/*caliente*-hot, *estranger*-foreign/*familiar*-local. These terms symbolise local perceptions of Scandinavian, British, and German visitors in contrast to their own Mediterranean stereotype. The northerners are blond, light, cold, strange, and foreign while southerners are dark, brown, warm, and familiar. These associations pervade everyday conversation. Not long ago a Mallorquin friend phoned to tell me she had become a grandmother. She said, '*No es nostra* (it is not ours). He is *rubia com sa mare* (blond like his Norwegian mother)'. 'Ours' would be dark like his father. The foreigners in the hotel were defined and contained through these simple references.

The cala road, highway, and Es Clot path form the boundary of the world known as Deià with its own values based on local experience. The roads symbolise the connections between Deià, the state, and foreigners as well as the links between Deianencs and the outside world. The recognition of the cala road as a link between known foreigners, the village, and the nation can be seen in the village council's conscious neglect of sign-posting the road. Although a thin line on maps of the area indicates a descent to the sea, there is no way that anyone driving through Deià would know where the road was except by asking someone along the way. The council's argument for not posting a sign was that the road was for the people of Deià and surrounding villages. They knew where it was. It was a road to be used by people that knew someone or something about Deià. The road department has twice put up signs and both have 'mysteriously' disappeared within days. As tourist development increases, more permanently installed government sign-posts are appearing on the highways and side roads.

The cala road once again became the focus of village attention and the subject of conflicting ideas just after the first democratic elections in 1977. The new mayor's projects included enlarging the cemetery, improving existing roads, modernising the cala road by filling in the bumps and holes, asphalting it, and building a new access road to Es Clot. The cemetery enlargement involved land exchanges between the City Hall and a foreign investor which benefited both parties. The cala road was widened at the point it joined up with the path from Es Clot to provide additional parking spaces which were marked out with white stripes on the black asphalt (a rather odd sight to behold as one descended by foot or car through rugged mountain terrain). This project brought forth a great protest from both locals and foreigners in the form of letters published in the local monthly magazine *S'Encruia*. The road improvements certainly made driving to the cala a great deal easier, safer, and less harmful to one's vehicle, but few seemed to find these advantages worthy of merit. One letter from a local man suggested that 'the only thing the mayor forgot to do was to draw circles on all the rocks of the cala to show people where to put their *culos* (bottoms)'.

The marking out of ordered parking places seemed absurd in a landscape where the human struggle to control nature is counteracted each year by the raging waters of the stream which washes away the stone terraces built and rebuilt over the centuries to support the olive trees twisted and gnarled by successive prunings and graftings. The mayor's concern with trying to make order where disorder prevailed was seen as a publicity stunt to attract outside respect for himself, at the price of neglecting his other obligations to the village. People felt the mayor had his priorities wrong. One letter pointed out that 'It was sufficient to note that hundreds of villages in Spain have running water and municipal sewage systems but as yet, have no paved streets'. Another letter implied that he was developing outside affairs and disregarding inside necessities. Furthermore, the project of road refurbishment had been imposed from above and outside (in conjunction with the Insular Council in Palma) rather than through village consensus. The mayor was accused of having the City Hall improved, new roads made, and old roads paved at the expense of the village taxpayers while ignoring the vital need for village-owned piped water and sanitation systems.[6]

He replied in the next issue of *S'Encruia* that the Insular Council had provided the funds especially for road improvements and that they would not have been available for other purposes. He was caught short on that when another writer explained that, 'Most of the residents of Deià pay *impuestos sobre la Renta* (income tax), *retenciones sobre el mismo* (witholdings on personal income), *sobre el patrimonio* (state tax), *Trafico de Impresas* (printing tax), and *Municipales* (city, town, or village tax). Additional taxes are included in the value of our purchases and transactions. All of these indirect taxes, which are higher everyday, are distributed by the state according to what it considers necessary priorities'. This writer was reminding the mayor that the funds distributed by the island council were drawn from taxes paid by the people of the villages on the island and therefore their voice in the use of that money was valid.

Another example of misplaced priorities was the City Hall's approval of the construction of a water-bottling plant on lands owned by the estate of Son Canals. The pipeline carrying water to the plant came from the fountain up at Ca l'Abat. It had two other outlets which were to be used to connect water to Ca'n Fusimanya and parts of the Puig. The only difficulty was that the plant drew all the pressure and the other areas never got any water. Further letters to *S'Encruia* accused the mayor of *trafico de agua, mas potenciada que el de droga* (trafficking in water, a substance with more potential gain than that of drugs). It was stated that the price to connect water to one's house was £500 and that the water itself was often non-drinkable and possibly infectious. The amount of money gained by two or three men from the sale and maintenance of water each year goes well into millions of pesetas. The 'right' to sell water comes from their tenant's rights to the waters of the fincas they managed in the past or in the present. The cost of connection runs from 25,000 to 100,000 pesetas (£125–£500) for houses within the village, and much more for those outside who have to lay pipes to reach the existing village connections. The complaint about the quality of the water is somewhat dubious given that the factory water is bottled from the same source and tested regularly before it can be sold around the island to hotels, bars, and shops with no complaints or casualties. However, the condition of water deposits or wells within each home can alter the quality of water. Many foreigners, for example, did not know that the water from the first rains should be diverted from entering wells as it carries all the debris that has collected on the roofs and in the water canals over the hot summer. This brings up the question of locally held ideas about the good and bad qualities of water sources which are based on social more than chemical determinants. An illustration of the way social values impinge on the use of water can be seen in the name and attitudes associated with the fountain named *Ses Mentides* (the lies). This water is considered to be non-potable because of the falsity of many of the agreements made about its use. Sa Font Fresca is believed to be no longer drinkable because it descends from the road where so many unknown people drop bits of rubbish. This implies that 'good water' is unspoiled by conflicts and out of the way of strangers and their dirt. Good water is that which has been used 'traditionally' without conflict or complications. According to local valuation, the 'best' water in the area where I live is from the *Font D'Òrfena* (The Orphan's Fountain). Its purity, name, and value suggest it is of an unknown underground source that belongs to Deià.

Further protests against the mayor concerned the formal opening of the new City Hall which was inaugurated during the fiestas of the village on St. John's Day, 24 June 1980. This time the criticism was about the reconstruction of the building which housed the City Hall and the village school. In the existing building there had been two large rooms. One was allocated to all administrative functions: secretarial work; record control of census, taxes, births, deaths; counselor's meetings; civil marriage ceremonies, etc. The other room was used by the school for six- to ten-year-olds. In the new building the school was enlarged, leaving one room on the ground floor for the administrative secretary and two other officials who carry on daily work in the City Hall. Two additional rooms were constructed in an area behind the school. One was a card room[7] now used as the mayor's office and the other a new surgery for the village doctor.[8] The latter has a separate entrance on the stairway up to the Puig. A wide tiled stairway with an elaborate wooden banister leads up to the first floor of the City Hall where there is a room for the archives, another for small meetings, and a third which is a large salon with the coat of arms of the village on one wall, a ten-foot long table and ten high-backed chairs against the back wall, and paintings of Deià by various artists on the remaining walls. This is where the council meets formally on the first Thursday of every month. Official gatherings, civil (non-Catholic) weddings, ceremonial presentations, and art exhibitions are also held here. The mayor holds informal meetings in the smaller room or will sit with one or two others in the secretary's office to discuss day-to-day matters.

The new City Hall was envisaged by the mayor as a centre for the village, providing bureaucratic services, medical care, social recreation, and cultural activities.

The grand opening of the new City Hall was scheduled as part of the village fiestas for 1980. After the usual mass, the congregation filled the street in front of the City Hall where visiting dignitaries and local people gathered to hear the fine words spoken by island officials and the local councillors. The doors of the new City Hall were opened and the dignitaries and councillors were directed to enter and go up the stairs to the main *Salon de Actes.* The doors closed behind the last official and everyone on the street looked up toward the balcony doors, anticipating the speeches. To their surprise, the balcony doors never opened and after about five minutes they heard applause from inside the building, announcing to them the end of speeches they had not heard. This was a strange introduction to the new democratic life so long denied them during the Franco regime. In the past, doors had been opened wide during official ceremonies, assuring everyone the vision of officials placed conveniently in front of the portrait of the Caudillo Francisco Franco himself. The mayor's vision of a City Hall that would unite the interests of the people, the bureaucracy, social and political groups, and encourage cultural activities and local identity certainly got off to a bad start.

The ceremony that accompanied the opening of the first City Hall in Deià in 1583 presents a further contrast to the 1980 dedication. The first City Hall was a small room with a large covered porch (hence the name of the area, Es Porxo – the porch). The entire ceremony took place in and around the porch where everyone could see and hear the visiting officials from Palma granting independence to the village of Deià after its many years under the Universitat de Valldemossa. A sword was given to the village leaders to symbolise the privilege of making decisions about their own welfare. Four hundred years later, despite many changes in the social, economic, and political life of the village and the new freedoms and autonomies of democracy, the villagers were excluded from participating in an act designed to celebrate their interests and welfare.

The fiasco of the inauguration of the new City Hall was added to the mounting number of criticisms being voiced about the mayor. The rudeness of the City Council, the intrusion of asphalted roads and multiple parking places in a 'primal forest', the erratic behaviour of the mayor who one day joked with his friends and the next became insulted if someone did not behave with the respect his position warranted were all subjects for letters to the village chronicle. *S'Encruia* also included council meeting agendas, the month's births, marriages, and deaths, and a bit of poetry and humour that wittily depicted the process of life in Deià. What the first democratically elected mayor and council of Deià lacked – involving the village in open discussions about controversial issues and a sense of humour – the monthly magazine *S'Encruia* supplied in abundance. Needless to say, the editorial board of the magazine was made up of a small group of friends (members of the PSOE [opposition party] and a number of foreigners).

Again in 1982, roads were the main focus of local gossip and conflict. The mayor presented the Ca'n Carindo[9] project, which proposed the construction of a new road descending from the highway and joining the Es Clot road where it crossed the stream. This project would necessitate cutting through privately owned land as well as covering a hundred yards of the stream bed in an area that passed in front of half a dozen houses. According to the mayor, the proprietor was willing to cede the land to facilitate lorry access to Es Clot which was quite restricted by narrow turns and deep gutters in the dirt road.[10] The covering of the area of the stream which had been the place where one could contemplate cascading waters in the winter and a myriad of morning glories in the early summer was seen as a desecration of the natural beauties of Deià by many local and foreign residents.

Most Deianencs were not sure if the project was at all necessary, but as one woman said, 'We won't know until it's done; maybe we'll find some use for it'. As in the past, passive acceptance was the way to deal with change when one felt one had no say in decision making. Most Deianencs had learned to swallow their personal opinions in the cause of village unity. No objections were made for fear of being different or experiencing some later reprisal. As permits for any kind of house or land reform had to be approved by the City Hall, most people felt obliged to protect their future interests by passive acceptance in the present.

A group calling themselves *Vecinos y Residentes de Deià* (Neighbours and Residents of Deià) sent a letter to the Arts Council (Belles Arts), criticising the plans and actions of the City Hall and expressing their fear that Deià was losing its picturesque and traditional qualities. The letter stated that

> The following illegal developments have taken place in Deià over the past seven years. The beauty and historical significance of the village of Deià is being destroyed, and if this is allowed to continue, it could soon become *a la Cala D'or*.[11] The developments include:

1. The recent construction of a number of houses in concrete and the use of stone facing (rather than the 'traditional' cut stone used in older houses).
2. The widening and paving of a road to the cala which has resulted in the construction of eleven houses, parking difficulties, and overcrowding on the beach.
3. The construction of a concrete water-bottling factory at the edge of the village where hundreds of blue plastic crates can be seen as one drives or strolls down the road that enters Deià.
4. The construction of houses within the village in areas of 'unspoiled' nature.
5. A plan to cover a large portion of the stream, a beautiful spot captured by artists and writers over the centuries and one of Deià's landmarks.

To counteract these problems and preserve the picturesque qualities of Deià, they requested that the following rules be established and maintained in all future building within the village and the municipality of Deià:

1. All houses should be built of stone.
2. No alteration of existing pathways and roads within the village either as a means to improve automobile transit or to provide access roads to undeveloped areas of the village.
3. No industry in Deià.
4. No high-rise buildings.

The letter was forwarded from the Arts Council to the village for its consideration and comments, and the City Council convened a special public meeting to discuss the matter. This was an unprecedented occurrence. Unlike the previous two years' activities behind closed doors, posters announcing this open meeting were placed in conspicuous spots around the village and everyone was encouraged to attend.

The Meeting

On 2 May 1982, an 'open meeting' of the City Council was held in the salon of the City Hall. However, the mayor did most of the talking and the few people who spoke did so to support what he was saying. He began the meeting by saying, 'After many years of living in a *societat controlada* (controlled society) it is surprising, now that there is democracy in Spain, that some people still have to deal with problems through third parties.[12] We consider this letter a denunciation, an insult and an intrusion in our affairs'. He went on to say that the letter was signed by very few people who were actually vecinos (registered voters) but rather by foreign residents in the village.

One of the few vecino signatories, a man from Santander who had resided in Deià for the past six years, tried to make clear that the letter was not meant as a denunciation but as a means of making contact with the Belles Arts to discuss the points listed in the letter. He said that the signatories had on various occasions tried to discuss the subject with the mayor but he had been unavailable or too busy. In response to this, the mayor explained that the statement in the letter that asserted that the actions by the City Hall were completely 'illegal' could only be read and interpreted as an insult. The audience shouted their agreement and additional angry comments ensued.

The mayor read the letter to the audience, making it clear both through the sarcastic tone of his voice and his gestures that most of the criticisms expressed were based on erroneous information or hearsay. He proceeded to note that almost all the people who had signed the letter had very definitely not observed the rules they were criticising: 'two of them were allowed to build houses without stone fronts and another has a concrete house that is an eyesore.' He reminded everyone that the road to the cala had been built originally in 1934 by a foreigner, Robert Graves, for his own personal gain, and the village had merely improved it for safety reasons.[13] The council felt that the improvements had brought about positive results. More people used the road, there were fewer potholes to cause breakdowns, and working people could drive down for a swim during their lunch break. Finally, the mayor pointed out that 'many who signed the letter use the road daily'.

The mayor explained that building styles had altered for a number of reasons: there were no stone masons left in the village, the cost of masons and construction workers had risen, and the time and money involved in transporting materials and labour to Deià had become prohibitive. Stone facing had become an attractive alternative which reduced costs considerably while retaining some resemblance to other village houses. He pointed out that when he had become mayor most of the men employed in the village were *picapedrers* (stonecutters).

> Not that there was anything wrong with that, but it was dangerous having an entire village dependent on work in construction and the care of absentee landowners' houses. We have managed to change that. During the past seven years there have been a variety of new jobs created. The water-bottling factory was opened and employs twelve

> village people. There is a pharmacy which employs one village person and two professional pharmacists from the city. There is a bank where pensioners can collect their monthly retirement[14] on time instead of having to wait weeks, money can be exchanged, loans made, accounts kept, etc., and here another job has been created for a Deianenc and a manager from the city. We now have an officially recognised administrative secretary in our City Hall as well as the auxiliary secretary of long standing. We have established a rubbish collection service and cleared the stream of filth and debris and employed two men to serve as Municipal police, handymen, town criers and rubbish collectors. A daughter of Deià[15] has returned from the city with her husband and two children to open a new bakery which transports fresh bread and newspapers from Palma each day. This represents nineteen new jobs that have been created to allow Deianencs to diversify and a new hotel is underway which will provide even more jobs for local people.

The mayor went on to say that the problem he hoped to deal with in this meeting was concerned with the sort of tourism Deià wanted to promote in the future and the control the village could assume in that choice. Until recently, the product Deià had to offer was Deià and its beauty. The vecinos maintained and supplied the product. But the future prospects for Deianencs had become more and more difficult as land prices rose beyond the means of most Deià-born people while work options decreased. The limited product and expanded demand had raised the prices of land, houses, rents, and the costs of building. Most Deianencs were now priced out of the market. Young people who wanted to marry and remain in Deià were unable to find skilled work or housing. They had been forced over the past twenty years to migrate to Palma or Soller to find work and housing. Thanks to the new jobs, road improvement, and the new hotel project, the situation was being redressed; the present generation of eighteen- to twenty-five-year-olds would not be forced to leave, as was the case with the previous generation. Unlike other parts of the island where all that remained were pensioners and foreigners, Deià was developing from within.

The mayor said the new Es Clot road had been built 'as a means to alleviate the difficulties of getting to the Clot for car drivers and lorries, especially those making essential deliveries of butane gas and foodstuffs to the grocer, as well as for rubbish collectors and sanitation trucks'. When asked how far the project to cover the stream would extend, the mayor said that, 'The actual project cannot be divulged until it is accepted by the council or it might create a degree of speculative buying that would make the lands which gained access rise in value again out of reach of any Deianenc. Once the project is approved then there is a time for criticism and/or amendments'. He was relying on passive acceptance.

The overall picture seemed to indicate that the Deianencs allowed the mayor to articulate their ideas and attitudes. Their loud agreements and comments throughout the proceedings were in accord with what the mayor was saying and openly angry and hostile to any replies made by what was clearly 'the opposition'. The City Council was composed of a building contractor, two of his construction crew, the butcher, two opposition councillors, and the mayor. It was common knowledge that the bank in Deià was a branch of the Banca Catalana in Palma where the mayor was a manager. The bank assistant in the new Deià bank was the mayor's sister-in-law. There was no doubt that she was the best suited for this position but many still saw this as one more sign of nepotism. The girls employed at the water-bottling factory were the daughters of influential men in the village and men who supported the mayor's party. Certainly these people reaped the benefits derived from supporting the mayor.

The excuse that the project to build the road over the stream had to be kept quiet until it was passed was clearly absurd since the most likely speculators were either the council members or those directly connected with the mayor. In fact, the project grew out of a landowner's wish to build three houses on his land and the necessity for an access road in order to carry out his plans. The mayor saw a way to combine the interests of the village with those of the landowner. If the landowner allowed the road to be cut through his property, the village would request the funding and permits for a public road. The landowner would have his access road and the problem of a wider road to Es Clot would also be solved.

In private conversations many Deianencs will concede that they did not fully agree with all aspects of the mayor's projects. They are aware that the mayor and a few entrepreneurs have benefited personally from the projects. However, the letter from the 'Vecinos y Residentes de Deià' had allowed the mayor to direct the attention of the villagers away from his manipulative strategies and focus it on the improvements he had introduced into the village. Foreigners were thus presented as detrimental to the progress of the village.

At the meeting it became clear that the term estrangers meant foreigners, outsiders, persons who did not have to be in Deià. The shouting and side comments ('Go home if you don't like it!') throughout the proceedings had made that clear enough. They were telling foreigners that they could pack up and leave if they no longer found the beauty, tranquillity, services, economy, and politics of Deià to their liking. Deianencs had to go on living there. Deianencs belonged to the place which held 'their ancestors', 'their history', 'their livelihood', and 'their future'. Its beauty was partly 'their creation' and largely the product of 'their efforts'. Deianencs were subject to the national economic and political system, and it was their prerogative to interpret, manipulate, maintain, or direct their actions within that system toward their own interests and future.

This was not the first time that foreigners had been criticised. Even the opposition socialist councillor had written a letter in *S'Encruia* commenting on the lack of participation by foreigners in village activities. Foreigners in Deià were obviously in an ambiguous situation: they were criticised if they stayed out of local activities and when they became involved. As the meeting progressed (or digressed) it became more and more evident that the problem was not really the contents of the letter but the new meanings behind the terms Deianenc and estranger and the rights of persons other than Deianencs to assume membership in the village. One Mallorquin woman, three mainland Spaniards, two Catalans, two Englishmen, three Americans, and two locally born foreigners who signed the letter 'Vecinos y Residentes de Deià' were being told they were not qualified as representatives of 'the village'. The composers and signers of the letter had assumed that being registered voters or residents with long-term standing gave them the right to call themselves vecinos of Deià. Their assumptions were based on their status as property owners, educated persons, and their long-term personal associations with a few Deianencs. They felt these qualities legitimated their comments on the development of the village. What they were ignoring was that their 'ideal' of the village no longer coincided with that of their hosts. In fact, it insulted Deianencs to realise that these people accused them of destroying their own heritage and judged them incapable of planning their own future.

As the meeting progressed, the mayor was quite careful and explicit in his choice of words when he said, 'This meeting is concerned with defining the sort of tourism Deià wants to promote in the future and the control the village should assume in that choice. Until now, Deianencs have supplied and served the product "Deià" as described and desired by others. Now we want to reidentify the product in our own terms; to put our needs, those of our children and their future in the forefront, before it is too late'.

The mayor convinced them that through his form of 'democratic' leadership Deianencs had begun to come out from under the dominance of governors, appointed mayors, senyors, and foreigners who had gained their status at the cost of the services given by Deianencs. Deianencs was the term which could express the solidarity and self-governing potential of the villagers. By identifying the opposition they were no longer to be victims of circumstances beyond their own control. They were well aware of their continued dependence on some forms of tourism, but until now the village had had no say in the sort of persons that settled or visited. Now that most people had economically viable means to maintain themselves, they felt confident to impose some limits and qualifications on the sort of tourists they wanted to attract in the future.

The mayor was suggesting that Deianencs reconsider their relationships with long-term foreign residents in light of the changing circumstances of local life. He pointed out that experience proved that quality services could attract quality tourism and a greater profit. Hotel Es Moli, the two pensions, and three of the restaurants in the village worked to capacity on a seasonal basis and closed for three to six months each year. Establishments that provided services necessary to the year-round maintenance of village life, i.e., bakery, pharmacy, post office, and food stores had begun to close twice weekly during the winter. Employment laws were designed for the tourist economy. Seasonal establishments could contract personnel for six- or nine-month periods. Unemployment benefit based on a percentage of the contracted wage was made available to cover the off-season. As long as one did not collect unemployment for eighteen consecutive months, a person could work half or three-quarters of each year and be paid unemployment for the remaining quarter or half. Perhaps further development of seasonal tourism could prevent the intervention of outsiders in village affairs.

The mayor's interpretation of the Vecinos' letter implied that it expressed a desire to maintain a 'paradise' envisaged by outsiders who assumed they knew better than the locals what was good for them. It implied that the local populace lacked aesthetic awareness and was not capable of making constructive decisions about their own village; that they should have remained 'quaint' villagers riding donkeys up and down narrow unpaved roads, living in simple peasant houses and providing the desired images and services, status and power to outsiders who, in exchange, provided them with their livelihood.

This had not been the intention of the writers. They felt they were expressing concerns shared by many people in the village. They accepted the realities of modern transport, the desire for upward mobility among the local population, and welcomed the advantages now open to young people in Deià. Rather, the letter was meant to deal with the negative problems created by modernity. The writers felt that many of the projects seemed to be planned by a few for the benefit of the few, while sanitation, water rights, and long-term public planning were neglected. Rather than directly accuse the mayor of corruption, by pointing out his personal involvement and potential profit from all the projects completed, they chose to list what they considered superficial problems and intended their letter to open a dialogue between the mayor, the council, and the dissenting public, with Belles Arts as mediators. Instead, they provided a perfect target which the mayor could use in order to divert attention from potential internal conflicts.

The mayor's presentation was forceful, authoritative, and calculated. He espoused the just cause of Deianencs to survive in a village which had seen such radical change during the past twenty years: 'It has moved from an agricultural backwater to a recognised beauty spot dealing with increased numbers of outsiders. However, the "natives" are just beginning to catch up with the changes.' He excited the emotions, the people's sense of identity based on the land they had occupied for generations and were trying to develop in a positive, constructive way for the future of their descendants. There was no room for the consideration of 'erroneous complaints that disregarded the livelihood and future of Deianencs'. He mentioned a number of projects which he and the council had rejected on the grounds that they would be detrimental to the landscape and beauty of Deià, thus dismissing the insinuation that Deianencs were not aware of the preservation of their environment and heritage. He cleverly twisted every word in the letter to enhance his position. Chuckles, sighs, and anger were produced from the audience in response to the intonations and inflections he used when reading some of the points highlighted in the letter.

An American signatory, who had been a resident for twenty years, tried to clarify the Vecinos' intentions but he was quickly silenced by shouts from the audience, including: 'If you don't like the way we do things here, go home. There are planes leaving every three minutes for all parts of the world.' Then the mayor opened a file and began to draw forth papers concerning the ten properties this man had registered in his name, the 'illegal' building that had taken place on those properties, the City Hall's leniency in ignoring these developments, and the absence of formal rent contracts verifying income from the properties he rented to 'friends'. The mayor called on the builder who was employed full-time by this man, to corroborate these details. The mayor's research had been thorough and his statements were verified by first-hand witnesses and

City Hall records. In contrast, the Vecinos' letter was shown to be full of inaccuracies and hearsay. The mayor succeeded in demeaning the content of the letter, the false superiority of its 'educated' writers, and their misguided advice. As the mayor said, 'If they were intelligent people they would have backed up their claims with examples'.

Until the receipt of this letter, the locals had 'turned a blind eye' to much that was going on in the foreign colony. As long as the personal desires of the foreigners had not been articulated in any public expression that presented them as a community in contrast to the collective interests of the village, they could live comfortably side by side. Unless something occurred which directly involved a local and a foreigner, everyone practised the adage 'live and let live'. At times, it seemed each group carried on as though the other were not there. There were occasional confrontations between persons who lived near one another but that occurred between locals and locals as often as between locals and foreigners. The verbal aggression and hostility expressed toward foreigners by some of the men at the meeting were evidence that discomfort had existed for a long time and had finally found an outlet.

It became clear that there was an absence of mutually understood values and socially accepted behaviour by which locals and foreigners guide their actions. The builder speaking out against his employer is an example of this. Traditionally, the bond between a builder and his patron went beyond their work relationship. In this case, the builder showed loyalty to the village over that toward his emloyer while the long-term resident employer assumed the 'old' values still held. In the past, the builder derived his social identity from the House he constructed and it was he who helped to prepare the grave for the patron and any members of his family. This particular builder was from Soller and had become known in Deià by his employer's House name, but he had come to realise he had been paid to do 'a job' not maintain a social relationship. The mayor cunningly used an effective device to show that when village unity is in question it will take precedence over any outside commitments. He made it clear that 'vecinos' were those who shared more than geographic space.

One man who spoke up many times during the meeting had recently returned to Deià after working for fifty years in France. He said: 'Men from Deià were forced to emigrate to South America, the United States and later to France. Many never came "home" and others like myself managed to return only for our final years. To us, "coming home" means participating, helping the village to maintain itself and grow.

Foreigners can stay, they should stay if they can help us today, not by idealising our past which may seem pleasing to them but was oppressive to us, but by taking an active part in securing our young people's future.' The meeting made it clear to all who attended that Deianencs meant those who belonged to Deià by birth and marriage but also through social, economic, and political commitment, and that this sense of belonging had been maintained with constant effort and against difficult circumstances.

Party Politics

The first democratically elected mayor served one and a half terms, during which time he managed to unite a pressure group that spoke louder and harsher than any opposition. Men who had previously stayed in the background were animated by the issues he addressed, improvements he instigated, his forcefulness, and the strength of his convictions. Although he was from mainland Spain himself, he had all the right credentials, was married to the daughter of one of Deià's oldest families whose father had been the longest standing mayor, was educated and a manager in a bank. Halfway into his second term, he resigned. He was appointed Director of the Foreign Department of Banca Catalana in Palma, and the demands of this position were seen by the bank to conflict with his responsibilities as a village mayor.

As mentioned in a previous section, he supported the opposition councillor (PSOE) in the special elections called to replace him but was overruled by his party members (UM) from Palma, who turned up in support of the UM candidate. There was a small body of PSOE (the opposition has been made up of members of the same two or three families for at least three generations) who at least had the opportunity to voice their opinions, but the long-entrenched conservatism and stubbornness of the voters from the other ten or twelve families won out.

The new mayor, elected in 1984, and the one who followed him two years later were brothers.[16] The elder was neither prepared for nor particularly interested in the job. Their family had been involved in village political life for generations which made them the obvious choice of the local conservatives. When the first brother was elected, there were only two parties to deal with. A cabinet of five conservative councillors (three men and two women) and one from the opposition was elected with him. The second brother had five parties competing with him so that the votes were more dispersed, but the councillors still ended up as five conservative and one from the opposition.

Road development continued to be the focus of local conflict during the first brother's term and was the main issue in the election campaign and party splits that occurred prior to the 1986 election of the second brother. This time the dissidents were mostly young Catalan residents of Llucalcari (the small hamlet along the road from Deià to Soller included within the jurisdiction of the municipality of Deià). In April 1986 they attended a council meeting where they presented their objections to a new road being cut through the pine forests that descended to the rocky cliffs and the many small coves below the hamlet of Llucalcari. The road was being built on private property but they asserted that it was being paid for by a company which was owned by the same parties as La Residencia Hotel.

The conflict was once again expressed in terms of insiders and outsiders; between 'the village' or 'Deianencs' and a group who presented themselves as 'ecologically informed' and wanted to preserve an idyllic way of life in a perfectly unspoiled setting. However, the village council made it clear that they had thoroughly considered the matter and felt it had its priorities straight and was not really interested in interventions from 'outsiders'. The only difference this time was that the people being called outsiders were legally entitled to their own opinions and to a vote in local affairs.

Catalans are seldom referred to as outsiders. They are forasters (Spaniards from other parts of the country), but they share a language and a heritage with those of the Balearic Islands. Despite these common features or perhaps due to them, Catalans are seen to be more of a threat to village cohesion than some foreigners. They have voting rights and many who have settled in Deià give the locals the impression that because they are educated they assume airs of superiority over Mallorquins. In times of conflict this sort of Catalan is referred to as an outsider. At other times, their support is cultivated.

The objectors filed an official complaint in Palma. Then in May, when it was to be brought up at the Deià council meeting, they were there to offer additional evidence in the form of documents and photographs to substantiate their claim that the road development was not just a narrow agricultural road (as stated in the permit issued to the constructors by the City Hall) but a wide expanse that had been formed by cutting down dozens of pine trees, blasting through large stone boulders, and destroying a major part of the natural landscape. Llucalcari was a favourite beach for residents and weekend visitors from other parts of the island. It was noted for its beautiful pine forest which led to the boulders and clear waters below where one could sunbathe, swim, and feel part of unspoiled natural surroundings. There were no bars, commerce, or construction anywhere in sight.

This meeting (in contrast to the previously described meeting of 1982 over the Ca'n Carindo road) was conducted with extreme protocol and exaggerated decorum. The secretary read out the day's agenda. Each article was discussed, voted upon, and a solution found. The last point to be addressed was the matter of the Llucalcari road. The socialist councillor read out the official complaint in a calm and articulate manner, interspersing at every possible occasion a direct comment to the mayor: i.e., 'and our respected mayor will recall' or 'at the time our esteemed mayor replied', etc. Little discussion followed as the mayor suggested the project be halted temporarily while the council reexamined the actual activities and construction that had been completed, and a full report was scheduled for the next meeting (to be held one month later).

On Sunday, 31 May 1986 (two weeks after the first meeting), the village held a *Romeria* (pilgrimage) to Llucalcari. Eighty-two Deianencs walked the four kilometers to Llucalcari and another hundred drove in cars. They were recreating the annual village celebration of the *mes de Maria* (Month of Mary) which had been neglected (even forgotten or never experienced by some) for the past fifteen or twenty years. Everyone was asked to bring a *truita de patates* (potato omelet known in English as a 'Spanish' omelet), and the City Hall provided tomatoes, peppers, onion, and olive oil to make a Mallorquin *trompo* (salad made from the above ingredients all finely cut and mixed with oil), and huge loaves of 'peasant' bread (made with heavy stone-ground flour). People brought homemade wine, olives, sausage, and fruit, and many women made *coques* (a pastry with vegetables or fruit on top). All the food was placed on a blanket in the middle of a flat area in the forest of Llucalcari and shared by all in attendance. After lunch the young went swimming and the older folk sat on cushions or chairs in the shaded area above the sea. A Palma businessman who rents a house in the forest brought out cognac and coffee after the meal, which made the group feel welcome in the spot it had so long neglected. At sunset, a mass was held in the small chapel at Llucalcari and the village was united in prayer to the holy Virgin. From the villager's point of view, the outing was a huge success. There had been a large turnout of people, old and young, to an event which reanimated a traditional religious celebration and expressed village cohesion through 'traditional' food, commensality, and ritual. It brought together those whose animosities had caused them to fall out with one another and reminded them of the spirit of community and belief in the virgin which unites them all.

The celebration had come about through the suggestion of a twenty-year-old village girl who commented that she had heard her grandmother and mother talk about the wonderful times they used to have when everyone walked to Llucalcari for the Month of Mary celebrations. It wasn't long before she and some friends had organised most of the village to join in and the date was set. This explanation of 'spontaneous enthusiasm' for traditional activities, seemed to coincide rather too closely with all the discussion concerning the road being built in Llucalcari. The village shared the mayor's view that the road did no harm and, in fact, was a great improvement. The forest had been badly neglected over the past few years and the prevention of forest fires had become a primary village concern each summer. The land was idle and the overgrowth out of hand, so what could be better than to have private interests take on the expense and responsibility of maintenance. In this way, the entire area would become another asset to add to the image of the village, its beautiful beaches, elegant residences, and well-kept landscape.

The Romeria was a perfect way for Deianencs to express the fact that Llucalcari was part of their world and that the decisions about what went on there were as important to them as anything in Deià. Their support of this controversial road project was symbolised in the act of pilgrimage (return to a traditional sight for religious observance) and through the participation of so many community members in the religious celebration that marked the occasion. The fact that the mayor was the first to drive his car down the new road as far as he could, and then joined the other villagers on foot, added the symbolic gesture that made the event appear to this participant-observer to be politics disguised as social and religious celebration. The political content was also evident in the absence of the opposition councillor, his parents, many aunts, uncles, and cousins. Had this been a political rally with supporters waving banners, it could not have presented a clearer picture – that of a unified body paving its way to the future by sharing community activities, food, nature, and God's blessings. The village, or at least a major part of it, approved of the road.

The Lluchalcari road project made it clear that the newly found power of Deianencs to assert their separateness or priorities over foreigners could be diminished if the opposition was made up of recognised voters, forasters, with whom, as Spanish citizens, they shared legal equality. It was important to keep Deianencs united and the combination of 'tradition' and religion gave local voters the impetus that was needed. However, the issue of the road continued to cause dissension within parties and among members of the various political parties. If Deianencs could not prevent internal disagreements from flaring up, they would have an even more difficult time controlling outside votes. If Deianencs could not get along with one another when faced with outside intervention, their 'Deianencness' would be more at risk than ever before.

In the summer before the elections, an article appeared in a major tabloid magazine called *Interviú* detailing the rise of Axel Ball as a major entrepreneur and developer in Deià and blaming him for the destruction of Llucalcari. Deià and its road project became a national issue. The matter of the road was discussed at the first meeting of the national parliament in September of 1986. The work was again halted until a decision was made. Local elections went ahead in June and the community of 340 voters (of which about 75 to 80 percent voted) had to chose from among thirty-five candidates representing five (UM, AP, PSOE, GOP and Communist) political parties. Proportional votes allotted seats to the candidates in order of their placement on their party's ticket and the number of votes that party received. The mayor and his councillors kept their positions when local conservatives won five seats, and the opposition retained its seat by only three votes, due to the dispersal of votes among the many parties.

Work and controversy over the road continued. By the end of 1987 the road was three-quarters finished and the discussions still heated. The work had been halted, fines levied and paid, and work begun again. The maximum penalty for not complying with a permit was a 25,000 peseta fine and halting of work for thirty days. New permits had then to be requested for slightly altered plans and, after the waiting period, work was resumed. Fines were imposed twice and, each time, the City Hall agreed to the altered plan. The road was completed by the spring of 1988.

A massive iron gate was installed at the entrance to the road. A bus brought guests from the hotel down to the beach below, where platforms had been built to hold beach chairs, and cold drinks and salads were served by a hotel employee. Every house registered in the village census was entitled to an entry card which would permit access to the Llucalcari beach through the hotel gate. However, few households knew this. A guard was employed by the hotel to control entry to those who carried pass cards, and two additional municipal policeman were hired to deal with the increased traffic during the 'summer season' in Deià. One of their new duties was to patrol Llucalcari during the day to keep 'the peace'. It was clear that Hotel La Residencia and the Llucalcari road were considered to be important additions to 'the village'.

The local opposition councillor informed the newspapers of the closure of the road, hoping to draw outside help in the fight to control this sort of privatisation of areas that once had public access. A large contingent of members of the Ecology Party (GOP) arrived in Deià, were joined by a few locals, and made their way to Llucalcari in an attempt to use the new road. When the guard asked for their passes, they said none were needed and continued to walk down the road exclaiming as they went, '*Que disastre, que horror*' (what a disaster, what a horror). The guard called the Guardia Civil to ask for help but they said that they were understaffed and, as the problem had occurred on private property, they could not intervene. The Ecologists carried on down to the beach, had a swim and some sun, and returned once again up the road, criticising the destruction of the natural environment caused by this project. It should be noted that the usual access for visitors was via a footpath through the forest to the sea, and this remained accessible throughout the discussions about the road.

The Romeria was celebrated again in 1988 and even more people attended than the previous year. Over half the people walked and the others drove their cars along the highway from Deià down the road to Llucalcari, where they were waved through the iron gate and onto the new road. When the group arrived at the picnic spot, they were surprised to find the gardener of La Residencia standing over an ice chest filled with ice and drinks for the group. There were also large rubbish bins in different corners to facilitate the cleanup afterward. These were both gifts from 'La Resi' (the local shortened form of Hotel La Residencia) to make the village outing more 'refreshing'. The hotel's designer-director Axel Ball was invited by the mayor and sat with him under a massive pine tree, sharing his lunch and the hotel's drinks. There had been notices placed around the village welcoming *tothom* (everyone) to attend, but Axel and myself were the only 'foreigners' present. Almost everyone asked me what I thought about the road and expressed their positive opinions. They all felt it was a vast improvement to a neglected area. A large number of villagers were once again celebrating their unity in social and religious terms, expressing their political views through the place they chose to celebrate and the guests they invited.

Mallorquins from the city, Catalans, other mainland Spaniards as well as foreigners have had to cut through olive or pine groves to gain access to land they purchased on remote areas of the mountainside. The cost of cutting access roads and bringing in electricity and building materials was as much or more than the cost of the property, but according to the buyers, the views and privacy they had warranted the additional costs. These are all private roads that individuals have built, sometimes with the agreement of neighbours whose houses were below or above and sometimes despite their objections. In one case, the neighbours have no access to a road that passes in front of their house. New complaints crop up now and again if one or the other user neglects to close a gate or leaves debris on the road, but they seldom reach village proportions. They are private problems among the few people concerned.

On the day of the Romeria in 1988 many foreigners were driving up a precariously winding mountain road that had been cut through olive groves and dry-stone walled terraces to reach the newly renovated, five-hundred-year-old house of an American resident. Recently retired, he had been attracted to the house by its solitude and the vast view of the village it afforded. He had purchased the house 'when things were cheap' (in the 1960s) and carried out the renovations over the years as he could afford them. It had become obvious by the early 1980s that the 'romantic' donkey trail that led to his front door would not make the transporting of building materials very economical. After a few years of negotiating to share the costs with the other three homeowners that might benefit, he succeeded in getting the road constructed. It is treacherous but manageable and certainly facilitates access to the few houses on its way to the top. The different reactions to these private roads and the Llucalcari road need to be understood.

It seems that individuals have a difficult time in seeing their own actions in a critical light. What is personally desired and attainable is acquired, often in spite of ecological or social repercussions. But those same people sit in judgement of others, criticising them for the same infractions they have committed themselves. The Catalan couple, who instigated the action against the Llucalcari road, built a road up to their own house on the mountainside above that hamlet. It is as though certain projects and people become the objects of criticism either because they are too open or public about what they are doing or because their projects arouse envy or greed among those who are feeling guilt or frustration from their own lives or actions. From the objectors' viewpoint, the fact that one cuts a road 'through the wilderness' and restricts use to oneself and one's family is quite different than cutting a road through land which has always had public access. Not only is the area privatised but it is being used for commercial gain. Ecological arguments are applicable to all of these examples but became an issue only in the latter case.

According to the general consensus among many foreigners and Catalans who live in Deià, it is all right to open 'a way into the wilderness' to reach a private dwelling, but it is not all right to build a private road for commercial use. The argument is that some areas must remain untouched at all costs to preserve the natural surroundings; but who is to decide to which areas this should be applied? The objectors agree that some expansion of the village and modern development is inevitable, but if there are no limits they believe the balance of life will be upset beyond repair. They do not see that the roads they have altered have also aided development. If a road is made to a single house in a remote area the land around that road increases in value and becomes more attractive to prospective buyers. If a new house is to be built in a remote area and a road is made to reach it, any land or houses that it passes on its route have access to its use. Graves had cut the road to the cala hoping to prevent large-scale development by restricting its use, but his hopes were dashed and his road has become a major artery bringing people from every direction into the little cala, where once only a few fishermen kept their boats and hung their nets and local people spent a quiet Sunday. The Ca'n Carindo road, which aroused such a heated confrontation, facilitates access to the lower village and has become the parking place for a dozen cars owned by persons living nearby, some of whom had been adamantly opposed to it.

The conflict of interests expressed in these various examples brought to light the ambivalence that had underlined coexistence for ages. The exclusion of the old men of the village from playing cards and taking up space in a local bar that tourists might occupy was only the first in a series of events that revealed the latent tensions. The mayor's personal dispute with a foreigner over the purchase of a house, and his efforts to impress officialdom beyond the village to secure his own professional advancement also served as catalysts to arouse village emotions, provoke discussion, and bring into focus 'local identity and values' in contrast to changing realities. The local tensions created by personal greed and ambition were seen to be the side effects of mixing too much with outsiders. Therefore, only by restructuring that relationship could the village survive.

The various disputes over roads made it clear that any decision concerning the future of the village and its development was tied to concepts of insiders and outsiders. However, it was also evident that the meanings of these terms were unclear. Some foreigners were considered to be more insiders than some Catalans or even other local villagers if their activities benefited the interests of the wider village. It was not just a matter of birth that made one a Deianenc. This identity marker could be extended to include or exclude people according to the circumstances. As a shifting identity, Deianenc is more an idea than a reality. The concept of insiders and outsiders or estrangers, forasters, or Deianencs are relational. When one is in agreement, is involved in decision making or investment, or passively accepts the decisions made by others in authority, one becomes part of the village. If one objects to decisions, he or she becomes marginalised. This can apply as much to locals as to foreigners. When public events and discourse suggest that insiders and outsiders, foreigners or Deianencs are fixed identities, the realities of everyday prove otherwise.

Ideas concerning identity, belonging, community, and the environment are social. Land once used for agriculture, owned by elites, cared for by locals, and converted into job-producing development was seen as a positive form of environmentally aware modernisation. The land and any building on it would once again be cared for by locals but under proper employment conditions that allowed them to reap the rewards of their labour. The village council and its members were no longer willing to 'wander without a clear direction'. If they planned correctly, the roads they approved would lead to a future of prosperity for the village and maintain the 'ethos of paradise' that the village had projected to the outside for centuries.The differences among people who live in the village today are drawn more in terms of those who want to 'open the village' to planned investment in construction which will produce jobs, housing, and livelihoods for their children and grandchildren and those who fear these activities will spoil 'their paradise'. Is there a means to encompass the realities of progress with the ideals of paradise?

Notes

1. This is the title of an article about the difficulties imposed by schools, the administration, the media as well as the demands and expectations of modern life on the teaching and use of Mallorquí/Catalan. Mallorquí/Catalan is used more and more in public circles but continues to be considered a second language by some people who relegate it to domestic and social uses because 'for important uses we have Castilian' (Grimalt 1980).
2. In the 1988 fiesta there was an exhibition of photographs taken before 1940. There were dozens of photos of dances, fiestas, musical recitals by the local band, as well as wedding, communion, and baptism celebrations, all of which were held in Es Porxo. This brought the past into the present. A sense of timelessness, generations of family ties, and social space were combined as one place and one time.
3. Reference has been made in Chapter 2 to the effects on the road caused by an influential landowner.
4. The stone bench on the main road at the entrance to Es Porxo was donated by an English woman who lived in the village from 1917 to 1925. Another farther along was donated by a Catalan artist who bought a house in Deià sixty years ago.
5. The publication of *I Claudius* in 1934 made him solvent again.
6. All water rights in Deià are privately owned. There was no sewage or waste system until 1994. Prior to that date, each house was meant to have its own septic tank. However, many old houses owned by locals and some foreigners have only pipes which run all waste into the streambed nearest their house. This is all thoroughly washed away in winter, but during the four to six months each year when there is no water in the stream there are obviously disturbing odoriferous repercussions in these areas. Sewage pipes have now been installed under the roads and a sewage processing plant is operative, but only about 30 percent of village houses have been connected. Each homeowner must pay the connection costs (£1,000) for his or her house.
7. I mentioned before that this room has never been used. There is only one small window and none of the hubbub of a café. The men who have gone to see it say it is too closed in.
8. Before this, doctors held surgery in their own houses. The present doctor, who lives outside the village, was always having to use the premises of friends. He used the lower room of an English woman's house for three years before it was refurbished and became an art gallery. By coincidence, this house has been referred to by the village as *Ca'l Metge* (House of the Doctor) for at least fifty years. The village doctor and his heirs lived there until the English woman bought the house in 1972. The doctor and his house are well remembered in village lore. There are three holes in the front door which are left over from the early years of the Civil War when the Guardia Civil came looking for a known rebel and mistakenly got the house of the doctor. In his fright, the doctor scurried out the bedroom window to hide in the hills and told his wife not to answer the door. When no one answered, the Guardia fired three shots at the door to make sure no one was inside.

9. This was the name of the House that originally owned the land on which the road was to be built. The land and House had been separated by partiple inheritance: one son got the land and another the House.
10. A law passed in 1975 required builders to cede to the City Hall a certain percentage of large land developments so that essential services – drainage, sewage, basic amenities – could be provided to the area. The City Hall has received land from projects given permissions since 1975, but none of the services have been provided.
11. Cala d'Or is a development on the southeast side of the island. The area has grown from a wasteland into a thriving tourist centre. The small indigenous population has either been bought out, moved away, or runs curio shops. The area is composed of high-rise hotels, bars, restaurants, apartments, and villas built by foreign investors, and most of those who own businesses and provide services are from other parts of the island, the mainland, and Europe.
12. Third parties: during the Franco regime people would often try to find a third party, an intermediary not directly involved in village politics, to act as a representative of faction interests (presented as village interests) to Palma officialdom. Outsiders or foreigners were ideal. The planners would thus remain anonymous while their concerns were given precedence over others within the village. Robert Graves acted as an intermediary 'third party' on a number of occasions.
13. It was full of gutters, holes, and narrow places where two cars could not pass, requiring one or the other to back precariously uphill or down.
14. When pensions were processed through the post office, there were often delays of two or three weeks.
15. Her mother was born in Deià and married a Palma man. Her daughter was born in Palma but spent every summer with her grandmother at Sa Fonda. She married a Palma man and they returned to Deià to set up this new business.
16. Early laws (1830) concerning the selection of candidates for municipal offices stipulated that siblings, first, second, or third cousins or affines of the retiring official could not run for that same office. This was intended to prevent 'conflict of interest'. There was a footnote that said 'except in the most extenuating circumstances'. Since the same families have dominated politics in Deià for years, I imagine there were many such instances.

Conclusions

The description of the changing social, political, and economic relations between local and foreign residents in Deià over the past 120 years presents a number of recurring patterns of struggle and conflict, albeit between different groups composed of people with changing attitudes, interests, and behaviours. These conflicts and the resulting compromises have provided a sense of local Deianenc identity. Tensions between locals and monks, tax collectors, landlords, tenants, or foreigners within the village seldom led to open confrontation. However, these recurring tensions served to increase a sense of local identity in contrast to 'opposition' and motivated a struggle for survival. Opposition has provided a purpose to those who have formed the village over time, and has aided them in constituting relationships and formulating a sense of identity. It has also helped to preserve and maintain some semblance of continuity despite the changes they have experienced. These tensions, which continually challenge the status quo, have enabled Deianencs to define, develop, and sustain their sense of belonging to a community where different cultural values and aspirations, brought in by a changing group of outsiders, have been a constant threat to any shared concept of local life. From the early days of monastic leaders to feudal lords and domineering senyors, local experiences have included 'outsiders', guests of artistic leanings and foreign developers of high finance. Deianencs' own lives, values, and experiences changed as the inside and outside influences merged, split, mixed, or confronted one another.

All the years of living with foreigners has shown them, at first hand, how disruptive life can be when people do not maintain some order in their lives based on long-standing values and rules. The threat from these other cultural values within the village has been confronted by creating a local sense of collective identity based on the values of marriage, family, a household, and relations with kin who share common experiences in Deià. The term Deianenc combines history, culture, ethnicity, and environment into a unity. Drawing on traditional aspects of their past, Deianencs have found ways to combat the disruptions caused by outsiders while taking full advantage of the social and economic opportunities offered by them.

Certainly, many of the developments within Deià were made possible by national and international events, growth, and advancement. The arrival of foreigners to the island and specifically to Deià was determined by the world events that affected the areas from which the visitors came. All those who found their way to Deià brought their 'cultural baggage' and particular predilections with them, and each found his or her own niche. The Archduke, displaced by a fallen monarchy, found solace among the trees and mountains of the Deià coast. Robert Graves, trying to overcome his Great War experiences, sought a peaceful spot for his and Laura Riding's 'ideal community'. On Graves's return after the Civil War with his wife Beryl and their children, Deià became 'a shelter, the place he chose to isolate himself from the literary circles of his time and the mechanisation of society' (L. Graves 1994). Later, German artists and philosophers seeking to understand their country's turmoil and American artists subsidised by their government for their participation in World War II were all allowed to move effortlessly into Deià life. These men and women found exactly what they were looking for, both aesthetically and emotionally: an imposing environment, as close to 'paradise' as one could be on earth, that combined the marvels of nature and a traditional culture where home, family, economics, religion, politics, and community were integrated. A place where one could be insulated from the outside world and yet not obliged to join those who formed the inside world.

The relationships, personalities, and characteristics of these foreigners, and the Deianencs they had dealings with, reflect the social, economic, and political structures of each period. The particular manner in which Deià developed and the process of change which has altered the social organisation, political and economic activities, gender relations, and the very concepts of 'the environment' and 'the village' have been greatly influenced by the various outsiders who have resided there over the past century. Mallorquin,

Catalan, European, and American businessmen, politicians and academics, mainland Spaniards, the Archduke, British poets, international artists, writers, musicians, hippies, and the nouveaux riches of Europe and America have had their impact on the village we find today.

Unlike neighbouring villagers who put on peasant costumes a few hours each day to 'act out the past' and entertain the tourists with folk dances and tours through rooms of ancient buildings where famous foreigners spent one brief *Winter in Mallorca*, the Deianencs have let the outsiders become part of their everyday lives. Today, most of local life is enmeshed with foreign residents. Some of the children born in Deià to foreign parents are now Spanish citizens, and in the municipal elections of June 1990 the Deià-born daughter of American residents was one of the proposed councilors on the Socialist Party ballot. Spaniards from Catalonia and other areas of mainland Spain have settled in the village and are taking an active interest in local politics. The power of Deianencs to assert their separateness or priorities over other recognised voters may be diminished in the future by the legal equality that all share as European Community citizens. Since 1992, any member of a European Common Market country residing in Deià can vote in municipal elections. Not many have used this opportunity to become informed or involved in the local decision-making process, but, in time, they may.

Over this century, the categories of insiders and outsiders have been contracted, expanded, and reinterpreted to fit the constantly changing realities of the society. Those included as insiders or outsiders are once again changing composition (F. Barth 1994). The boundaries and definitions of Deianencs as insiders and foreigners as outsiders will continue to shift back and forth according to the circumstances that arise in the future. The challenge will be to find a means of creating mutual tolerance between people of different ideologies. The greatest fear for Deianencs is that in twenty-five years' time, foreigners will outnumber Deianencs and the concept of insiders and outsiders may be reversed.

In all events, both insiders and outsiders have histories that give them a sense of being part of Deià. History can be structured by the victors and the vanquished or their experiences can be interwoven to create one 'local' history. Local identity or insider status, in the future, may well be based on 'local history', on knowledge of the landscape, names of Houses, streets, and people both living and dead. The myths of the past, of art and poetry, success or failure in paradise may be added to other pasts to add new dimensions to the stories told to future generations and each new visitor to Deià.

'Paradise' comes by way of ancient Persian to Latin. It refers to an enclosed garden: a 'cloister' (from Latin *clostrum*), an enclosed park or green, the pleasure park of Kings. Enclosed gardens are safe places to play, a place of freedom within set boundaries. In such a paradise one is both inside and outside. The boundaries are clear, the space is known, the people are familiar, the mysteries and fears of a wider world are contained. Life in Deià has served as paradise for many. When we speak of paradise we are considering questions of creation, nature, progress, technology, freedom, right and wrong. These are the issues that Deianencs are dealing with every day. By observing the complexity of the concepts of insiders and outsiders in Deià, we consider the contrasts, contradictions, and interactions of local and foreign values, hopes, and dreams and the 'realities' that prevent them or make them possible. For many in Deià, the ideal of paradise and the reality of everyday coalesce. Long-term residents and Deianencs have a commitment to the place and people with whom they share a past and a future. The village has been able to continue as a community with its own symbolic boundaries not despite outsiders but because of their presence. The rare fascination the landscape has exercised over the imagination of generations of outsiders has paved the way into the future for Deianencs.

The impact of world affairs is reflected in the changing concepts of insiders and outsiders in this small village. Insiders and outsiders have had different meanings at different times, and the conflicts and resulting compromises have provided a sense of history which allows each group to define, develop, adapt, and sustain their sense of belonging to a community where different social values and aspirations have been a constant threat to any shared concept of local life. The growth of the village and its path into the future will depend on the continued coexistence of resident locals and foreigners. If they are able to coalesce on major decisions concerning the village while respecting individual independence, there can be progress without destroying the fabric of local life or the environment they all value so highly.

Bibliography

Aceves, J. 1971. *Social Change in a Spanish Village.* London: Schenkman.

——— and W. Douglass (eds.). 1976. *The Changing Faces of Rural Spain.* Cambridge: Schenkman.

Adán, J.C. 1975. *La Historia de España Vista por Estranjeros.* Barcelona: Editorial Planeta.

Alcover, M.A. 1965. *Rondalles Mallorquines.* Mallorca: Editorial Moll.

Alomar, E.G. 1979. *Historia de las Islas Baleares, hasta el año 1800.* Mallorca.

Antoun, R.T. 1968. 'On the Significance of Names in an Arab Village'. *Ethnology* 7:58–170.

Ardener, S. (ed.). 1981. *Women and Space.* London: Croom Helm.

Arimany, M. 1965. *Diccionari Catalá General.* Barcelona.

Atholl, Duchess. 1938. *Searchlight on Spain.* London: Penguin.

Ayala, F. 1986. *La Imagen de España.* Madrid: Editorial Alianza.

Bailey, F.G. 1973. *Debate and Compromise.* Oxford: Blackwell.

Barcelo, M. 1975. 'Comentaris a un text sobre Mallorca del geograf, Al-Zuhri'. *Mayurqa* 14. Mallorca.

Barcelo Pons, B. 1970. *Evoluciòn reciente y estructura actual de la población en las Baleares.* Madrid: Consejo Superior de Investigaciones Cientificas.

Barrera González, A. 1990. *Casa, herencia y familia en la Cataluña rural.* Madrid: Editorial Alianza.

Barrett, R.A. 1978. 'Village Modernization and Changing Nicknaming Practices in Northern Spain'. *Journal of Anthropological Research* 34:92–108.

Barth, F. 1994. [1969] *Ethnic Groups and Boundaries: The Social Organisation of Cultural Difference.* Oslo: Universitetsforlaget.

Behar, R. 1986. *Santa María del Monte.* Princeton: Princeton University Press.

Bennassar, B. 1979. *The Spanish Character.* London: University of California Press.

Bernanos, George. 1938. *Le Cimetière Sur la Lune.* Paris.

Bestard, J. 1986. *Casa y Familia.* Palma, Mallorca: Institut d'Estudis Baleàrics.

Bisson, J. 1969. 'Origin y decadenciá de la gran propriedad en Mallorca'. No. 665. BCCIN – Boletin de la Camara de Comercio, de Industria y Navegación de Palma de Mallorca.

Bloch, M. and S. Guggenheim. 1981. 'Compadrazco, Baptism and the Symbolism of Second Birth'. *Man* (N.S.) 16, 3:376–86.

Blok, A. 1981. 'Rams and Billy-Goats: A Key to the Mediterranean Code of Honor'. *Man* (N.S.) 16, 3:427–40.
Boissevain, J. 1974. *Friends of Friends*. Oxford: Blackwell.
———. 1979. 'Towards an Anthropology of the Mediterranean'. *Current Anthropology* 20, 1:81–94.
Bonner, A. 1980. *Plantas de les Balears*. Palma, Mallorca: Editorial Moll.
Borrow, G. 1899. *The Bible in Spain*. London: John Murray.
Bourdieu, P. 1977. *Outline of a Theory of Practice*. Cambridge: Cambridge University Press.
———. 1984 *Distinction*, London: Routledge and Keagan Paul.
Brandes, S.H. 1975. *Migration, Kinship and Community*. London: Academic Press.
———. 1981. 'Gender Distinctions in Montero Mortuary Rituals'. *Ethnology* 20, 3:177–190.
Braudel, F. 1975. *The Mediterranean and the Mediterranean World in the Age of Phillip II*. Vols. I and II. London: Fontana.
Braunstein, B. 1936. *The Chuetas of Majorca: Conversos and the Inquisition of Majorca*. New York: Columbia University Press.
Brenan, G. 1964. *The Spanish Labyrinth*. Cambridge: Cambridge University Press.
Brettet, C. 1986. *Men Who Migrate, Women Who Wait*. Princeton: Princeton University Press.
Capellà, L. 1977. *Mallorca i El Món Obrer*. Mallorca: Editorial Moll.
Caplan, P. 1987. *The Cultural Construction of Sexuality*. London: Tavistock.
Caro Baroja, J. 1946. *Los Pueblos de España*. Barcelona: Editorial Barna.
Carr, R. 1980. *Modern Spain 1875–1980*. Oxford: Oxford University Press.
Cela Conde, C. 1979. *Capitalismo y campesinado en la Isla de Mallorca, Siglo XXI*. Madrid: Editorial.
Chamberlin, F. 1927. *The Balearics and Their Peoples*. London: John Lane.
Christian, W.A. 1972. *Person and God in a Spanish Valley*. London: Seminar Press.
Coad, E.D. 1995. 'Painting and Sculpture: The Rejection of High Art', in H. Graham and J. Labanyi (eds.). *Spanish Cultural Studies*. Oxford: Oxford University Press.
Cohen, A. 1974. *Two Dimensional Man*. London: Routledge and Keagan Paul.
Cohen, A. P. (ed.). 1982. *Belonging: Identity and Social Organization in British Rural Cultures*. Manchester: Manchester University Press.
———. 1985. *The Symbolic Construction of Community*. Chichester: Ellis Harwood.
Collins, Roger. 1986. *The Basques*. Oxford: Blackwell.
Donat, F. 1983. *L'Arxiduc i El Criat*. Mallorca: Col.lecció Miramar.
Du Boulay, J. 1974. *Portrait of a Greek Mountain Village*. Oxford: Clarendon Press.
———. 1984. 'The Blood: Symbolic Relationships between Descent, Marriage, Incest Prohibitions and Spiritual Kinship in Greece'. *Man* (N.S.) 19, 4:533–566.
Fernandez, J. 1976. 'Poetry in Motion'. *New Literary History* 8:459–483.
Ferra, B. 1948. *El Archiduke Errante*. Mallorca: Ediciones La Cartoixá.
———. 1961. *Chopin y George Sand en Mallorca*. Mallorca: Ediciones La Cartoixá.
Foucault, M. 1976. *La Volonté de Savoir*. Paris: Gallimard.
Freeman, S. F. 1967. 'Religious Aspects of the Social Organisation of a Castilian Village'. *American Anthropologist* 69:34–49.
———. 1970. *Neighbours*. Chicago: University of Chicago Press.
Gasett de Saveur, A. 1901. *Voyage aux Iles Baleares et Pitiusas*. Paris: Hachette et C[ie].
Geertz, C. 1988. *Works and Lives*. Cambridge: Polity Press.
Geertz, H. 1979. 'The Meaning of Family Ties', in C. Geertz, H. Geertz and L. Rosen (eds.). *Meaning and Order in Moroccan Society*. Cambridge: Cambridge University Press.
Gilmore, D. 1980. The *People of the Plain*. New York: Columbia University Press.
———. 1982. 'Some Notes on Community Nicknaming in Spain'. *Man* 17, 4.

———. 1985. *From Franco to Constitutional Monarchy.* London: Quarter Books.
———. 1987. *Aggression and Community*. New Haven: Yale University Press.
Ginard, P. 1976. *Rondalles.* Mallorca: Arxiu de Tradiciones Populars-José J. de Olañeta.
Gould, S.J. 1982. *The Mismeasure of Man.* New York: Pelican Books.
Graham, H. and A. Sanchez. 1995. 'The Politics of 1992', in H. Graham and J. Labanyi (eds.). *Spanish Cultural Studies.* Oxford: Oxford University Press.
Graves, R. 1929. *Good-bye to All That.* London: Penguin.
———. 1948. *The White Goddess.* London: Faber and Faber.
———. 1953. *Collected Poems.* London: Penguin.
———. 1965. *Collected Short Stories.* London: Penguin.
———. 1972 'The Devils Advice to Storytellers', in *Collected Works.* London: Penguin.
Graves, R., and P. Hogarth (eds.). 1965. *Majorca Observed.* London: Cassell.
Greenwood, D. 1976. *Unrewarding Wealth.* Cambridge: Cambridge University Press.
Grimalt, J. 1979. 'Els Personatges De La Rondalla Meravellosa', in *Lectures Mallorquines.* Vol. I. Mallorca.
Harding, S. F. 1984. *Remaking Ibieca: Rural Life in Aragon Under Franco.* North Carolina: University of North Carolina Press.
Herzfeld, M. 1985. *The Poetics of Manhood.* Princeton: Princeton University Press.
Hirschon, R. 1981. 'Essential Objects and the Sacred: Interior and Exterior Space in an Urban Greek Locality', in S. Ardener (ed.). *Women and Space.* London: Croom Helm.
Hobsbawm and Ranger (eds.). 1984. *The Invention of Tradition.* Cambridge: Cambridge University Press.
Iszaevich, A. 1980. 'Household Renown: The Traditional Naming System in Catalonia'. *Ethnology* 19, 3:315–325.
Janer, M. G. 1980. *Sexe i Cultura a Mallorca: El Cançoner.* Mallorca: Editorial Moll.
Kenny, M. 1961. *A Spanish Tapestry.* London: Cohen and West.
Kenny, M. and D. Kertzner (eds.). 1983. *Urban Life in Mediterranean Europe.* Illinois: University of Illinois Press.
Kirkegaard, 1968. *Concluding unscientific postscript.* (trans. D.F. Svenson). Princeton: American Scandinavian Society.
Laurens, 1840. *Souvenir de un voyage d'art a Majorque.* Paris: A. Bertrand.
Lee, L. 1971. *As I Walked Out One Midsummer Morning.* London: Penguin.
Lévi-Strauss, C. 1968. *Elementary Structures of Kinship.* London: Ayre and Spottiswoode.
Lienhardt, P. 1975. 'The Interpretation of Rumour', in J. Beattie and R.G. Lienhardt (eds.). *Studies in Social Anthropology.* Oxford: Clarendon Press.
Lison-Tolosana, C. 1983. *Belmonte de los Caballeros.* Princeton: Princeton University Press.
———. 1988. 'The Beatae: Feminine Responses to Christianity in Sixteenth Century Castile', in W. James and D. Johnson (eds.). *Vernacular Christianity: Essays in the Anthropology of Religion.* Oxford: JASO.
Lourie, E. 1970. 'Free Moslems in the Balearics Under Christian rule in the Thirteenth Century'. *Speculum*, XLV, 4:624–649.
Lyttleton, A. 1973. *The Seizure of Power: Fascism in Italy.* London: Cape.
MacCormak, G. 1976. 'Reciprocity'. *Man.* Vol. 11, No. 1, March, pp. 89–103.
March, J. 1976. *El Archiduke.* Mallorca: Editorial Moll.
———. 1977 [1944]. *Jacks or Better.* New York: Harper and Row.
Massot i Muntaner, J. 1978. *Cultura i Vida a Mallorca Entre La Guerra i La Postguerra (1930–1950).* Barcelona: Publicaciones de Labadia de Montserrat.
Masur, A. 1984. 'Women's Work in Rural Andalucia'. *Ethnology* 23, 1.
Matthews, T. 1936. *The Moon's No Fool.* Deya: Seizin Press.

Moll, I., and J. Suau. 1979. 'Senyors i Pagesos a Mallorca (1718–1870)'. *Estudis d'Història Agrària,* 2:95–170. Barcelona: Curial Editions Catalans.

Montaner, P. 1989. 'The Islander'. *Insight Guides Mallorca and Ibiza: Menorca and Formentera.* Singapore: APA Publications Ltd.

Moore, H. 1986. *Space, Text and Gender.* Cambridge: Cambridge University Press.

Moore, K. 1976. *Those of the Street: The Catholic Jews of Mallorca.* Indiana: Notre Dame.

O'Prey, P. (ed.). 1982. *Broken Images. Selected Letters of Robert Graves 1926–1946.* London: Moyer Bell Ltd.

———. 1984. *Between Moon and Moon. Selected Letters of Robert Graves, 1946– 1972.* London: Moyer Bell Ltd.

Ott, S. 1981. *The Circle of Mountains: A Basque Shepherding Community.* Oxford: Clarendon Press.

Paul, Elliot. 1939. *The Life and Death of a Spanish Town.* London: Peter Davies.

Pericot Garcia, L. 1972. *The Balearic Islands.* London: Thames and Hudson.

Pina-Cabral. 1986. *Sons of Adam Daughters of Eve.* Oxford: Clarendon Press.

———. 1987. "Paved Roads and Enchanted Mooresses". *Man* (N.S.) 22, 4:715–735.

Pi-Sunyer, O. 1982. 'Two Stages of Technological Change in a Catalan Fishing Community', in E. Smith (ed.). *Those Who Live by the Sea.*

Pitt-Rivers, J. 1954. *The People of the Sierra.* Chicago: University of Chicago Press.

———. (ed.). 1963. *Mediterranean Countrymen: Essays in the Social Anthropology of the Mediterranean.* Paris: Mouton & Co.

———. 1971. 'On the Word Caste'. F.O. Beidelman (ed.). *The Translation of Culture.* London: Tavistock.

———. 1977. *The Fate of Shechem or the Politics of Sex.* Cambridge: Cambridge University Press.

Pons, J.P. 1976. *Notas para la Historia de Deià.* Mallorca: Ayuntamiento de Deià.

Porcel, B. 1987. *Los Chuetas.* Mallorca: Editorial Moll.

Poveda i Sanchez, A. 1983. 'La Toponímia Arabo-Musulmana de Mayurqa', in *Estudis de Prehistoria de Mayurqa i d'Historia de Mallorca.* Mallorca.

Prat, J. 1977. 'Una aproximaciòn a la bibliografia antropologia sobre España'. *Ethnica,* 13.

Quadrado, J. Mª 1930. *Informaciòn judicial sobre els adictes a la Germania.* Mallorca.

———. 1939 'Refutation of George Sand' from *La Palma* Reprinted in R. Graves's 1956 translation of G. Sand's *Winter in Majorca.* Mallorca: Ediciones Valldemosa.

Richards, M. 1995. '"Terror and Progress": Industrialization, Modernity, and the Making of Francosim', in H. Graham and J. Labanyi (eds.). *Spanish Cultural Studies.* Oxford: Oxford University Press.

Rossello Bordoy, G. 1968. *l'Islam a les illes Baleares.* Mallorca: Museo de Mallorca.

———. 1973. *Los Siglos Oscuros de Mallorca.* Mayurqa 77–97.

Rossello i Verger, V.M. 1981. 'Canvis de propietat i parcellacions al camp Mallorqui entre els segles XIX i XX'. *Randa* 12:19–60.

Rossello Vaquer, R. 1980. *Notes Per a La Historia de Deià* (IV) Segle XIII-XVI. Mallorca: Ayuntamiento de Deià.

Rusiñol, S. (1905) 1958. *Mallorca: The Island of Calm.* Barcelona: Editorial Pulide.

Sabater, Gaspar. 1986. *Roberto Gravés.* Mallorca: Imprenta Politecnica.

Sabrafin, G. 1982. *Leyendas, Tradiciones, Cuentos, Fabulosos y Otros Relatos Fantasticos de Las Islas Cabrera, Formentera, Eivissa, Menorca y Mallorca.* Mallorca: Arxiu de Tradiciones Populars-José J. de Olañeta.

Salvador, Archiduque Luis, 1869. 6 vols. *Die Balearen in Wort Und Bild Geschildert,* 6 vols. Leipzig.

———. 1955. *Los Pueblos de Mallorca . El estribo Norte de la Sierra y sus cumbres.* Mallorca: Edicion de Baleares Sa Nostra.
———. 1959. *Mallorca Agrícola.* Mallorca: Edicion de Baleares Sa Nostra.
———. 1981. *Costumbres de Los Mallorquines Artesania y Folklore.* Mallorca: Arxiu de Tradiciones Populars-José J. de Olañeta.
Salve, P. 1984. 'L'estructura de la proprietat a la serra', in *Randa* 12:72–85. Mallorca: Universitat de L'Illes Balear.
Sand, George. (Dudevant, A.L.) 1845. *Histoire de ma vie: Un Hiver à Majorque.* Paris: Edicions Garnier.
———. 1956. *Winter in Mallorca.* (trans. R. Graves). Mallorca: Ediciones Valldemosa.
Sanmartin, R. 'Marriage and Inheritance in a Mediterranean Fishing Community'. *Man* (N.S.) 17, 4:664–685.
Sartre, J. 1957 (1943) *Being and Nothingness.* London: Metheun.
Schalekamp, Jean A. 1976. *Mallorca L'any 1936.* Mallorca: Prensa Universitaria.
Segalen, M. 1983. *Love and Power in the Peasant Family.* Oxford: Blackwell.
Segura i Salado, J. 1977. *Deià en el Segle XVI.* Mallorca: Banca Catalana.
———. 1979. *Notes Per a La Historia de Deià (III), Cases Fortificades.* Mallorca: Banca Catalana.
Seymour-Smith. 1982. *Robert Graves: His Life and Work.* London: Hutchinson.
Shanin, T. 1971. *Peasant and Peasant Societies.* London: Penguin.
Simmel, G. 1953. *Conflict in Modern Culture and Other Essays.* New York: Free Press.
Smith, M.E. 1977. *Those Who Live from the Sea.* New York: West Publishing Co.
Smith, V. 1977. *Hosts and Guests: The Anthropology of Tourism.* Philadelphia: University of Pennsylvania Press.
Snipes, K. 1979. *Robert Graves.* New York: Frederick Ungar Publishing Co.
Soto, 1982. *Estudis de Prehistoria de Mayurqa i d'Historia de Mallorca.* Mallorca.
Strathern, M. 1981. *Kinship at the Core: An Anthropology of Elmdon, Essex.* Cambridge: Cambridge University Press.
Thomas, Hugh. 1961. *The Spanish Civil War.* London: Eyre & Spottiswoode.
Turner, V. 1982. *Celebration.* Washington, D.C.: Smithsonian Institute Press.
Vargas Ponce, J. 1787. *Descripciones de las Islas Pithiusas y Baleares.* Madrid: Ibarra.
Vila, A. 1984. *Almanac Balear.* Mallorca: Diario de Mallorca.
Villalonga, J. 1938. *Bearn.* Mallorca: Editorial Moll.
Viullier, G. 1893. *Les Iles Oubliées. Les Baléares. La Corse et la Sardaigne.* Paris: Hachette et Cie.
Waldren, J. 1988. 'House Names As Metaphors for Social Relations'. *JASO*, Vol. XIX, No. 2: 166–169.
———. 1990. 'An Artists' Colony in Mallorca', in *Insight Guides: Mallorca, Ibiza, Menorca and Formentera.* Singapore: APA Publications.
———. 1990. *Historia de Las Baleares.* Fasicules 61–70. Mallorca: Editorial Fomentor.
Waldren, W.H. 1982. *Aspects of Balearic Prehistoric Ecology and Culture*, I-III. Oxford. B.A.R.
Wallman, S. 1979. 'Ethnicity at Work', in S. Wallman (ed.). *Social Anthropology of Work.* London: Macmillan Press.
Whelpton, E. 1952. *The Balearics: Majorca, Minorca, Ibiza.* London: Robert Hale.
Wood, Charles. 1888. *Letters from Majorca.* London: Richard Bentley and Sons.

Index